AMERICAN HISTORY

IT'S MORE THAN THE *CRAP* YOU LEARNED IN HIGH SCHOOL

ROBERT MACDOUGALL

WORD ASSOCIATION PUBLISHERS
www.wordassociation.com
1.800.821.1903

Printed in the United States of America.

ISBN: 978-1-63385-162-7

Library of Congress Control Number: 2016913567

Designed and published by

Word Association Publishers
205 Fifth Avenue
Tarentum, Pennsylvania 15084

www.wordassociation.com
1.800.827.7903

TABLE OF CONTENTS

PREFACE

If you are the least bit interested in revisiting the things you learned in your high school American History class, then you will enjoy reading this book. You will also like it if you really never learned much at all in your history classes and would now like to catch up a bit on what you missed. My goal is to summarize American history, from the American Revolutionary War to the present, in a way that is both satisfying and clear, and for you to come away with a better understanding of the history of our country.

This subject matter is dear to my heart, and through sharing its value and importance in the pages of this book, I hope to help you become able to find new ways in which history might illuminate *your* life. If you approach the people and events of the past wondering what you can learn from them, you will enjoy the study so much more, because it will mean something to you.

You may *not* enjoy this book if you disliked history class in school and continue to be bored by anything that has happened since. In the introduction, I describe my encounter with a hairdresser named Tina. I doubt that Tina would be interested in this book, which is a shame, because, if she would only give history a chance, it could possibly help her lead a more fulfilling life. One of the major themes of this book is that history will help you out—if you let it.

At the start of my high school U.S. History class each year, I ask this question of my students: Do you think that most of what you will learn about U.S. History will be useless crap you will never have any need for, as long as you live? A few of them boldly raise their hands, and I know they will probably be the ones who are the hardest to reach, or possibly the real independent thinkers in the group. I then tell them I will try very hard to do the following:

A. not make them learn anything that is useless "crap"; and

B. help them see the utility of the stuff I do want them to learn.

I make those same promises to you. In this book, I have tried to share *only* the good stuff, and I have tried to show you how that good stuff has been useful to me and might be useful to you.

> **Note:** *You may experience a bit of déjà vu as you read because several events, such as the Watergate scandal, appear in different contexts. Be aware that you are not losing your mind, and I haven't lost mine. Certain events are sometimes great examples of several lessons we can learn.*

ACKNOWLEDGEMENTS

'll begin by giving some credit for the direction of my teaching career to Mr. Paul Simon. After I had been teaching American History for a few years, his song "Kodachrome" gave me a slap on the side of the head with the opening: "When I think back on all the crap I learned in high school, it's a wonder I can think at all." From the moment I heard those words I pledged not to be a purveyor of "crap" or a teacher who left his students unable to think. Thanks to Paul for waking me up to my responsibilities.

My students, during my fifty years of teaching, have been terrific. They have been generous with praise when classes went well and forgiving when classes flopped. I never worked a day in my life because I had the pleasure of teaching history at Southfield High School in Southfield, Michigan, Tewksbury Memorial High School in Tewksbury, Massachusetts, Northern Essex Community College in Haverhill, Massachusetts, and Central Catholic High School in Lawrence, Massachusetts. The students at my last post, Central Catholic High School, have been especially encouraging and helpful with many ideas for what to include and what – please! – to leave out. Thank you, students, for your enthusiasm and brutal honesty.

For decades my family has put up with my rants about how my classes were going at school . . . or not going. On many occasions they have offered good ideas both for my teaching and for this book. My wife, Diane, in particular has always been there for me with helpful suggestions and emotional support. Thank you, family, for helping me be the best I could be.

The people at Word Association Publishing have been very helpful in putting this book into its current form. I am grateful to Tom and Francine Costello, the founders of Word Association, for their enthusiasm and encouragement. Pam Greer, my editor, worked assiduously to whip my writing into shape and to avoid snobby words such as "assiduously." April Urso did a great job researching and creating the images for the cover. In all, Word Association did superb work creating this book and any shortcomings in it are totally my fault. Thank you, Word Association, for putting out a book I can be proud of.

Finally, every writer needs a special place where he does his best thinking and scribbling. I found such a place in Town Market, a first class general store and coffee shop at the corner of Main Street and Rattlesnake Hill Road in Andover, Massachusetts. I composed many of the words in this book by the fireplace in that cozy environment. Many thanks to Tom Walsh and his partners for creating a great place for me to write.

INTRODUCTION

So you don't know who Robert E. Lee was, and you think Abraham Lincoln had a cell phone. Is that a problem? Is it a disgrace that you don't know that the Vietnam War was *after* World War II and not before it? To get laughs, late night TV shows interview "people on the street" to ask them what they know about American history. "Was it Roosevelt?" a man will say when asked who was president during the Civil War. After learning the answer was Lincoln, he shrugs his shoulders and walks off, presumably on his way to a six-figure job in finance. He appeared to be stupid during a thirty-second segment on a television show, but did his ignorance of history have any effect on his life? Did it reduce his income? Did it ruin his relationship with his family and friends? Would knowing who was president during the Civil War help him earn more money or make his family love him more? Certainly not. So why should he care to know any American history?

In my early years teaching American history in high school, I assumed that my students and I recognized there was value in knowing history, even if it was boring, and I forged ahead every year, teaching everything from the colonies to the hippies, trying to make it as interesting as possible. We made the best of it. They had to take history class—it was required; I had to teach it—it was my job. Lately, however, I have become troubled by the sickening thought that we are all wasting our time if there really is no value in knowing American history. Maybe American history is the "crap (we) learned in high school," as a popular song once proclaimed. If we cannot figure out why we are learning it, and if we don't have some really good reasons for knowing it, then perhaps we should just give it up and forget about it. After all, there are millions of people who are leading happy, productive lives who have no clue that the United States once fought a war with Spain and took over the Philippine Islands. Be honest, now ... did you know that?

As I reach the end of my teaching career, I have become a little desperate to prove to myself and to all the unfortunate people who had to endure my classes, and millions like them across the land, that history is not just "the crap (you) learned in high school," that it has real world value. To get started on this quest, I have asked people—college graduates, high school graduates, high school dropouts—to give me any good examples of how knowledge of American history might be useful to them or might actually improve their lives in some tangible way.

A typical conversation was one I had with Tina, a twenty-year-old woman who had dropped out of high school to become a hairstylist. We talked while she was cutting my hair at a local shop.

"So, what do you teach?" she asked.

"American history," I replied. Her scissors started to snip much faster.

"I always hated history," she snarled.

"Maybe it would have helped you to think of history as a story with interesting characters, rather than just a long list of names and dates to memorize," I offered.

"How interesting could old guys in powdered wigs who lived over two hundred years ago possibly be?" she asked, gesturing with a comb and flashing the elaborate rose tattoo on her arm.

I guessed her interest in hair helped her remember that those "old guys" wore powdered wigs, and I was impressed that she accurately placed them at over two hundred years ago. Hopeful, I ventured on.

"Can you think of anything that you learned in history that has helped you in your life?" I asked, warily.

"No!" she stated emphatically. "That's why I dropped out of high school. I wanted to learn stuff that would help me make money."

As I endured the rest of the haircut, I tried to think of ways Tina could make money from knowing American history. All I could come up with was that she could teach it; several schools have paid me huge piles of cash to do so; she could be a tour guide at a historic site; I hear the camera-toting Civil War buffs at Gettysburg tip very well; or she could go on *Jeopardy*. When Alex Trebek says, "He signed the bill creating the Transcontinental Railroad," she could slam her buzzer and blurt out, "Who was Abraham Lincoln?" and win thirty thousand dollars!

I knew none of these scenarios would be very convincing. There's not a lot of money to be made from knowing American history.

Later, at the cash register, I dropped three ten-dollar bills on the counter to pay for the haircut. The bills lay there with Alexander Hamilton's face staring at us. Knowing full well that what I was about to say would be nerdy, I nevertheless could not resist.

"Look at that. I'm dropping Hamiltons like I'm Aaron Burr!"

"What?"

"Burr killed Hamilton in a duel," I explained.

She performed a world-class eye roll and scooped up the money. I almost said, "They were wearing powdered wigs at the time," but I decided to let it go. It was obvious that Tina could not wait for this incredible dweeb, who reminded her way too much of her uncomfortable past, to leave the shop.

Clearly, Tina was a lost cause, but I had to go down fighting. "Hamilton was the first secretary of the treasury," I informed her as I left and the bells on the door sang their happy little song.

Desperate for affirmation, I talked to my wife, Diane, who is a counselor with a master's degree in psychotherapy and is interested in everything.

"Why do you think it is useful to know history?" I asked.

"I like to know the back story of what's happening in the world," she said.

"Ah, yes, the 'back story,'" I concurred. That is the standard answer to the question "Why learn history?" It helps us better understand the world in which we live and the events that are taking place around us. The problem for most is that *their* real world only includes their families, their jobs, their friends, their quest for fun—countless issues that do not have any obvious relationship to current events, let alone to history. Diane counsels people every day who have problems in their lives, and I would guess that she never brings history into her discussions with them. What troubled client would respond to her saying, "Your situation is very similar to what Lincoln went through during the Civil War?"

Yet, as I write this, I *can* recall how I have made use in my own life of how Lincoln managed many issues, including the decision to free the slaves during the Civil War. The abridged version of Lincoln's story goes like this: At the start of the Civil War, many people in the North, and in his own administration, wanted Lincoln to free the slaves immediately. Some powerful political figures, such as Senator Charles Sumner, visited the White House almost daily to demand that Lincoln take action and to warn him that the people of the North would not support a war that would only put down the southern rebellion without freeing the slaves. Lincoln knew, however, that the war could not be won if the four slave states that had not seceded were to decide to join the Confederate States of America. Kentucky, Missouri, Maryland, and Delaware—the border states—all had slavery, and their loss to the Confederacy would make the task of winning the war almost impossible. Announcing that the war was being fought to end slavery would almost surely drive those states into the arms of the Confederacy. For more than a year, Lincoln held firm, convinced that his path was correct. Finally, almost two years into the war, when it was clear that the Union forces had secured the border region, Lincoln announced his Emancipation Proclamation. He had held firm in the face of incredible pressure, and his policy ultimately proved correct. The Union won the Civil War and slavery was ended in large part because the border states had remained in the Union during the first two years of the fighting.

There are many times in our own lives when we would profit by following Lincoln's example. We would do well not to let the people around us pressure us into making a rash move that we know would not be a good idea. We would be well advised to wait until we knew all the facts before taking an important step. Have I ever actually used this in a practical way? Well, yes. It may seem strange, but I thought of Lincoln's emancipation stand on a night when I went to a well-publicized "career opportunity" meeting at a large hotel in Detroit. The men in charge of the meeting, all of them well dressed and flashing expensive watches, promised a golden future for enterprising young people hoping to make huge incomes with *almost* no financial risk. The "opportunity" was a catalog of cosmetic products to sell, but the point was that I, a future millionaire entrepreneur, would not actually sell the creams and lotions. I would sell *franchises* and build my own little empire of franchise owners, and then sit back and let the cash flow in as more and more franchises were sold and I got a cut from each. The pressure on me to sign up for this deal and buy a franchise was tremendous. At one point, five men who were already franchise owners sat me down at a round table, bought me a drink, and regaled me with tales of all the money they had already made. One especially aggressive salesman even pulled a thick wad of cash out of his pocket to demonstrate that he literally had bundles of money! He told me that if I did not write a check right then to buy a franchise, I was a small-minded man who could not think big and, therefore, would never be rich.

I cannot always claim to have followed Lincoln's example in every situation in which I've found myself, but in this case, I thought about Lincoln and acted like Lincoln. I ignored the pressure, the imputation that I would be missing a chance in a lifetime if I let this opportunity get away. I brushed off the insulting remarks that I was a small thinker who would never make much money, and I resisted the urge to get it over with by just agreeing to what these men wanted. My model was Lincoln, who looked his cabinet members and powerful senators in the eye and said, "No, I will not make this a war against slavery until I am ready!" I finally looked the salesmen in the eye, said one last emphatic "No!" and walked out. Summoning my "inner Lincoln" had enabled me to do the right thing and avoid a possible disaster.

A few months later, I had the satisfaction of reading that the state attorney general's office had prosecuted the company for operating an illegal pyramid scheme, and several of the "big thinkers" who had pressured me were now in court facing serious criminal charges.

Right now you may be thinking, "My God, this guy goes around thinking he's Lincoln!" Let me assure you, I am actually quite normal—most people would support me on that—but I can see the world with a unique historical perspective. I can think of numerous other ways my knowledge of American history has served me well in my life, so I have decided to make this book a testimonial to what knowing history has done for *me* and to suggest that it might do the same for you. Of course, not all of the same historical people, themes, and events that resonated with me will necessarily resonate with you, but perhaps by sharing how American history has influenced my life, I might encourage you to learn more about history and how you can apply it to your life.

To begin, I have described the basics that a decent American history course would cover. In short, I dish out the *crap*; however, I have tried to do it in an interesting way. For example, the two hundred forty years since the Declaration of Independence was signed in 1776 would be covered by four lifetimes of approximately sixty years each. It's strange to think of it this way, isn't it? Only four lifetimes encompass the whole history of our country, and those are relatively short lifetimes of sixty years each. I have chosen to tell the story of what happened in our country through the voices of four individuals. James Madison, who lived from 1755 to 1836, will describe the years 1776 to the year of his death; Mark Twain, who lived from 1835 to 1910, will take the story from 1836 to 1900; Alice Roosevelt, who lived from 1884 to 1980, will narrate events from 1901 to 1961; and, finally, I, who was born in 1944, will cover events from 1962, the year I graduated from high school, to the present.

After we have reviewed the stuff you probably learned—or were supposed to have learned—we will go on to see what might be gained from knowing all that crap! I have formulated eight ways my knowledge of American history has helped me in my life. I will devote a chapter to each. If after reading all eight chapters and making an honest attempt to think about history in ways that might apply to your own life you still think American history is the crap you learned in high school, then I will have wasted my time not only writing this book, but in having taught American history in high school for forty-nine years.

My eight reasons why American history has not been crap for me are as follows:

1. It has helped me better appreciate how people who came before me lived their everyday lives. It has shown me that in the three lifetimes that have spanned the years from the birth of the nation to our present day, our lifestyles have gone from small towns and horses to big cities and jets. (Yes, we *could* divide the years since independence into *three* lifetimes. They would be eighty years each, and I know many people who have lived that long.) Each lifetime has witnessed increasingly faster and more dramatic changes. It is important to know those changes so that you don't picture your grandfather getting a *text message* that his daughter (your mother) was just born.

2. It has introduced me to magnificent men and women whom I have adopted as role models in my life. None of them is perfect, but they all have provided me with invaluable guidance on how to lead my life.

3. It has introduced me to rogues and shown me cautionary tales, stories about people who had character traits, values, or attitudes that I want to avoid, stories about people who did things that I find repulsive and would not want to emulate in the slightest way.

4. It has introduced me to some of the greatest leaders of all time, people from whom I have learned leadership principles that have served me well whenever I have been in leadership roles or whenever I have participated in choosing leaders.

5. It has shown me the power of words by providing stimulating examples of how books, speeches, or simple pithy phrases have transformed a nation and have dramatically changed the course of events. It has also provided me with an awareness of how effective writing and speaking is done. And it has given me quotes and expressions that I have used very effectively in key moments.

6. It has shown me the power of images, pictures that have defined the way people thought about an event or a person. Some images have changed the course of history, and those examples are a guide to what might be important in our own times.

7. It has shown me the causes for which Americans have been asked to die, and it has made it possible for me to evaluate what I think have been worthwhile causes and what I think have been foolish misadventures. Armed with this knowledge, I have been able to make informed decisions about what I would be willing to put my own or my family's

lives on the line for. The study of the United States' twelve major wars has given me plenty of fodder for thought as the nation heads toward future military involvements.

8. And, yes, history does give me the *back story* for what is happening in the world. At the conclusion of this book, I will show how history helps me understand recent news stories that affect our lives in important ways. I will show that with history, I have a clue about what is going on, I have a good idea about who will receive my vote, and I am not easy meat for any dishonest egomaniac who is running for office.

In all my years of studying and teaching American history, I have loved the subject simply for what it is. I think it is a terrific story filled with interesting characters and amazing plotlines. Not everyone feels this way, of course, but I am hopeful that the stories told will help you to live your life with more awareness and enthusiasm.

CHAPTER I

WHAT HAPPENED IN
THE YEARS 1776-1836

ACCORDING TO JAMES MADISON

James Madison lived from 1751 to 1836. He owned a plantation (Montpelier) in Virginia and kept hundreds of slaves. During the Constitutional Convention of 1787, he served as a delegate from Virginia and took copious notes on the proceedings. Many of his ideas made it into the final constitution and the subsequent Bill of Rights—the first ten amendments. To facilitate ratification of the Constitution, he, along with Alexander Hamilton and John Jay, wrote a series of essays called "The Federalist Papers." During the first twelve years of the new government, Madison served as a member of Congress from Virginia and helped start the first political party, the Republican Party (the forerunner, ironically, of today's Democratic Party). When his friend Thomas Jefferson was president, Madison served as secretary of state. From 1809 to 1817, he was President of the United States. His administration was focused primarily on the troubles with Britain and the subsequent War of 1812.

 n 1776, I was a member of the Virginia state legislature, where I was closely allied with my friend and neighbor, Thomas Jefferson. In the spring of that year, the Continental Congress meeting in

Philadelphia decided to declare independence from Great Britain, and they asked my friend Jefferson and four other members to write a declaration to send to the king. Thomas's Declaration of Independence was adopted on July 4, 1776, and, of course, it has since become one of the world's most famous documents.

Declaring independence was one thing, but winning it was quite another. Britain was not going to let her American colonies go without a fight. We had to fight the British Army for six years, and our cause did not always go well. General Washington suffered many defeats; his soldiers kept deserting; over a third of the colonists were actually loyal to the British government; one of Washington's best generals, Benedict Arnold, became a traitor and switched sides; and the British took over New York (our largest port) and Philadelphia (the capital city of our new country). Still, Washington kept an army in the field, the French came to our assistance, and after Washington defeated General Cornwallis at Yorktown, the British government decided the fight wasn't worth what they were spending on it and they gave up. The Treaty of Paris in 1783 gave us our independence and established our borders at the Great Lakes in the north, the Mississippi River in the west, and Florida in the south.

These boundaries made our new nation one of the largest countries on Earth in terms of land area; however, there were many problems. We were thirteen disunited states who couldn't seem to agree on much of anything. All of the territory west of the Appalachian Mountains was vulnerable to invasion by the Spanish, from the south and west, where they controlled Florida and the Louisiana Territory, and the British from the north, where they controlled Canada. The land was mostly wilderness, inhabited by Indians who, quite naturally, opposed our presence in the area. The government we had set up during the war very quickly proved to be unable to cope with all of these vexing issues.

The Articles of Confederation established the government, giving almost total sovereignty to every state over all of its affairs. The states could even print their own money! The country was supposedly governed by a congress in which each state had one vote. There was no chief executive and no national court system. Nine states had to vote for any law to be passed, and the states were given the sole power to enforce any legislation that went into effect. They usually didn't. Needless to say, the so-called nation quickly descended into chaos. King George III described the situation rather bluntly when he told John Adams, who was our ambassador to England, "Frankly, Mr. Adams, my government finds it impossible to deal with a creature that has thirteen arms and no head!"

The only significant laws the congress was able to pass while the Articles of Confederation were in effect were the Land Ordinance of 1785 and the Northwest Ordinance of 1787. The Land Ordinance divided the territory north of the Ohio River into townships of thirty-six square miles and decreed that in each town, one of those thirty-six would be set aside for public education. The Northwest Ordinance said that three to five territories would be created in that region and that they would be eligible to become states—equal to the thirteen original states—as soon as their populations reached sixty thousand people. The ordinance also stated that slavery would be prohibited in those territories. Eventually five states were created: Ohio, Indiana, Illinois, Michigan, and Wisconsin. Their admission to the union as states equal in status to the original thirteen was a big deal. It meant we were not going to make *colonies* out of our new territories … not yet, anyway.

In 1786, Shays' Rebellion in western Massachusetts showed even the most complacent Americans that something needed to be done to strengthen the central government. Shays and his followers, mostly farmers, were protesting their taxes and other grievances, and they raided courthouses and attacked an arsenal. There was no United States Army to deal with the situation, and it took quick organization of a volunteer militia to route the rebels. Clearly, the country needed a stronger central government that could manage the economy and create a national army.

In the summer of 1787, a convention of delegates from the thirteen states met in Philadelphia to amend the Articles of Confederation. I was a delegate from Virginia, and I played a leading role in the proceedings. Actually, I played such an important role—taking notes on all the debates, proposing the major plan that formed the nucleus of the new government, and doing much of the actual writing—that I am often referred to as the Father of the Constitution.

We immediately decided not to amend the Articles, but rather write a whole new constitution, a rather bold, but necessary, decision. The document we came up with, after tedious debate in the horrific summer heat, was brilliant. Its principles of "separation of powers" and "checks and balances" have served the country magnificently. No single person has ever emerged as a dictator, and the nation has dealt with expansion of territory, a huge growth of population, and dramatic changes in technology, without having to scrap the work we did in 1787. What I am most proud of is that my "Virginia Plan" allowed the *people* to be represented equally in the House of Representatives and the *states* to be represented equally in the Senate. This resolved a heated argument we had at the convention between the large states who wanted all representation in congress based on the population of each state and the small states who wanted each state to have the same number of representatives, regardless of size. We didn't realize at the time that the biggest fight in the years to come would not be between the large states and the small states, but rather between the states that allowed and protected slavery (slave states) and those that did not (free states).

The ratification of the new constitution was very close in several of the large states. New York approved it by a vote of thirty to twenty-seven. To make the case for the new charter, Alexander Hamilton, John Jay, and I wrote a series of essays called "The Federalist Papers." My essay, Federalist paper number ten, had a major impact on the voters in New York, because I persuasively argued that a federal republic in which each state chose representatives to a legislative assembly would best assure perpetual democracy. Also, Mr. Hamilton and Mr. Jay agreed that a federal bill of rights would be added to the constitution to allay any fears that the new government would be tyrannical.

The Bill of Rights that we added to the constitution became the first ten amendments. Those clear statements of specific rights for all citizens, especially the ones pertaining to those people accused of crimes and the ones protecting freedom of speech and religion, have been the primary guarantees of our liberties ever since they went into effect in 1791. I wrote them, and I think they are my biggest contribution to the success of the new government. I must say, it's pretty awesome being the guy who wrote the Bill of Rights.

Much of the credit for getting the new government off to a solid start should go to George Washington, who served as the first president from 1789 to 1797. He established the first cabinet, which consisted of the secretaries of state, war, and treasury, the attorney general, and the postmaster general. His treasury secretary, Alexander Hamilton, put an economic plan in place that I think favored the rich: a tariff to protect domestic manufacturers, a national bank to collect taxes and issue bank notes (paper money), and a policy of paying off all the federal and state debts. It might seem that paying off all the debts would be a good thing, but the fact was that Hamilton's wealthy friends would get all their bonds paid back with interest and the poor people in the country would have to pay taxes to make that happen.

My friend Thomas Jefferson and I opposed what Hamilton was doing and we believed he was overreaching the national (federal) government's powers. There is nothing in the constitution that says anything about creating a national bank. By the end of Washington's first term, Jefferson and I were forming a political party that we called the Republicans, or the Democratic-Republicans. Hamilton and his supporters were calling themselves Federalists. Thus, a two-party system was born. Political parties are not mentioned in the constitution, and yet here they were.

President Washington also established a foreign policy that was going to endure for decades. A war was being fought in Europe between the French and the British, and Washington was determined that the United States would stay out of the fight. He issued the Proclamation of Neutrality, and both Jefferson and Hamilton, rivals on most everything, supported the idea. With three thousand miles of Atlantic Ocean between Europe and our shores, why should we have to concern ourselves with the Europeans' annoying squabbles?

John Adams, who was Washington's vice president, won the presidency in 1796, barely defeating my friend Jefferson. Adams was a Federalist, but he stood up against his Federalist friends—and most of the American people—in 1799, when they wanted to fight a war against France because of the attacks the French Navy was making against our ships on the high seas. He believed it would be a mistake to fight at that time, and he was probably right. That was Adams for you, always pompous and annoying, but almost always right.

I admire him for keeping the peace, but I don't like the Alien and Sedition Acts that he and his friends in congress enacted. The Sedition Act made it a crime to print criticisms of the president (the pudgy Adams hated being called "his rotundity!"). The Alien Act required immigrants to reside in the United States for fourteen years before they became citizens. I think the Federalists wanted this because immigrants tended to vote for Jefferson's Republican Party candidates. Jefferson and I wrote resolutions saying that these laws were unconstitutional violations of the First Amendment and that any state that agreed with us could nullify those laws (refuse to enforce them) within their boundaries. Virginia adopted my resolution and Kentucky adopted Jefferson's. Our so-called Virginia and Kentucky Resolutions set forth the concept of nullification, which, sadly, South Carolina was going to use thirty years later and again sixty years later, with horrific consequences—a major civil war.

In 1800, Jefferson took on Adams again, only this time he won. However, Aaron Burr, Thomas' running mate, got the same number of electors' votes and, so, technically, tied for the presidency. It took the House of Representatives thirty-six votes to finally elect Jefferson over

Burr, because some of the Federalists wanted to vote for Burr, who had no strong Republican Party loyalty, and would make deals with them, rather than vote for Jefferson, the leader of the Republican Party. It was Hamilton who convinced Federalists in Congress to vote for Jefferson, even though Jefferson was his rival, because he didn't think Burr was trustworthy. Burr would one day make him pay for that.

Four years later, Hamilton again opposed Burr, this time when Burr ran for governor of New York. Calling Burr a dangerous man not to be trusted, Hamilton provoked a challenge from Vice President Burr, and they met on the dueling field. Burr killed Hamilton in one of the most famous duels in American history.

Before I leave John Adams, I have to give him credit for something, even though I hate to do so. In 1801, he did foresee the power of the judicial branch of the government. While he and his party, the Federalists, still controlled congress and the presidency, they passed the Judiciary Act of 1801, which increased the number of judges. This enabled Adams to appoint several Federalist justices and get them confirmed by the senate before he left office. We called these appointments "midnight judges" because Adams was supposedly still signing their commissions at midnight of his last day in office. That story can't be true; Adams never stayed up that late.

One of Adams' appointments in the last months of his presidency was naming John Marshall to be the new chief justice of the Supreme Court. That man would sit in the center chair at the court for the next thirty-five years and make numerous rulings that favored the Federalist concepts of strong central government and pro-business policies. After Adams, the Federalists never again controlled the executive or legislative branches, but they held the judicial, and that was a lot! Damn! When we wrote the Constitution, we never should have given federal judges *life* terms! What were we thinking?

Meanwhile, when Jefferson took office, he appointed me to be secretary of state, and in his first term, we had some notable successes. We refused to pay the traditional bribes that the Tripoli pirates were demanding from all ships traveling in the Mediterranean Sea. This brought on a war with the pirates that we eventually won. We also were able to purchase the Louisiana Territory from Napoleon for fifteen million dollars, a real bargain, because it almost doubled the size of the country. Jefferson was especially enthusiastic about the maps and specimens brought back to him by Meriwether Lewis and William Clark, whom he had sent on an expedition to explore our new Louisiana Territory.

Everything seemed to be going very well, but in Jefferson's second term (1805-1809), we ran into big trouble with France and Britain, especially Britain. Because of the war they were fighting with each other, they were both trying to stop our ships from reaching European ports. The British were doing even more. They were taking sailors off our ships and impressing them into the British Navy. At first, we tried an embargo—stopping all trade—to keep our ships out of harm's way and to deprive Britain and France of our products, especially cotton. But that hurt our own merchants more than it did Britain and France, so we gave it up.

It was about this time that Aaron Burr was caught trying to lead some sort of military expedition down the Mississippi River and into Texas. No one knows exactly what he was up to, but he was tried for treason. The trial was a farce. There were not enough witnesses against Burr and he was acquitted. It was all very strange, but ever since the duel, we had come to expect outrageous behavior from Mr. Burr. Since Burr was universally regarded as a scoundrel because of the Hamilton duel and now *this* tawdry episode, he left for Europe in self-imposed exile. I felt especially bad about the direction the man's life had taken, because Burr was an old friend and it was he who had introduced me to my wife, Dolly.

While all these things were happening, the Supreme Court was beginning to make its presence felt. John Marshall was a very clever man, and he very quickly made the Supreme Court an equal branch of the government, along with the president and the Congress, by taking on the power of *judicial review* (the power to declare laws passed by

Congress and signed by the president to be unconstitutional and thus null and void).

Sadly, I was a player in the case that allowed Marshall to grab this power. As secretary of state, I withheld a judicial commission from a man named William Marbury because he was a Federalist and I didn't want him to become a judge. Marbury went to court to seek a court order (a writ of mandamus) that would force me to hand over his commission. We all expected Marshall would order me to give Marbury, a fellow Federalist, his commission, but Marshall fooled us. In *Marbury v. Madison*, he denied Marbury's request because the part of the Judiciary Act of 1789 that gave the Supreme Court the authority to issue writs of mandamus was unconstitutional; thus, he took on the power to declare laws invalid. In this great political game of chess, Marshall sacrificed the pawn, Marbury, in order to take the queen: judicial review. I wished I had just given Marbury his papers and not handed Marshall this golden opportunity to grab power. Now the court was in position to make all kinds of pro-Federalist decisions, such as upholding the constitutionality of the National Bank.

In 1808, I was elected president, and so I inherited the problem of maintaining our neutral rights during the endless war that was going on between Britain and France. There was a group of congressmen from the western states, Representative Henry Clay from Kentucky, in particular, who were screaming for war with Britain, not only because of the impressment issue, but also because Britain was supplying the Indians along the frontier with weapons to attack our settlements. Clay also claimed he could lead an army of rugged frontiersmen into Canada and add that huge territory to our country. I called these congressmen War Hawks, and their calls for war were pretty hard to resist. I began to realize how solid and principled John Adams had been when he resisted calls for war against France twelve years earlier.

Finally, in June of 1812, I could no longer resist, and I asked congress to declare war against Great Britain. We call it the War of 1812 now, but it was just a war with Britain at the time. It did not go well at first. Our attempts to invade Canada failed miserably, and in 1814, the British attacked Washington and burned down the president's house (the White House, as it was later called). I had to leave town in a hurry to avoid capture, and my wife, Dolly, whom I had left behind, got out just in time before the British showed up with their torches. Why did I leave town in a hurry and leave my wife behind to face the British without me? If they had captured me, we would have lost the war; if they had captured her, we would have lost Dolly. She is a strong woman who tolerates no nonsense, and I'm sure they would have gladly released her within a few hours.

Fortunately, the British had bigger fish to fry than us; they were fighting Napoleon at the time. So they made peace with us at Ghent, Belgium. The Treaty of Ghent provided for no exchange of territory and said nothing about the rights of neutrals on the high seas, the major reason we went to war. But we didn't *lose* the war, and the treaty arrived home just at the time the public was hearing about Andrew Jackson's big victory over the British Army at New Orleans; thus, everyone felt as if we had won.

The five years after the War of 1812 were happy and prosperous. The Federalist Party disappeared because we Republicans adopted most of their ideas—a tariff and a second national bank—and they couldn't come up with any good candidates for president. In 1816, another friend of mine, fellow Republican James Monroe was elected president, and I went back to my plantation, Montpelier, in Virginia. Monroe's eight years in the presidency went pretty smoothly, especially the first four, which some people called The Era of Good Feelings, because there seemed to be political agreement on just about everything.

In 1820, however, storm clouds appeared on the distant horizon. Missouri applied for admission to the Union as a state. Situated on the west bank of the Mississippi River, Missouri straddles the place where the Ohio River enters the Mississippi. Since the Ohio had long been the boundary between the slave states and the free states, Missouri's status—slave or free?—was very much in question. Compounding the problem was the fact that there were eleven slave states and eleven free states in the Union, so whichever section, North or South, got Missouri, that section would have two more votes in the United States Senate.

The Missouri debates in Congress got very heated and it almost seemed, at times, that there would be fist fights on the floor of the House. Finally, Henry Clay, a congressman from Kentucky, a border state between the North and the South, saved the day by proposing a compromise whereby Maine would enter the Union as a free state along with Missouri, which would enter as a slave state. That would keep the balance between slave states and free states at twelve and twelve. The southern border of Missouri, the 36°30' line of latitude, would be the boundary between slave territory and free territory in the rest of the Louisiana Purchase, with all territory north of that line being free except for Missouri itself.

The country breathed a sigh of relief when Congress passed the so-called Missouri Compromise; however, my friend Jefferson wrote in his diary that the Missouri debates had awakened him "like a fire bell in the night" and filled him with dread. He feared there would be many more conflicts over slavery in the future. In a very colorful metaphor, Jefferson said that with slavery, "we had the wolf by the ears and could not safely hold on or let it go."

Near the end of his eight years in office, James Monroe included a statement in his annual message to Congress that didn't seem to be that big a deal at the time, but it proved to be a major cornerstone of American foreign policy in years to come. Monroe said that the Western hemisphere was no longer open to European colonization. He also reiterated what George Washington had said thirty years earlier: the United States would not interfere with European affairs. Monroe made this statement as a way of saying that the United States would defend the newly created republics in South America against any attempt by Europe to reverse the recent revolutions and restore them to Spanish rule. From this point on, the United States would be the protector of Latin America. We didn't have much military power with which to do it in 1823 when Monroe announced his Monroe Doctrine, but at least the policy was in place.

Just as Monroe was completing his successful terms as president, a very significant internal improvement project reached its conclusion in Upstate New York. In 1816, Governor Dewitt Clinton had convinced the New York legislature to appropriate money to build a canal from Buffalo, at the eastern end of Lake Erie, to Albany, on the Hudson River. The canal would connect the Great Lakes with New York City and make it possible for farmers and manufacturers as far west as Minnesota to ship their goods to New York and from there to Europe. I admired Clinton's vision and his courage in keeping the difficult construction going for eight years while people mocked him and laughingly referred to the project as Clinton's ditch. He had the last laugh in 1825 when he ceremoniously scooped up a bucket of Lake Erie water, traveled by barge the entire three hundred twenty-five-mile length of the canal to Albany and down the Hudson River to New York. At New York harbor, he dumped the Lake Erie water into the Atlantic, thus symbolizing the magnificent connection the canal had achieved.

The canal was just the kind of economically beneficial project that John Quincy Adams, John Adams' son and Monroe's secretary of state, would enthusiastically promote. Adams was elected president in 1824 in a hotly disputed contest with the hero of New Orleans, Andrew Jackson. Four years later, after Jackson had spent Adams' entire presidency campaigning against him and making it almost impossible for JQA to achieve any of his internal improvement goals, the old warrior defeated Adams in one of the dirtiest presidential elections of all time. Jackson's people called Adams a snob and a corrupt politician, and the Adams supporters called Jackson an adulterer and a murderer. As usual with these kinds of things, there was a shred of truth in each side's allegations. Adams *was* kind of a pompous ass (just like his father), and he probably *did* make a deal with Henry Clay to get Clay's votes for president in 1824 in return for a promise to appoint Clay secretary of state. Jackson *did* marry his wife, Rachel, before she was legally divorced and was, thus, *technically* an adulterer, and he *did* shoot Charles Dickinson dead, but it was in a duel.

After his defeat, Adams went back to Massachusetts, and to his credit, he returned to Washington as a member of Congress from his Massachusetts district. I would never have done that. When I returned to Virginia after being president, I gave no thought to running for a seat in Congress! I was content to settle down with Dolly, the rest of my family, and my slaves.

Andy Jackson was the last president I observed in my time on earth; I died during his last year in office. He gave me quite a show for my last years. One thing was certain; everyone knew where Andrew Jackson stood on all things. He never sugarcoated his message!

Jackson's Indian policy was to throw them out of the East and send them to Indian Territory on the other side of the Mississippi. He pursued that policy throughout his years in office and even defied the Supreme Court to get it done. He killed a lot of Indians during his military career; he probably killed even more with his removal policies and the ensuing Trail of Tears while he was president. Hundreds of Indians died in the thousand-mile trek during the winter to their new homes on the wind-swept plains of Indian Territory.

Jackson despised the Bank of the United States and vetoed a bill for its re-charter. When he was reelected over Henry Clay, who favored the Bank, Jackson took his victory to mean the people supported him, and he proceeded to remove all the federal government money from the Bank and leave it in ruins.

On the issue of states' rights, Jackson generally stood with the states, except when he didn't. When John C. Calhoun, Jackson's vice president, led South Carolina in its nullification of the Tariff of 1832, Jackson threatened to hang Calhoun and lead an army into South Carolina and hang every nullifier he could find. Jackson was more than ready to start a civil war with the Palmetto State, and it was only another compromise by Henry Clay that allowed cooler thinking to prevail. Clay proposed a ten-year tariff that would start out high to protect new industries in the North, but gradually diminish to reach eventually the low levels the South favored. Jackson accepted this, and so, thank God, did South Carolina.

In my last years, I felt a little sad and guilty that my concept of nullification had been used to create such divisions in the country. I passed from this earth hoping that Jackson's strong stand would make it unlikely that any state would try nullification again.

The biggest thing I hated about dying, besides leaving Dolly and all my loved ones, was that I didn't get to see how all the problems I dealt with in my life turned out. In the last years of my life, I was particularly concerned about the slavery issue. Eli Whitney's cotton gin enabled cotton growing to spread across the South, and by the 1830s, slavery was firmly planted in the region and generally regarded as the labor system necessary to produce cotton. John C. Calhoun of South Carolina, who I always thought was an unlikeable hothead, led the way in proclaiming that slavery was not a "necessary evil," as we had always said, but a "positive good" for both races. As property, he said, the slaves were cared for much better than they would ever be as free laborers. The year before I died, William Lloyd Garrison was nearly lynched in Boston for his anti-slavery views, but I wondered at the time if northern opinion would remain on the side of the slave owners. I, myself, was becoming very ambivalent about an institution that so grossly contradicted the Bill of Rights that *I* had written. I was fearful that my friend Jefferson had it right when he said that with slavery, "we had the wolf by the ears."

C H A P T E R 1 1

WHAT HAPPENED IN
THE YEARS 1836-1901

ACCORDING TO MARK TWAIN

Samuel Clemens, who went by the pen name of Mark Twain, lived from 1835 to 1910. He grew up in Missouri, and as a young man, he engaged in many careers that took him all over the country and, indeed, the world. He was a printer's apprentice, a riverboat pilot, a prospector for gold, a newspaper reporter and, eventually, a writer of stories and a public speaker. Eventually, he settled into a career of writing books and produced an impressive library of twenty-six volumes, including the classics The Adventures of Tom Sawyer and The Adventures of Huckleberry Finn. Many of his works, especially his later ones, savagely lampooned the excesses and arrogance of the idle rich people. He also viciously attacked American imperialism: the takeover of the Hawaiian Islands and the Philippines.

I came into this world with Haley's Comet in 1835 and I left it when the comet came back in 1910; my books were set in just about every decade in between those years, so I guess I'm pretty well qualified to be your guide for a life that spanned 1836 to 1901. I could tell you about those last nine years, but a lot of bad things happened to me and to my country then, so it's probably best I leave them to a more objective observer. That will be Alice Roosevelt, and come to think of it, I'm not so sure she *will* be objective, since her father was Teddy, her cousin was Eleanor, and her distant cousin was Franklin. It seems to me she might be inclined to give their presidencies favorable treatment. You will have to be the judge of that. Now, on to my story.

In the 1840s and 1850s, none of us had any idea about the horrible civil war that awaited us in the 1860s, but we should have had an inkling if we observed what was going on with any more thought than a jackass might invest. I was growing up in Hannibal, Missouri, smack in the middle of the United States. From my perch, I was able to see a lot of what was going on in the country, and I took it all in; I was a child, but an observant one. Even I could see some bad stuff was coming.

We had slaves in Hannibal (Missouri was a slave state), and I saw many of the poor creatures sitting on the dock in chains waiting for the boats that would take them to the Deep South and to the tortures of life on the big plantations. I have never seen a more miserable looking group of human beings in my life. Every week, huge steamboats loaded with slaves and cotton pulled up at Hannibal on their way to New Orleans. The South was totally wedded to a cotton-slave economy. Even the most ignorant child could see that.

Meanwhile, energetic people were coming through the town on their way to the West. Manifest destiny was taking hold, and thousands of folks wanted to go to Oregon or Texas to start new lives. It was a dynamic time, and I wanted to be part of it. I wanted to pilot a steamboat, and when I was twenty-four, I did!

In 1844, the people elected a president who promised to expand the country even further. James K. Polk was ready to fight Mexico to get Texas and California, and he would throw a fight with England into the mix to get Oregon. Fortunately, he settled the Oregon question by splitting the difference with the Brits, satisfying himself with owning Oregon up to the forty-ninth parallel. Then he provoked a war with Mexico. Many young men from Hannibal went off to fight in the

Mexican War because it was a chance for adventure and a chance to join the great enterprise of expanding the country to the Pacific Ocean. I was only twelve, so I stayed home.

The war went well for the United States, and we got California and made Mexico throw all the land between California and Texas into the bargain as well. Some yahoos even wanted Polk to take over *all* of Mexico, but he wisely declined. Now there seemed to be only two questions: How quickly could we settle California? What goodies would we find there? Very few people were asking the tough question: Would slavery be allowed in the new land we had taken from the hapless Mexicans?

At first, it was all about gold. A guy in California found some nuggets in a stream and the next thing you knew, thousands of people were coming through Missouri on their way to the California gold fields. The prospectors of 1849 (the 49ers) filled the territory up pretty fast, and, suddenly, California had a large enough population (sixty thousand souls) to become a state.

I went to California to look for gold long after the '49 rush was over, but even when I got there twelve years later, it was a rough place. There were drunks, swindlers, thieves, and desperados of all descriptions, all looking to take your money. I wrote a book about my experiences out there called *Roughing It*.

When the Californians applied for statehood in 1850, they wanted to be a free state, not because they hated slavery, but because they hated Negroes, and they didn't want any around, slave or free. Nice folks, those Californians, all of them. In Congress, the Southerners declared that their states would leave the Union (secede!) if slavery were not allowed into California. So there it was, a full-blown crisis, and we hadn't even had time to count the gold yet.

In those days, whenever we had a crisis, we all turned to Henry Clay, the great senator from Kentucky, to come up with a way we could keep from killing each other. Poor old Henry was getting on in years, but fortunately he still had most of his marbles and was able to come up with yet another compromise. His so-called Compromise of 1850 made California a free state, which sent the southern congressmen into catatonic fits, but he gave them a strong federal fugitive slave law requiring all Americans, even Northerners, to return runaway slaves, and the Southerners took their prize and declared themselves mollified.

All would have been well except that the people of the North refused to obey the Fugitive Slave Law. Instead of returning runaways as the law required, they acted like Huck Finn with Jim and helped the slaves to escape. Southerners felt they were being swindled out of the one valuable thing they got in the compromise, and they were ripping mad.

Then, in 1852, Harriet Beecher Stowe put out her book *Uncle Tom's Cabin*, and the South got even madder. The story ends with the villainous slave owner Simon Legree ordering his overseer to whip the slave, poor saintly Tom, to death. Southerners were totally outraged at this portrayal of slavery. Years later, Harriet lived next door to me in Hartford, so I got to know her. I never met a kinder or gentler person in my life. It was hard to believe she was the one who caused such a fuss.

For the rest of the decade it seemed as though every year brought a new outrage that ratcheted up the tension between the North and the South.

In 1854, Senator Stephen Douglas from Illinois opened up Kansas and Nebraska to settlement. That wouldn't have been a problem except that he repealed the 36°30' line that kept slavery south of Missouri. Douglas' law opened new lands for slavery and Northerners were outraged.

In 1855, Northerners who oppose the extension of slavery into Kansas formed the Republican Party, which opposed slavery in the territories. The existence of a political party that wanted to deny them the right to bring their "property" anywhere they pleased really upset Southerners, and they were outraged.

In 1856, settlers in Kansas from the North and South began killing each other in a fight over what kind of state Kansas would be: slave or free.

The territory became known as Bleeding Kansas. Both Northerners and Southerners were outraged.

In 1857, the Supreme Court declared that slavery could not be banned from the federal territories because slaves were property. This seemed to open the way for the court to rule that all states, even northern ones, would have to allow slavery. The North was outraged.

In 1859, a Northerner named John Brown raided the arsenal at Harper's Ferry, Virginia, presumably to get guns for a slave revolt. Even though Brown was captured and hanged, the South was outraged.

By 1860, outrage was very fashionable.

Then, in the minds of Southerners, came the ultimate outrage. Abraham Lincoln, a Republican who wanted to keep slavery out of the territories, won the presidency without a single southern vote. Now many Southerners were more than outraged; they were ready to leave the Union and fight a war for their independence. South Carolina led the way, as she always did. Those fanatical slave owners in South Carolina had been threatening to secede for thirty years and now they saw their chance to actually do it and bring many other slave states along with them. By the time Lincoln took office, seven slave states had seceded. They had declared themselves the Confederate States of America; they had written a constitution; they had chosen Jefferson Davis as their president; and they had established their capital at Montgomery, Alabama.

When Lincoln sent ships to resupply Fort Sumter in Charleston harbor, the Confederacy fired on the fort. Lincoln called for volunteers to form a Union Army to put down the southern rebellion; with that, four more slave states joined the Confederacy. The South defiantly moved its capital to Richmond, Virginia, just ninety miles south of Washington. Now the fight everyone had been dreading for fifty years was on. Many political leaders had predicted that if war came between the North and the South, it would be very bloody. The Civil War fulfilled their predictions many times over. It was the bloodiest war of the nineteenth century, perhaps of all time.

I spent two weeks fighting in the Civil War … or, I should say, wandering the Missouri countryside with a gun during the Civil War. In the first weeks of the war, I enlisted in a local brigade for the Confederacy, and my cronies and I were on the prowl looking for action. When we heard news of a Yankee regiment nearby, we decided to quit soldiering. I lit out for the territories, and it was then that I went to the gold fields. I understand the leader of the Federal troops in the area at the time was Ulysses S. Grant. It was fortunate for the Union cause that I didn't stay and fight. I might have taken out the man who won the war for the Union before he even got started.

The Union forces got off to a slow start in the Civil War, failing in three attempts to take Richmond. Finally, Lincoln decided the Union could not win the war unless he freed the slaves. He needed to show the world, especially England, that the war was a noble fight for freedom that they should support. He also needed black soldiers. So, on January 1, 1863, he issued the Emancipation Proclamation, freeing the slaves in the Confederacy. Of course, the Confederates ignored his edict, but from that day forward, everywhere the Union armies drove the Confederate troops back, the slaves walked.

After four years, the South had run out of everything: ammunition, food, soldiers, and even their fighting spirit. Grant took Richmond, Lee surrendered at Appomattox, and it was all over. Meanwhile, Congress had passed the Thirteenth Amendment, which freed *all* the slaves. In April of 1865, it was clear that for the South, secession had been the worst idea imaginable. Slavery was dead, most of the southern cities were random piles of bricks, and plantations by the hundreds were charred ruins. To achieve this, over six hundred thousand men had been killed. Never in the history of man has a civilization fallen so far so fast.

Sadly, President Lincoln only had five days to savor the Union victory he had worked so hard to achieve. John Wilkes Booth murdered perhaps the greatest man who ever lived, and he left the country to lesser humanoids to piece it back together and to deal with the four million black souls who were now free but also without land, money, or education. For a few years, the Radical Republicans did a few things to help the freedmen. They passed the Fourteenth Amendment, which gave them citizenship and guaranteed their equal treatment under law, and the Fifteenth Amendment, which gave them the vote. They also denied former Confederates the right to vote for a while, and so some freedmen got to savor political power when they were elected to state legislatures and even to the U.S. Congress.

Of course, the whites really hated all this, and they planned for the day when they would get back in control and "put the Negro in his place." One thing they did in the 1860s was organize a band of thugs called the Ku Klux Klan. Men wearing white bed sheets would ride around at night and terrorize black folks who might have gotten *uppity*. The Klan was greatly feared until, in 1872, President Grant sent the Army down to put a stop to the terror, at least temporarily.

The whites in the South were not to be denied, however, and in the 1870s, they got the vote back and began figuring out clever ways to shut the blacks out of power. By the 1890s, blacks held no political offices and were very rarely even able to vote. Literacy tests, poll taxes, and outright fear of violence kept most blacks away from the polls. It was a white man's country once again.

Meanwhile, every southern state passed segregation laws (Jim Crow laws), which required separate facilities for blacks in all public places: railroad cars, schools, restaurants, hotels, etc. In 1896, the Supreme Court said that these laws did not violate the equality provisions of the Fourteenth Amendment because the facilities offered to blacks were "separate, but equal." The separate but equal doctrine was a complete fraud, of course, but most whites bought it and blacks knew they had no choice but to accept it. In my memory, no black person ever fought back against abuse and went on to live a long and happy life.

To compound the losses the South suffered during the war, Congress passed two laws the South had opposed for years. Southern congressmen had gone with their states into secession, so while the cats were away, the mice played, so to speak. The northern congressmen passed the Pacific Railway Act to build a transcontinental railroad from Omaha, Nebraska, to Sacramento, California. This was the northern route the Southerners had always opposed, but they had lost their vote by seceding, so there it was. When the war ended, work on the railroad proceeded rapidly, and by 1869, it was finished. It was now possible to travel from New York to California by rail in a week. When I went to the gold fields in 1861, I went by stagecoach, and it took over a month of bone rattling torture to get there.

Congress also passed the Homestead Act, which offered one hundred sixty acres of land to anyone who would stake a claim, build a house on it, and farm it for five years. The goal was to populate the West, and within a few years, thousands of homesteaders were moving out onto the prairies to stake their claims. Civilization was on the march.

Of course, the American Indians were directly in the path of this progress and their final demise was assured. They had a brief moment of success when Chief Sitting Bull's warriors wiped out Custer and his men at the Battle of the Little Bighorn in 1876, but, for the most part, they were slaughtered by the thousands and their buffalo were decimated. By the end of the century, the poor devils were shunted onto reservations set up on the poorest land in the country.

As the nation's Indian and black populations slid down into oblivion, the country as a whole surged forward as never before. The war had spurred the creation of large industrial factories to make war materials, and now those factories were poised to provide consumer goods and make many people prosperous. Simultaneously, huge numbers of immigrants were arriving every day, and those people would provide the labor the factories would need. Amassing huge fortunes, or trying to, was the order of the day, and a few people did become obscenely rich.

I wrote a novel about the people who were trying to make big money, and I called it *The Gilded Age*. A gilded object is something that is basically ugly, but it is covered with a gold paint, a gild, that makes it look good. The gild in the decades after the Civil War was the upper class society, with their fine mansions, stylish clothes, and genteel manners. The base material underneath was the abject poverty and the political corruption that was so rampant during those years. In my view, much of the gross inequality of wealth was due to the greed and selfishness of the business tycoons. In an open letter I wrote to Cornelius Vanderbilt, the plutocrat who made a fortune in steamboats and railroads, I said, "All I wish to urge upon you now is that you crush out your native instincts and go and do something worthy of praise; go and do something you need not blush to see in print."

The big business tycoons were not necessarily bad people, although I don't have much good to say about a few of them, such as Vanderbilt and Jay Gould. They were just unable to really feel for the plight of the millions of people who made it possible for them to be where they were. Andrew Carnegie was a good friend of mine. As a lad, he worked in a textile mill and he built his fortune through hard work and clever management of his steel mills. But by the time he was very wealthy— he sold his steel company for $400 million—I don't think he could remember at all what it had been like to be putting in twelve-hour days, six days a week, doing hard physical labor, for just pennies a day. Once he became part of the gild, he thought everyone else should be able to do what he did, unless they were too stupid or lazy. And Carnegie was one of the nicer tycoons! He gave away most of his fortune to libraries, other public foundations, and schools.

The workers who toiled in the factories during the Gilded Age were a sorry lot. Twelve-hour days, six-day weeks, miserable pay, and dangerous and filthy work conditions were all standard. Almost every attempt by workers to unionize and go on strike for improvements met with bitter defeat. The employers held all the cards. So when Carnegie's steel workers struck at Homestead in 1892, the state militia came in and the strike and the union were busted. When George Pullman's workers went on strike in 1894, President Cleveland sent in the Army, the strike was crushed, and the leaders were thrown in jail. The public saw strikers as terrorists and outlaws; the government acted accordingly.

By 1896, big businessmen were securely in charge. Farmers in the Midwest formed the Populist Party to try to elevate the poor and lower class people, and they put forth several ideas to accomplish that. They wanted to have the government coin silver, as well as gold, for money (free and unlimited coinage of silver) so there would be more money available, and they wanted to have the government take over the railroads so farmers would no longer be at the mercy of men like Vanderbilt, who only cared about profits. But their ideas seemed too radical to most voters and they were never able to get very many of their people into office.

William Jennings Bryan took up their cause of free silver at the Democratic convention in 1896 and ran for president on a *free silver* platform, but as great an orator as he was, he was not able to defeat the big money that pushed Bill McKinley and the Republicans into power that year.

McKinley and the Republicans, and quite a few Democrats, were keen on expanding our nation's borders beyond our natural boundaries. It wasn't enough that we had pushed our way to the Pacific, that we had given the Indians a nasty thrashing and pushed them onto reservations, and that we now controlled millions of square miles of land that we could never settle in a hundred years. No, now they wanted to expand across the oceans, to Cuba and Puerto Rico in the Caribbean, to Hawaii and the Philippines in the Pacific, and even further if they got the chance. In 1898, we fought a war with Spain, a splendid little war that lasted four months, netted us most of Spain's empire, and made Teddy Roosevelt a hero who would be president. The dreams of the imperialists, those who wanted to take over distant territories, were realized. Now we could civilize and Christianize the backward natives and take their resources when they weren't looking. I was against it. It contradicted everything we supposedly stood for and it led to the unholy slaughter of innocent people. I was an anti-imperialist and proud of it.

Of course, by 1900, no one was listening to me anymore. The country was changing faster than an old geezer like me could comprehend. When I was a kid, the telegraph that sent messages by Morse code was the wonder of the age, and railroad locomotives could travel at the unheard of speed of twenty miles per hour. As an old man, I saw people talking on the telephone to other people hundreds of miles away and trains moving at sixty miles an hour. God only knows what the new century, the twentieth century, will bring. But it is not my century, and all I can do is wish it well. I will now take my leave and turn you over to Alice. Alice is Teddy Roosevelt's daughter, and let me tell you, she is quite a handful. She's a free spirit who says and does whatever she takes a mind to. Teddy once said, "I can run the country or I can control Alice, but I can't do both." Enjoy your time with Alice; most everyone does.

CHAPTER III

WHAT HAPPENED IN THE YEARS 1901-1961

AS TOLD BY ALICE ROOSEVELT

Alice Roosevelt was born in 1884 to Alice Hathaway Lee Roosevelt and her husband, Theodore. Two days later, baby Alice's mother died. It was Valentine's Day, and Theodore Roosevelt was devastated. In the same house, his mother also died on the same day. For the first two years of his daughter's life, Theodore was out in Dakota Territory living the life of a rancher and trying to get over his grief. When he returned, he remarried and had five more children. Alice, consequently, was a bit of an outsider, felt herself to be an outsider, and became a teenage rebel when she was seventeen and her father became president. After flirting with many suitors—the men flocked to her because she was very vivacious and quite pretty—she finally married Congressman Nicholas Longworth in a White House wedding. Her marriage only slowed her down a little. She spent the next seventy-four years as one of Washington's leading social figures. She lived until 1980. Right to the end, she could always be counted on for a wisecrack or a pithy saying that would reveal the truth about a person in an amusing way.

n 1901, my father, Theodore Roosevelt, became president after an anarchist assassin shot poor William McKinley. I was very proud of the way Father handled the situation. He was careful not to get too excited about being president and played a subdued role in the ceremonies for McKinley. That must have been difficult for Father because he had such an ego. He always wanted to be the center of attention, the bride at every wedding and the corpse at every funeral.

When our family moved into the White House, it was quite a change for the staff. We had my half-brothers (four rambunctious boys), my half sister, Ethel, and me. The boys were constantly on the move, doing crazy things like bringing a pony onto the elevator. I was seventeen and couldn't wait to get out of the house and into the Washington social scene. I must admit, however, that living in the White House with all the servants and visiting dignitaries, a lot of them fine looking young men, was quite a hoot.

In spite of all the hubbub, Father was able to accomplish a great deal as president … a lot more, I must say, than any of the bearded stiffs who had come before him. On the domestic front, he was far more active than any president since Lincoln. Although he was a leader of the Republican Party, he began to call himself a progressive, a political person who believes government should play an active role in helping the country progress toward more democracy, more equality, and a better standard of living for everyone. He mediated the coal strike and did not automatically take the side of the mine operators, as most presidents before him would have done. In the negotiations, he got a square deal for the miners. He took on the wealthy financier J.P. Morgan and used the Sherman Anti-Trust Act to break up his railroad monopoly. He got Congress to pass the Pure Food and Drug Act to make sure we all were not poisoned by what we ate, and the Hepburn Act, which gave the Interstate Commerce Commission real power to control what the railroad companies were doing.

He got these laws passed in 1906, the same year I got married to Nicholas Longworth. Naturally, Father had to stand next to Nicky and me in our wedding picture. I'm not sure what gave him more satisfaction that year, his new laws or getting me married off.

His most notable accomplishment, in my estimation, was his work for the conservation of natural resources. He set aside millions of acres of land for the national park system and stopped the rape of the environment by the commercial interests. In all these actions, he was trying to put the government on the side of the people.

Father's foreign policies were, shall we say, energetic. He got the Panamanians to revolt against Colombia so he could negotiate a treaty with an independent Panama for a canal zone across the isthmus. When that was accomplished, he proceeded to build the Panama Canal, and Father couldn't resist the urge to go down to Panama to watch the work and even take a try at operating a steam shovel. Of course, he had to have his picture taken wearing a white suit and sitting in the machine.

Because there was a chance the European powers might try to move forces into the Caribbean to collect debts owed to them, Father announced what became known as the Roosevelt Corollary to the Monroe Doctrine. Essentially, he proclaimed that any intervention in Latin America that needed to be done would be done by the United States. We, and no one else, would police Latin America. Latin Americans since then have resented this policy, but, realistically, some country had to keep order, and I'm sure, when it came right down to it, they fared better under us than they would have under any other country.

Theodore Roosevelt made his reputation in war, but he really did want peace. He won the Nobel Peace Prize in 1905 by mediating the war between Russia and Japan. In 1908, the last year of his term, he sent the United States Navy around the world on a mission of good will. Our warships, all painted white (they called it the Great White Fleet) made port in many different countries and, actually, may have done more than engender good will; they may have stirred envy and belligerence. The Japanese, in particular, took note of our power and resolved to match it.

That was going to be a problem for my distant cousin, Franklin, when he was president.

When Father chose not to run for another term in 1908 and went big game hunting in Africa instead, his old friend William Howard Taft won the presidency. Taft also considered himself a progressive, and he continued breaking up the large trusts; however, he started to undo some of the conservation work Father had done, so when Teddy came back from Africa, he decided to challenge Taft for the Republican presidential nomination. That resulted in a nasty fight between the two old friends. Father won most of the primary elections, but Taft had the Old Guard party people behind him, so he got the nomination. In a rage, feeling he'd been swindled, Father ran for president as a third party candidate. He called his party the Progressive, or Bull Moose Party. Unfortunately, Father's candidacy split the Republican vote and the Democratic candidate, Woodrow Wilson, won the election and took office in 1913. Any politician thinking of splitting his party and running for president as a third party candidate could learn a lesson from what Father did in 1912. As popular as he was, Father was only able to win six states.

I almost lost my father during the 1912 campaign. As he was getting out of a car to deliver a speech in Milwaukee, a deranged assassin shot him in the chest. The bullet passed through his glasses case in his pocket and a folded copy of his speech. Fortunately, it was a long speech, so the wound was not mortal. Naturally, Father went through with his performance before allowing himself to be taken to the hospital. He could never pass up the chance to prove his bravery and be the drama king.

By this time, my cousin Eleanor Roosevelt had married a distant cousin of ours, Franklin Roosevelt. Yes, she was Eleanor Roosevelt Roosevelt, and Father joked that we liked to keep the name in the family. Wilson appointed Franklin to be Assistant Secretary of the Navy, a position Father had once held. Franklin, of course, was part of the Upstate New

York Roosevelts and was a Democrat. The two branches of the Roosevelt family were really very different.

Wilson continued the Progressive Movement by signing the Clayton Anti-Trust Act to outlaw monopolies, the Federal Trade Act to regulate truth in advertising, and the Federal Reserve Act to answer the age-old question, how do we best determine the money supply? I always wondered how it was possible to have too *much* money, but sometimes the Fed, as they called it, saw inflation going on and they raised interest rates and, thus, decreased the amount of money people could borrow.

The Wilson Administration couldn't stay focused on domestic legislation for long because there was a huge war going on in Europe. We immediately declared neutrality, as we always did, and President Wilson asked us to be neutral in thought as well as in action. For two years, we stayed out of the terrible fighting that was going on between the Central Powers (Germany and Austria-Hungary) and the Allied Powers (Britain, France, and Russia). It wasn't easy. In 1915, the Germans torpedoed a British passenger liner, the Lusitania, and one-hundred twenty-eight Americans drowned. Wilson protested against this violation of our rights as neutrals and eventually Germany apologized and pledged not to sink unarmed passenger ships. Wilson was able to get reelected using the slogan "He kept us out of war."

Then, in 1917, Germany resumed unrestricted submarine warfare, German subs sunk several American merchant ships, and Wilson was compelled to ask Congress to declare war. The American Expeditionary Force that landed in France in June of 1917 was the first American force ever to fight in Europe. Waging war as a separate unit rather than combining with the British and French forces that were already in the trenches, our troops distinguished themselves in several battles and succeeded in turning the tide of the war against the Germans.

Our family suffered a grievous loss in the final months of the war. My half-brother Quentin, who was a pilot, was shot down over France and killed. My father, who at long last saw the awful suffering that war causes, was so heartbroken that he died four months later.

On November 11, 1918, Germany signed an armistice, and the long, terrible war was over. The deadly new weapons—machine guns, poison gas, tanks, airplanes, and long-range artillery—and the horrific trench warfare tortured President Wilson, and he was determined to see that this would be the "war to end all wars." To that end, he went personally to Europe to negotiate the final peace treaty. He was armed with his fourteen-point plan for a "just and lasting peace." Unfortunately for Wilson, our British and French allies were in no mood for a treaty that would be lenient on the Germans. The Treaty of Versailles that resulted from their negotiations required Germany to give up its colonies, cede several thousand square miles of territory to its neighbors, admit guilt for starting the war, pay billions of dollars in reparations, and disarm. Only Wilson's plan for a League of Nations made it into the treaty, but the president thought this might be enough to make the treaty workable if the United States would join.

Wilson's Republican opponents in the Senate, led by Henry Cabot Lodge, wanted a guarantee that the United States would not be dragged into any military action without congressional approval. This seemed to me to be eminently reasonable. A very good friend of mine, Senator William Borah of Idaho, supported Lodge in opposing the treaty unless it contained the Lodge proposals. Wilson was bullheaded and refused to accept this condition, and the treaty went down in the Senate. We never signed the treaty and we never joined the League of Nations. During the next twenty years, Germany suffered dismay and depression, Hitler ultimately seized power, and he vowed to gain revenge on the allies. The League and the former allies were ineffectual, to say the least. By the mid-1930s, a rejuvenated Germany was ready to launch another war.

Meanwhile, here in the United States, we went through a period right after the war known as the Red Scare. The communists (Reds) had taken over in Russia, there were active communist movements in other European countries, and we were afraid there were Reds in our own country as well. On September 16, 1920, a bomb planted in a truck exploded in front of the offices of J.P. Morgan and Company on Wall Street. The horrific explosion killed thirty-eight people and rocked the whole financial district. Investigators were never able to fix the blame, but they believed the bomb was the work of communists. Coming as it did, just a year after other bombings, most notably an explosion at the home of Attorney General A. Mitchell Palmer, this event convinced many of us that there were radical agitators in our midst who would stop at nothing to overthrow our capitalist system and our government.

Many believed the Reds were coming into our country from southern and eastern Europe, particularly Italy and Russia. Adding fuel to this belief was the case of Nicola Sacco and Bartolomeo Vanzetti, who went on trial in 1921 for the murder of a guard and a payroll master during a robbery at a shoe factory in Braintree, Massachusetts. Because they were known to be radical socialists, Sacco and Vanzetti did not get justice. The judge was reported as saying, "Those anarchist bastards, of course they're guilty." The jury took only a few hours to convict the two men and they were sentenced to die in the electric chair. Six years of appeals followed, but, finally, in 1927, they were executed.

In the atmosphere created by the Red Scare and the Sacco and Vanzetti case, Congress passed new immigration laws in 1921 and 1924. These laws pointedly limited immigration from Italy and eastern European countries. It seems it only takes a couple of incidents to dim the light in Lady Liberty's torch.

Corresponding to the anti-immigrant movement was the incredible growth of the new Ku Klux Klan during the twenties. Men in this organization looked ridiculous in their pointy-headed bed sheets, but they terrified black people when they rode at night to beat up or even kill "uppity niggers." I wished my father were still president. For all his faults, he would have known what to do about the Ku Klux Klan.

The country pulled back from the world's problems during the twenties and focused on enjoying our prosperity here at home. Republican administrations under Harding, Coolidge, and Hoover gave full rein to laissez-faire capitalism. Business boomed and it seemed like everyone was having a good time. Jazz music, the Charleston dance craze, women wearing short skirts, and people drinking alcohol in blatant disregard of prohibition all symbolized the new era. It felt to me like the world had finally caught up to me. Recently invented appliances such as radios, washing machines, and refrigerators, not to mention the automobile, were making life easier and giving people more time to live it up. We called it the Roaring Twenties, and it seemed as if the party would go on forever. I, for one, hoped it would.

There were, unfortunately, many people who could not join the party. Farmers were suffering from low prices for their crops and were experiencing their own economic depression long before the general depression hit in the 1930s. I could never have made it as a farmer, although I would have liked the moonshine part.

My cousin Eleanor and her husband, Franklin, were certainly not poor, but they had their own problem during the twenties and it was a big one. In 1921, Franklin came down with infantile paralysis (polio), which took away his ability to walk. He and Eleanor spent most of the twenties working on his rehabilitation, to get him to the point where he could stand on his own and perform a very slow form of walking with his leg braces and crutches. By the end of the decade, he was ready to reenter political life, and just in time.

In 1928, Franklin ran for governor of New York and won. He was following in the footsteps of my father, who had also been governor of New York. The parallels in their careers were striking, but, of course, Franklin had no heroic military adventures in Cuba in his resume like Father had.

In 1929, the Stock Market Crash wiped out many banks and the savings of millions of people. The country fell into a deep economic depression, which led to emotional depression, as millions of people lost their jobs, their farms, their homes, and their hope. By 1932, the country was on the brink of total collapse. President Hoover seemed at a loss as to what to do about the problem. Franklin got the nomination of the Democratic Party to run against Hoover, and at the convention, he promised a New Deal for the American people. The election was a choice between the dour Hoover, whom many people blamed for the economic mess in which the country found itself, and FDR, who had a flamboyant style and ready smile that people loved. The people wanted to see what his New Deal would bring, so they elected him in a landslide.

Inauguration day was gloomy and rainy, and I sensed the desperation of the people. They were hanging on to the new president's every word for signs of hope. Cousin Franklin did not disappoint. "The only thing we have to fear is fear itself!" he said in his clear, ringing voice. The people responded, and the New Deal was off and running.

Franklin's approach was very pragmatic; he would try anything to see if it worked. During his first one hundred days in office, he asked Congress to pass over a dozen pieces of major legislation. There were jobs programs, such as the Civilian Conservation Corps (CCC), the Public Works Administration (PWA), and the Civil Works Administration (CWA). There was a whole new electric power operation for the South called the Tennessee Valley Authority (TVA). There were reform programs such as the National Industrial Recovery Act (NIRA), with its codes for fair competition and its blue eagle symbol. And there were emergency relief programs to give federal money to the desperately poor and unemployed. Franklin went on the radio to give fireside chats to explain his programs to the people. At last, everyone had the feeling that the president cared about them and that his government was doing something to fix the problems.

For many people, the New Deal and the Republican opposition to it laid the foundation for the debates between liberals and conservatives that were to dominate political discourse for years to come. That view is a little simplistic because, as I said, Franklin would try anything, regardless of the label it had on it, if it would work; however, it is mostly accurate to say that the new dealers were liberals who favored strong action by the federal government to help the working and lower classes, even if that meant direct relief payments. The Republican opponents of the New Deal were conservatives who believed the economy should rely on private enterprise and poor people should improve their condition through their own efforts. Laborers and labor unions tended to favor the liberals while big business people favored the conservatives.

I personally believed that Franklin was going off the deep end with his spending and make-work programs. His wife, Eleanor, however, was fully supportive and even went around the country to report back to him on how the New Deal programs were going. Her only criticism of what Franklin was doing was that he did not take specific steps to relieve the suffering of the Negro people in the South. She thought he should push for a federal anti-lynching law, but he told her that doing so would cost him southern support for his other programs, and he couldn't afford to lose those votes. "I sympathize with your view," he told Eleanor, "but we have to play the game skillfully or we won't get anything for anybody." Poor Eleanor; she was so earnest, but so impractical. She did, however, have courage—more than he did, I'm afraid. Franklin was one-third mush and two-thirds Eleanor.

In spite of FDR's lack of effort on civil rights, the African-American people in the country shifted their allegiance away from the party that had set them free—the Republican Party—and to the party that had once fought to keep them as slaves but now offered them economic hope, the Democratic Party. It took another generation for white Southerners to realize it was the Republican Party, rather than the Democratic Party, which they had supported with a vengeance for over one hundred years, that best represented their conservative views on a strong military, state power over federal power, and limited federal government interference with race relations.

The Depression was very stubborn and the New Deal only made a dent in the unemployment. There were several demagogues in the land, most notably Senator Huey Long of Louisiana, who were leading movements to overthrow the system and adopt very drastic measures.

Long's program, Share Our Wealth, called for taxing inherited fortunes at one hundred percent and guaranteeing everyone an income of a thousand dollars. He was a dangerous man and he was gaining quite a large following. By 1935, Franklin felt compelled to spend even more federal money on work projects, so he created the Works Progress Administration (WPA) to spend eight billion dollars on various projects across the country. He also started the Social Security system to provide benefits to people who were old or disabled. These programs, along with what he had done earlier, as well as his charming personality, got FDR reelected by a landslide in 1936. He won every state in the country except for Maine and Vermont!

At that point, I think Cousin Franklin's head got a little swollen. He probably thought they should be preparing a place for him on Mount Rushmore. He was so egocentric that he thought Congress would pass anything he asked them to.

The Supreme Court had been annoying him for years by declaring some of his most important laws unconstitutional. In 1937, fresh off his electoral hurrah, he proposed a court reform bill. This law would allow him to appoint six new justices to the court, bringing the total number of justices to fifteen. This was a radical proposal, and for once, Franklin had miscalculated. He didn't understand the loyalty many congressmen had to the principle of checks and balances. Even members of his own Democratic Party didn't want the president to have both the Congress and the court in his hip pocket. They called his bill "court packing" and voted it down. Poor Cousin Franklin! He had never tasted defeat before, and it was bitter!

By the end of the decade, after nine years of hard times, things were finally starting to look better. But that was hardly because of FDR's expensive programs; it was because we were gearing up for another war. Actually, come to think of it, war itself (or preparation for it) is just another expensive government program that makes jobs for people.

Adolph Hitler took power in Germany just six weeks before FDR took the oath of office in 1933. While Franklin was putting his New Deal in place, Hitler was building up Germany's armed forces in violation of the Versailles Treaty. In 1938, he took over Austria and then Czechoslovakia with no opposition from the British or French. Franklin sensed the danger, but Congress passed neutrality laws to make sure we stayed out of any new war, and Franklin felt compelled to sign them because the people were heartily opposed to any involvement in a European conflict. They had gotten into the fighting in 1917 and they were not in the mood to fight again.

When Germany invaded France and Britain and France declared war on Germany, Franklin had no choice but to stay neutral, even though he despised Hitler and thought Germany was a true menace. He did get Congress to allow Britain and France to buy weapons and carry them home in their own ships as a *cash and carry* program.

The year 1940 was probably the most horrible year the world has ever seen. Hitler conquered most of Europe, including France, and began massive air raids over London in preparation for invading Britain. The British people were stalwart as they endured the German blitz, but it was problematic how long they could hold out. Meanwhile, the Japanese, who had invaded China in 1937, were extending their conquests not only in China but in French Indo-China as well. With the world in flames, Franklin believed he should stay on the job, and he was reelected to a third term in the fall of 1940, the first time any president had ever been elected three times. I thought it was a bit egocentric of Franklin to think the country could not go on without him. I guess my father did not have a monopoly on huge egos.

In 1941, to keep Britain from going under, Franklin came up with the Lend-Lease idea. We would simply lend or lease weapons and equipment to any country fighting Hitler and they could pay us back later. Good luck with that! The isolationists, led by Charles Lindbergh, who still did not want to get involved, screamed in outrage, but Franklin got the Lend-Lease Bill passed and we became the arsenal of democracy.

Finally, on December 7, 1941, after we had cut off shipments of steel and oil and had frozen their assets in American banks, the Japanese started war with us by attacking our naval base at Pearl Harbor. Franklin was totally shocked and was barely able to pull himself together enough to give a rousing speech to Congress the next day, asking for a declaration of war. Three days later, Hitler declared war on us, and so we were in it at last.

World War II was a global war. We fought the Germans on the sands of North Africa, in the mountains of Italy, on the beaches of Normandy, in the snows of Belgium, and in the streets of European villages, all the way to Berlin. We fought the Japanese in New Guinea, Guadalcanal, the Solomon Islands, the Philippines, Iwo Jima, and on Okinawa, the doorstep of Japan itself. Eleanor went all over the world wearing that silly khaki uniform and ridiculous hat with the big visor. She visited our troops in places as far flung as islands in the Pacific and England.

The war sapped Cousin Franklin's health, and by 1944, when he got reelected to yet another term, he was at death's door. Those of us who knew him could see it. He died on April 12, 1945, just a few weeks before Germany surrendered. His passing left the handling of the war's conclusion to his vice president, Harry Truman.

As the war was drawing to a close in 1945, two horrors sucked the joy out of all of us. One was the horrendous death camps our soldiers were liberating as they drove the Nazis back in Europe. The ghastly rumors we had been hearing for years about mass extermination and crematoriums were true. Hitler and his henchmen had tried to eliminate the entire Jewish population from Europe, and they had come awfully close to succeeding. Six million people were murdered in the camps and many thousands more were sick and emaciated when our soldiers arrived. After the war, the United Nations put the Nazi leaders (those who were still living) on trial in Nuremberg, Germany, for war crimes. The hunt for the Nazis who led the Holocaust, as the horrors came to be called, will go on as long as there is the slightest chance any of the perpetrators is still alive.

The other horror was the complete annihilation of the Japanese cities Hiroshima and Nagasaki. Franklin Roosevelt had started atomic bomb research—the Manhattan Project—back in 1939, when Albert Einstein warned him that the Germans were at work developing an atom bomb. When Cousin Franklin died and Harry Truman became president, he was shocked to find out there was such a bomb and that it was nearly ready for use. In July of 1945, Germany had surrendered and Truman was in Potsdam, Germany, holding meetings with Churchill and Stalin when he got the news that the bomb had been successfully tested in New Mexico. He issued a statement to the Japanese government warning them to surrender or they would suffer the destruction that would be wrought by a very powerful new weapon. The Japanese did not respond to the president's "Potsdam Declaration," so, on August 6, an American plane dropped an atomic bomb on the city of Hiroshima. The city was incinerated and more than one hundred thousand people died. When the Japanese did not surrender, another bomb was dropped on Nagasaki, killing another seventy thousand civilians. On August 14, the Japanese government finally agreed to surrender unconditionally and the war was finally over.

There has been a lot of controversy over Truman's decision to use the bomb. I personally think he had to end the war quickly and save thousands of lives. I always remember what one GI said after he returned from the war in the Pacific: "We used to pray we'd see the Golden Gate in '48. Thanks to the bomb, we're home alive in '45!"

One of the most visionary things Cousin Franklin did during the war was get Congress to pass the Serviceman's Readjustment Act, usually referred to as the G.I. Bill of Rights or G.I Bill. Once again he was committing billions of federal dollars to programs, but these dollars were going to soldiers who were returning from the war. They would be rewarded for their service by getting money for education, or to start a new business, or to buy a new home. This was not wasted money. It was a great investment in the future because we would head into the post-war world with an educated and motivated workforce of men and women who had already proven their willingness to work hard and serve their country. Even Republicans were willing to support this expensive program because it would pay big dividends in the future. It is one of Franklin Roosevelt's greatest legacies.

Just before Franklin died, he was working on his proposal to create a new world peace organization. President Truman took up the cause and the new United Nations (UN) was set up. I doubt that it will be any more effective than the League of Nations was, but this time we would be a member and even have the headquarters located in New York. I noted that the UN legislation included reference to congressional approval for United States involvement in UN action, the same kind of authority Senator Lodge and my lover, *er*, friend, Senator Borah wanted to include in the League of Nations bill in 1920. Franklin and Harry Truman did not repeat Wilson's mistake.

After the war, we found ourselves with a new enemy. The Soviet Union, having driven the Nazis out of Eastern Europe, installed communist governments in those countries and planted communist movements in countries of Western Europe as well. President Truman's response was to adopt a policy of containment, whereby we would move to prevent the spread of communism to any country threatened by a communist takeover either from an attack by an outside force or a movement within its borders. In 1947, he asked Congress to create a program proposed by Secretary of State George Marshall of aid to war-torn Europe. This Marshall Plan helped restore the economies of Western Europe so they could stave off communist movements. When the Russians blockaded West Berlin, Truman ordered a round-the-clock airlift of supplies to the beleaguered city that lasted a year and prevented the Soviets from taking over.

In the midst of dealing with this new Cold War with Russia, Truman ran for election to the presidency in his own right. His chances of winning seemed almost hopeless. People couldn't forgive him for not being Franklin Roosevelt, and there was a lot of talk about corruption in his administration. The Republican candidate, Governor Thomas Dewey of New York, was a dapper man with a black mustache. I opined that he looked like the little groom they put next to the bride on wedding cakes. That got quite a laugh, but all the pollsters had Dewey winning the election by at least ten percentage points. Despite the polls, Truman campaigned like a demon, lambasted the Republicans at every railroad stop, and was called Give 'em hell Harry. The actual election results knocked all of the pollsters on their butts. Truman won handily in the biggest upset in presidential election history.

After the election, in 1949, Truman formalized containment in Europe by organizing NATO, the North Atlantic Treaty Organization, a treaty that requires the signatories—the nations of Western Europe, Canada, and the United States—to go to war to defend any member who falls under attack. This was the first time our country had ever committed itself to defending a whole list of countries before any war had even started, and I believed Mr. Truman was taking a huge step into the unknown. Now even an attack on Iceland would have us at war.

By 1950, our defensive perimeter in Europe was very clear. In Asia it was not clear at all. In 1949, the communist leader Mao Zedong won the civil war against Chiang Kai-Shek and took power. That was a big blow to containment, and it wasn't clear which countries in Asia we would fight to protect. The Russians had installed a communist government in North Korea. If it attempted to cross the thirty-eighth parallel (the dividing line between North and South Korea) and take over South Korea, would the United States respond? The communists decided to find out.

On June 25, 1950, North Korea attacked South Korea and quickly overran Seoul, the capital city. President Truman ordered American troops into Korea from where they were stationed on occupation duty in Japan. The UN Security Council voted to send a United Nations force to defend South Korea, and the UN force was all under the command of the American General, Douglas MacArthur. Truman saw the North Korean attack as a clear cut case of containment; if we allowed the communists to take this small country that would be as ill-advised as it was to allow Hitler to take Czechoslovakia in 1938. So here it was … war again.

At first, the war went badly, and the South Korean and UN forces were almost driven into the sea at Pusan on the southern tip of the Korean peninsula. MacArthur turned the situation around by brazenly landing a force at Inchon, well behind the North Korean lines, and launching a counter attack from Pusan that drove the communists out of the South in a few days. The UN and President Truman authorized the general to go after the North Korean Army into North Korea, but not to get too close to the Chinese border. Just when it seemed as though the war would be over by Christmas, the Chinese came in with two hundred fifty thousand troops and drove MacArthur all the way back to the thirty-eighth parallel.

At this point, we found out what my cousin, Franklin, meant when he said Douglas MacArthur was the most dangerous man in America. MacArthur wanted to bomb Chinese bases north of the Yalu River (the boundary between Korea and China), expand the war into China, and even use atomic bombs. The president disagreed. He did not want a third world war with China and/or the Soviet Union. He ordered MacArthur to keep his opinions to himself, but MacArthur went public with his criticisms of his commander-in-chief. By April of 1951, Truman believed he had no choice but to remove MacArthur from his command.

MacArthur came back to the United States as a hero to sixty percent of the people. He toured the country proclaiming the righteousness of his point of view and saying time and time again, "There is no substitute for victory." Fortunately, cooler heads prevailed, the people began to see how dangerous MacArthur's policy could be, and the old general finally faded away.

Meanwhile the war in Korea dragged on and settled into a stalemate along a line very close to the original thirty-eighth parallel line. In 1952, Dwight D. Eisenhower, the man who had led our forces in Europe during the war, won the presidential election, partly on his promise to end the war in Korea. Eisenhower personally went to Korea and quickly realized there was no way to achieve victory without substantial increases in bombing and troop commitment. He sought a ceasefire to end the fighting and got one in July of 1953. Combat in Korea ended with an armistice that has remained in place in Korea ever since. We had lost more than twenty-two thousand men in combat, but we had met our responsibilities under the containment policy.

Eisenhower, the first Republican president since Hoover, proved to be competent but unremarkable. People associate his eight years in office (basically the 1950s) with peace and prosperity, and I suppose those years were pretty placid. Cousin Franklin's twelve years in office—his handling of the Depression and the world war—had left the country in good shape. Eisenhower's signature achievement was the Interstate Highway Act, which I always tell everyone was a bigger and more expensive public works project than anything Franklin ever proposed. There was a recession starting in 1957, and, basically, what Eisenhower did was to put the country to work with a huge New Deal type project.

Eisenhower's early years were marred by the headline grabbing antics of Senator Joe McCarthy of Wisconsin. McCarthy seemed to claim there were communists everywhere: in the State Department, in the Army, even under his own bed. I wouldn't know if any existed there because his was one bed I never visited. Anyway, his accusations were totally without foundation, and they reminded me of the Red Scare of 1920. The man was such a jerk that I had to put him in his place. At a party, he tried to call me Alice, and I told him the man who picked up my trash could call me Alice, but he, Joe McCarthy, could not. Finally, McCarthy made a fool of himself on television in the Army-McCarthy hearings, and we stopped hearing about him. However, the idea that there were communist agents everywhere persisted for the next ten to fifteen years.

Eisenhower's biggest failure, at least in the opinion of Cousin Eleanor, was the same as Cousin Franklin's: He didn't do enough to give the black population in our country hope. I disagree with Eleanor, as she was always a bit self-righteous and overly idealistic on this subject. Ike did have a civil rights record. It was an Eisenhower appointee to the Supreme Court, Chief Justice Earl Warren, who led the Court in its nine-zero *Brown* decision, striking down "separate but equal" in public schools. I don't think Eisenhower was entirely happy that Warren had decided the Brown case the way he did, but he went ahead and enforced the ruling. When Dr. Martin Luther King achieved national fame by leading a successful boycott against Montgomery, Alabama's segregated bus system, Eisenhower was very sympathetic to the movement and called his cabinet together to prepare civil rights legislation.

In 1957, Eisenhower signed a civil rights act. It wasn't a very potent piece of legislation, but it was the first civil rights act passed since the Era of Reconstruction. It stated that black citizens could appeal to a Civil Rights Commission if they felt their voting rights were being unconstitutionally denied. Ike knew he couldn't go too far with new laws at this point; the racial prejudices were too deeply ingrained. Even this mild law provoked a record-breaking filibuster by southern senators opposed to it.

That same year, when the governor of Arkansas used the National Guard to keep nine black students from integrating Little Rock Central High School, Eisenhower sent a thousand troops (the One Hundred First Airborne) into Little Rock to enforce the court's integration order. When Eisenhower decided to act, he always did so with overwhelming force. No white racist in Little Rock was about to challenge a thousand determined soldiers, bayonets at the ready, as they escorted the black students into the high school.

It is true that Ike did not deliver any major addresses on race relations, and he didn't use his popularity to push for further gains in civil rights. For these failings, I suppose he could be faulted, but I think Eleanor was too judgmental of him. Eisenhower actually did more for civil rights than her own husband did.

As the fifties drew to a close and the Eisenhower era was about to end, I, for one, was glad to see him go. Even I, an old lady, could see we needed young and vigorous leadership, and in the election of 1960, we were sure to get it either with the forty-seven-year-old vice president, Richard Nixon, or the young senator from Massachusetts, John F. Kennedy. As a lifelong Republican, I voted for Nixon, but I was not altogether unhappy to see the very handsome and energetic young Kennedy and his beautiful family move into the White House. Father was only forty-two when we moved into the White House after McKinley died, but at forty-three, JFK was the youngest man ever elected president.

It was like a fresh breeze had wafted across the country when John F. Kennedy took office in 1961. One sensational aspect of the new president was that he was the first Roman Catholic ever to be elected president. It was simple blind prejudice that made Americans oppose a Catholic president, but if you pinned them down for a specific reason, they would tell you they were afraid that if a Catholic were president, the pope would run the country. That was nonsense, of course, and Kennedy put the whole thing to rest by reminding people that no one asked him his religion when he served his country by putting his life in jeopardy as a soldier. Once Kennedy was elected, I began to wonder when the next barriers would be broken—perhaps a woman in the White House, or impossible to imagine, a black man?

Kennedy was not without his faults, however, and I must say I was a little dismayed at some of the things I was hearing about him. I was fond of holding social gatherings at my home on DuPont Circle, and I often entertained glitterati of all types: members of Congress, diplomats, and even presidents. I kept a cushion on my couch that was embroidered with the words "If you can't say something good about someone, sit right here by me." I was not kidding about that, and I heard all sorts of things about the whole lot of them. What I heard about the Kennedy men would make your hair stand on end. John Kennedy and his brothers were certainly, shall we say, interesting. I was too old to be invited to some of the White House pool parties; more's the pity.

I was a little disheartened by some of the events in John F. Kennedy's first year. He ordered an invasion of Cuba by an ill-prepared group of anti-Castro Cuban exiles in April 1961, and the whole thing was a flop. All of the invaders were killed or captured in the Bay of Pigs invasion, and our new president looked weak and ineffective. As if to take advantage of that, Nikita Khrushchev, the big, fat Russian dictator, ordered the construction of a wall around West Berlin in the summer of 1961. This actual embodiment of the Iron Curtain seemed to make the division of Germany permanent and radically heightened tensions between the world's two major powers. Things were about to get really tense, but I'll leave that story to the next person.

I lived for nearly a century and didn't check out until the year Ronald Reagan was elected president (I went from Grover Cleveland to Ronald Reagan!), but I've covered all the things that happened when I was in my glorious prime.

CHAPTER IV

WHAT HAPPENED IN THE YEARS 1962-2016

AS TOLD BY ROBERT MACDOUGALL

I was born in 1944 and grew up in the halcyon days of the 1950s. I remember Eisenhower as president and events such as the Little Rock School integration incident, but I don't remember events with clarity until about the time I started high school in 1959. I spent the sixties finishing high school, going to college at the University of Michigan, and beginning my teaching career. I saw the sixties as a young adult who disliked the conservative views of my parents, but who never flipped out and became a radicalized hippie. From 1966 to 2015, I taught history in several high schools and at a community college. Throughout that entire period, I tried to hold a balanced view of politics and the social issues of the times, largely because I always thought it was important to give my students all sides of the issues rather than indoctrinate them.

In 1962, I was a freshman at the University of Michigan. I had grown up in the prosperous and placid 1950s, but I do remember feeling some anxiety, even as a kid, about the possibility that the Russians would hit us with an atomic bomb, blow us all to bits, and cover the world with a blanket of deadly radiation. When the schools ran air raid drills with loud sirens and teachers shouted at you to crawl under your desks and put your arms over your head, it was understandable that we would all worry a bit. By the sixties, we all knew that the United States and Russia had missiles aimed at each other and that one missile could wipe out an entire city.

In October 1962, President Kennedy reported to the nation that the Russians were installing intermediate range nuclear missiles in Cuba, just ninety miles off the coast of Florida. All of us sitting in the dining hall of the dorm where we had assembled to hear the president's broadcast were terrified. The president told us he was ordering a blockade, or quarantine, of Cuba to prevent any further introduction of missiles; he demanded that Chairman Khrushchev remove the missiles that were already there; and he warned that an attack on any country in the Western Hemisphere would be regarded as an attack on the United States, requiring a nuclear response against the Soviet Union.

For the next several days, the country waited anxiously to see what the Russian response would be. We all knew Khrushchev was a volatile man with a hot temper and that an attempt by Russia to run the blockade or even a nuclear attack on the United States was a distinct possibility. Our first line of anxiety was removed when the Russian ships headed for Cuba turned back. Then, a few days later, when Khrushchev agreed to remove the missiles from Cuba in return for a U.S. pledge not to invade the island, the world breathed a collective sigh of relief. We had been to the brink and had not fallen into a war that would have incinerated the world. We all believed that Kennedy had gone eyeball to eyeball with Khrushchev, and Khrushchev had blinked. We did not know yet that Kennedy had also agreed to remove the missiles the United States had stationed in Turkey.

President Kennedy was suddenly elevated to the status of a great president and his popularity soared. For the next year, he was really on a roll. His good looks and beautiful family now had solid achievement to go with them. The newspapers and magazines were full of stories, replete with many photos, about the Kennedy White House being the land of Camelot, where everything was perfect. Of course, nothing is ever as good as it seems, and in due time we found out some of the seamy aspects of the Kennedy years: extra-marital sex, heavy drinking, and tensions between Jack and Jackie.

Kennedy's reputation, of course, could not rest on his handling of the Cuban Missile Crisis, and he had several other issues to deal with in 1963. In the South, Dr. Martin Luther King's peaceful protests against racial discrimination were meeting violent reactions from white counter-demonstrators and the police. On June 11, Kennedy went on television to announce he was sending to Congress civil rights legislation that would outlaw segregation and other forms of racial discrimination. That very night, just a few hours after the speech, Medgar Evers, a black civil rights leader in Jackson, Mississippi, was shot and killed in his driveway by a white racist who had been waiting in ambush across the street. (Assassin Byron De La Beckwith wasn't convicted until 1994. He avoided conviction for the murder because of hung juries for thirty years.)

Throughout the summer of 1963, the country debated the idea of federal civil rights legislation. The standard objection of southern conservatives was that states should have the right to determine their own social customs, and that no government should have the power to force a private businessman—hotel owner, restaurant manager, etc.—to serve people he objected to serving. In August, Dr. King and others staged a massive march on Washington to lobby for passage of Kennedy's bill. As thousands lined the reflecting pool in front of the Lincoln Memorial and millions watched on television, Dr. King delivered his *I Have a Dream* speech. The speech was very moving and it touched many of us. Most of us felt that momentum was building for passage of the Civil Rights Act; however, there was strong resistance in Congress, and as the fall wore on, it seemed as though little progress was being made toward getting the bill passed.

In foreign policy, Kennedy produced a major achievement when he got a nuclear test ban treaty with the Soviet Union. He gave a passionate speech for peace and a nuclear test ban on June 10 at American University, just a day before his televised address on civil rights legislation. Clearly, he was moving forward vigorously on all fronts. The treaty that emerged ended nuclear testing in the atmosphere and gave all of us some relief from the anxiety we had been feeling about fallout—radiation from nuclear explosions that was raining down on us all and causing cancer. Now all testing of nuclear bombs would be done underground.

Then there was the problem in Southeast Asia, in a country most of us had heard very little about, Vietnam. It seemed like a Korea-type situation, where communists in the north were trying to take over the south, and we had soldiers in the south to help the South Vietnamese fight off the Reds. Kennedy was reassuring when he said that "in the final analysis," it was their problem, the South Vietnamese against the communists. We could advise them and give them weapons and equipment, but they were the ones who had to win it or lose it. It did not seem to me at the time that this was going to be a war the United States would have to fight. I had recently registered for the draft, and I was not enthusiastic about the idea of being called up to go fight in the jungles of Southeast Asia.

As we passed the one-year anniversary of the Cuban Missile Crisis and headed toward Thanksgiving 1963, most of us were pretty sure Kennedy would be reelected the following year. He had a decent record of achievement to go along with his charisma, so it seemed like just a precaution Kennedy was taking when he went to Dallas in late November to meet with Democratic Party leaders, to make a few public appearances, and to make sure the Democrats stayed united and carried the state in 1964.

It was the biggest shock of our lives when we heard the news on Friday, November 22, that Kennedy had been shot to death while riding in a motorcade in Dallas. I may have been the last person on Earth to hear the news because I had locked myself in my dorm room at eleven in the morning to work like crazy on a major paper I had to finish by Thanksgiving break. I didn't emerge from my room until almost six o'clock and only then got the terrible news that people had been talking about for four hours. I staggered to the TV room to join the others watching the sad commentators tell the country that the Dallas police believed the assassin was Lee Harvey Oswald. Two days later, on Sunday afternoon, we were all watching when the police brought Oswald out to transfer him to another jail, and right before our eyes, a man named Jack Ruby, a Dallas nightclub owner, came up to the handcuffed Oswald and shot him in the stomach while the shocked police looked on. Oswald's sudden death deprived the police and the world from getting any information from him—he was still saying he didn't do it before Ruby killed him—and the door was opened to all kinds of conspiracy theories that persist to this day.

Looking back on the 1960s, it is clear now that the Kennedy assassination marked a turning point for most of us. It certainly marked an end to our innocence. I remember standing on the sidewalk in Ann Arbor the morning after the assassination and staring in disbelief at the newspaper I had just bought. Its giant headline read KENNEDY KILLED. From that day on, the world got messier. We got deeper into Vietnam, and it was very ugly. The Civil Rights Act passed—segregation was outlawed—but it didn't bring a new era of improved race relations; in fact, it seemed to usher in an era of intense racial conflict and tension. During the next several years, the relationship between the generations, baby boomers like me who were coming of age, and the older generation who had survived the depression and World War II, became strained and, in many cases, downright hostile.

In the summer of 1964, Lyndon Johnson, who had been elevated to the presidency when Kennedy died, responded to an attack by North Vietnamese gunboats on two of our ships in the Gulf of Tonkin, off the coast of North Vietnam, by asking Congress to pass a resolution authorizing the president to use military force to protect American interests in Southeast Asia. In a sense, he was asking for a blank check to increase our military commitment. Congress passed the Gulf of Tonkin Resolution by a wide margin (four hundred sixteen to zero in the House, eighty-eight to two in the Senate), and now Johnson had his green light to act.

In the presidential election of 1964, Republican candidate Barry Goldwater, a senator from Arizona, advocated stronger military action than what we were currently using in Vietnam. He even suggested using tactical nuclear weapons. The voters thought they were choosing between a very sober, rational policy in Vietnam (Johnson) and a policy of all-out war (Goldwater). Johnson won by a huge margin, sixty to forty percent, and it seemed as though the war in Vietnam would be a low-key, back burner affair.

Imagine our shock the next year when the United States began bombing North Vietnam and sending thousands of combat troops into the country. During the next three years, our troop levels kept escalating until, by 1968, we had more than five hundred thousand soldiers fighting in Vietnam. The war was very nasty and difficult to fight. The Vietcong—South Vietnamese communists—and the regular North Vietnamese troops used guerrilla tactics and often had the support of the local population; therefore, they could attack our forces by night and blend into the scenery as innocent peasants by day. The South Vietnamese government that we were propping up was corrupt and unpopular. North Vietnamese leader Ho Chi Minh was a communist, but the peasants didn't care; he looked like one of them, and they believed they could trust him. As the war slogged on, American casualties mounted, sometimes reaching a thousand in a week, and it seemed there was no end in sight.

By 1968, there was an active and growing anti-war movement protesting the war in Vietnam on college campuses and in the streets of major cities. The anti-war protesters kept their hair long and wore colorful clothing that looked outrageous to the older generation, who spat when they heard or said the word hippies. Occasionally the protesters wore military fatigues and carried American flags, but only to mock them. In many homes, there was friction between the fathers who had served their country in the war and the sons who had long hair and planned to leave the country and go to Canada if the draft called them. Like every other male my age, I have a story to tell about this, and I will do it in Chapter XI of this book.

Concurrent with the anti-war protests, and in some ways linked to it, was the growing discontent in the black community. Starting in the Watts section of Los Angeles and moving on to Detroit and other major cities, race riots erupted as black people took to the streets to vent their displeasure about police violence against blacks, particularly young black men, and black economic inequality. The demonstrations in the streets of St. Louis, Chicago, and elsewhere in 2015 by groups such as Black Lives Matter were exactly the same as the demonstrations of the late sixties. The only difference was that by 2015, white people were watching the angry protesters in color on high-definition big screen TVs rather than in black and white on small analog sets. It might surprise some white people to know that the racial demonstrations of the sixties were much more violent, probably because they came after a century of total degradation, humiliation, and frustration. I lived near Detroit in 1967 and saw the burned out city blocks after the Motown riots of that summer.

Along with the riots in the sixties came a fast growing movement called Black Power. Before he was assassinated in 1965, Malcolm X called on black people to shed their feelings of inferiority and take control of their lives and their futures. Groups such as the Black Panthers organized to engage in "armed defense of the Ghetto." Their aim was to keep an eagle eye on the "pigs" (police) and to protect their black brothers and sisters with violence, if necessary. Today, it would probably be a good idea to organize some new black defense teams to patrol the streets of the black communities. These defenders would be armed, not with guns, but with cameras to record everything that happened between the police and the black population. Dash cams and cameras on police uniforms are often in place, and sometimes random bystanders take videos, but these *armed* patrols I'm speaking of would add another level of protection for the people ... and verification for the police if their actions were warranted.

A brief distraction for Americans from the racial tensions and the Vietnam War was a war in the Middle East that was going to have ramifications far beyond the issues we were dealing with at the time. Israel struck first. Correctly sensing an Arab attack was in the making in June of 1967, Israel wiped out the entire Egyptian air force on the ground. There followed a war pitting the Arab countries (Egypt, Syria, Jordan, and the Palestinian Arabs) against tiny Israel. Shockingly, Israel delivered crushing blows to all of them in only six days. The Israelis drove the Egyptians out of the Sinai Peninsula all the way back to the Suez Canal; they took the Golan Heights from Syria; and they took the West Bank from the Palestinians and Jordan. When the smoke and dust cleared, Israel occupied lands on all sides of her borders, and the Arab states had been humiliated.

At the time the Six-Day War occurred, I was teaching at Southfield High School in Southfield, Michigan, a school that at that time had a very large Jewish population. The students were very upset when the Middle East war began in early June. Some of the seniors said they would go to Israel to help fight, but the war ended before they graduated. In that one-week period, I got a brief but profound view of the devotion to Israel felt by the Jewish people all over the world. When I read how the Arab countries reacted to the defeat, I also realized that this would not be the end of anything, but rather the beginning of an Arab payback vendetta. The conclusion many Muslims reached as they contemplated their disaster was that they had lost the Six-Day War because they had not been true to Islam. They vowed to be more devoted to Islam in the future and to destroy Israel.

Nineteen sixty-eight proved to be a pivotal year in Vietnam and in race relations. The Vietcong, who we thought was on the ropes because it hadn't launched an operation in months, suddenly launched powerful attacks on the lunar New Year called Tet. The Tet Offensive involved Vietcong fighters going into almost every city and major town in South Vietnam and showing they still had plenty of fighters and lots of firepower. For a brief time, they even got into the American embassy in downtown Saigon. The attacks were a shock, but the Cong were ultimately defeated in every town, so in that sense, the Tet Offensive was a failure, but the victories were very costly for the American troops and our South Vietnamese allies. In the city of Hue, which is a university town in the northern part of South Vietnam, hundreds of buildings were leveled, and the American commander in the area said, with very little sense of irony, "We had to destroy the city in order to save it." Increasing numbers of Americans were beginning to think that statement could apply to the whole country. Clearly, the war as it was currently being fought was going to continue much longer, and Americans were getting very sick of it.

In February 1968, the Tet Offensive was going to set off a cascade of shattering events that would take place over the next four months. In March, President Johnson, weary of the war and probably convinced he could not be reelected, withdrew from the presidential race. Bobby Kennedy, JFK's younger brother, then became a candidate and looked to be the likely nominee of the Democratic Party on an anti-war platform. In April, Dr. Martin Luther King was assassinated by a white man in Memphis and the country experienced a new round of race riots. Then, in June, Bobby Kennedy, who had just won the California primary, was assassinated in Los Angeles. In the space of one hundred days, the war in Vietnam got significantly worse, and two of the foremost leaders in the country were killed.

In the fall of 1968, Richard Nixon, who had reemerged from his defeat to John F. Kennedy in 1960, was elected president. People voted for him partly because of his promise that he had a plan to get the United States out of Vietnam. In 1969, the plan turned out to be Vietnamization. The United States would gradually withdraw our forces and Vietnamize the conflict by increasingly turning the fighting against the Vietcong and the North Vietnamese over to our South Vietnamese allies. In essence, we would return to the policy we had been following in the early sixties, when we supplied and advised but did not fight. Looking back on Nixon's policy now, two things seem obvious:

It was the only way out of Vietnam short of simply abandoning the South to the communists; and

The policy was essentially the same as that followed by Barack Obama in getting U.S. troops out of Iraq and Afghanistan.

The Vietnamization policy worked, but not quickly enough for most of the anti-war protestors. When Nixon ordered a brief incursion into Cambodia in April of 1970, riots broke out on college campuses across the country. At Kent State University in Ohio, students burned down the ROTC building, and the next day, soldiers from the Ohio National Guard fired their rifles into a crowd of students, killing four of them. The event became known as the Kent State Massacre, and like the Boston Massacre exactly two hundred years earlier, it had its own set of iconic images. I will discuss one of those, in particular, in Chapter X.

In the area of race relations, Dr. King's murder was a profoundly tragic event because he was such a strong force for moderation and peace. By the 1970s, relations between blacks and whites were still tense. There were hopeful signs though: the "whites only" signs were long gone; more black people were voting because of the Voting Rights Act of 1965; and there were more black faces on television. But black-white relations were always on the brink of violence. Confrontation was going to happen again, this time in the North.

In 1974, racial violence came to Boston, the Cradle of Liberty. A federal judge decreed that Boston's schools were in effect segregated because of neighborhood patterns and the failure of the school committee to locate schools at the junction of neighborhoods so students from both races would attend each school. He now ordered Boston schools to begin integrating by means of mandatory busing. Black students from Roxbury High School would be bused across town to the all-white (mostly Irish) South Boston High, and some South Boston High students would be bused to Roxbury. On the first day of school that fall, a mob formed in front of South Boston High School to meet the buses coming from Roxbury—meet them with jeers and rocks. As Southerners were quick to point out, the scene was reminiscent of Little Rock in 1957, when an angry white mob confronted a group of trembling black students attempting to enter a school. It was the beginning of a violent fall that saw black students harassed every time they arrived at the previously all-white schools. Many white parents took their children out of the Boston public schools and put them in private schools, or moved right out of the city to lily-white suburbs.

My wife and I had no children in 1974. We were quite liberal-minded on the race issue, and so we supported the busing program, but because we lived twenty miles outside of Boston, no one much cared what we thought. Later, after having had two children and watching them grow up and go through school, I now realize I probably would have opposed busing if I had been a parent in South Boston in 1974. Busing to achieve racial balance was a crazy idea; I think almost everyone agrees about that now. They certainly should not have bused high school students right away. Perhaps a program of one or two grades at a time would have worked the concept up in a way that would have allowed people to get used to it—maybe.

During the busing crisis in Boston, we were also buzzing about what had just happened that summer to President Richard Nixon. He had been forced to resign the presidency, the first president ever to have that happen to him. The story that led to his resignation had all the makings of a Greek tragedy: pride and a fatal flaw leading to downfall.

In 1972 no one saw tragedy coming because Nixon was reelected by a huge margin. He won big for several reasons:

He had reduced our troop commitment to Vietnam and the number of casualties each week by a significant amount. It was clear we would be out of the fighting before too much longer;

Concurrently, he had opened diplomatic relations with China, had visited China, toasted the Chinese leaders, and started a thaw in our

Cold War relations with a country many of us considered to be very dangerous;

He had visited the Soviet Union and signed an arms limitation agreement with the Soviet leader, the dour Leonid Brezhnev; and

His Democratic opponent, Senator George McGovern of South Dakota, was a likeable but very liberal man who favored an immediate pullout from Vietnam and proposed expanding the welfare system dramatically. American presidents always get elected from the middle of the political spectrum. In 1964, Goldwater was way too far to the right to get elected; now McGovern was way too far to the left to get elected. Both men received about forty percent of the vote, which is the standard, it seems, for candidates too far out of the mainstream.

With his reelection so likely, what Richard Nixon and his top staff did seems almost impossible to comprehend. Some members of the White House staff ordered burglars to break into the offices of the Democratic National Committee in the Watergate Hotel and Office Complex and install listening devices in the telephones. On the night of June 17, 1972, the burglars were caught red-handed. There were questions right away about whether the White House was involved in the break-in, but top Nixon officials denied it, Nixon himself vigorously denied it, and so the election took place without any Watergate issue factoring in. I had voted for Nixon in '68, but I had decided by '72 that he was a shady character and that McGovern was a person of solid morals who would be a good president, so I became a McGovern campaign worker in Massachusetts. I manned the telephones, stuffed envelopes, and, of course, brought victory to my man in the state. Unfortunately, he lost in all the others; Nixon won forty-nine states. After the whole Watergate mess was over, people in Massachusetts sported bumper stickers that said "Don't blame me; I'm from Massachusetts."

In 1973, the Nixon Administration's denial about Watergate involvement began to unravel. A special committee in the Senate began investigating the charges a few people were making that the orders to conduct the break-in had come from the White House and that hush money had been paid to buy the silence of the five burglars. When it came out that an oval office taping system had been in place during the whole Watergate period, the special prosecutor who had been appointed to investigate the case, subpoenaed the tapes of oval office conversations so he could prove, one way or the other, whether the president knew about the break-in or the attempt to cover up White House involvement. Nixon refused to hand them over, citing executive privilege, and the dispute over the tapes, *Nixon v. United States*, ended up in the Supreme Court.

In late July 1974, the Court ruled that Nixon, even though he was the president, was not above the law and that he must turn over the tapes. It was quickly discovered that a tape of an oval office conversation on June 22, 1972 (five days after the break-in), revealed a conversation between Nixon and one of his top advisors, in which Nixon ordered him to use the CIA to thwart the investigation of Watergate and to pay hush money to the burglars. Here was the president, organizing an obstruction of justice: a felony and certainly an impeachable offense.

Events moved quickly. The House of Representatives prepared to vote articles of impeachment against the president. Nixon talked to a few friends he had in the Senate and asked what his chances were of being acquitted in the Senate trial, as Andrew Johnson was in 1868. The senators told him there were 98 to 99 votes for guilty, far more than the two-thirds necessary for conviction. With that news, Nixon decided to resign and left office with a tearful farewell to his staff on August 9, 1974.

The Richard Nixon Presidential Library and Museum in Yorba Linda, California, the town where Nixon was raised, is surprisingly candid about the Watergate scandal and Nixon's role in it. There is an entire room devoted to it, including excerpts from the tapes. The tragedy of the museum is the contrast between that room and the others: his boyhood home (which is right next door), a very modest little house, his incredible foreign policy achievements, and some lesser known accomplishments as president, such as the creation of the Environmental Protection

Agency. The man could have been one of the greats, but he fell into total disgrace. I'll discuss this more in the chapter titled "Rogues and Cautionary Tales."

The new president in 1974 was Gerald Ford, former house minority leader and congressman from Michigan. He was a very self-assured, genial man, who quickly moved to settle the country down. "The long national nightmare is over," he said, and most of us believed that at least honesty had been restored to government. Within a month, however, he did something that made many people cringe with frustration and anger and resume their cynical thinking about government. Ford gave Richard Nixon a pardon for all crimes he may have committed while president. He offered as his reason that we needed to put Watergate behind us, that we had many pressing problems that needed to be resolved. A series of long, drawn-out trials would distract the country from the problems of inflation and energy shortages we needed to confront. Many people rejected that explanation and suspected a deal had been cooked up between Ford and Tricky Dicky. They resented the fact that they would not get to see Nixon sitting as a defendant in a courtroom and ultimately going off to prison in an orange jumpsuit. I tended to agree with Ford. Also, it did seem that Nixon had suffered enough by having to leave office and go off to exile in disgrace. That was pretty awful for a man who had spent his whole adult life struggling for power and prestige.

Meanwhile, back in January 1973, just as the Watergate scandal was starting to heat up, two major events occurred. The Supreme Court handed down an earth shaking decision and the Vietnam War ended, at least for our combat troops.

The court ruling was *Roe v. Wade*. In this decision, the Supreme Court said that no state could prohibit a woman from choosing to end a pregnancy by abortion during the first two trimesters. At this time, most states outlawed the abortion procedure, but all those laws were struck down by the argument that they violated a woman's right to privacy, which is not specifically spelled out in the Bill of Rights but is implied by the Fourteenth Amendment's right to liberty and the Fourth Amendment's right to protection against unreasonable searches and seizures. The judges split seven to two in this case, and the country split as well. Those who opposed the Court's ruling argued that the Fourteenth Amendment also protects life, and an unborn child is a life entitled to the states' protection. Both sides on this issue were passionate right from the start, and the debate has raged ever since 1973. Conservatives, mostly Republicans, have tried for four decades to overturn *Roe v. Wade*, or at least limit the right to choose in order to protect the lives of the unborn. Liberals, mostly Democrats, have fought to protect a women's right to make her own choice regarding her reproductive health.

The Vietnam War ended for us with a peace agreement signed in Paris by the United States, South Vietnam, North Vietnam, and the Vietcong. Under the agreement, the United States would remove its remaining forces from Vietnam and the North Vietnamese authorities would return American prisoners of war. There would be a ceasefire in place, and North Vietnam would be permitted to keep its forces in South Vietnam. That last provision was the killer; even the average citizen, like me, could see that. If there was ever a face-saving for a country, this was it. Leaving the North Vietnamese troops in the South was tantamount to leaving a rattlesnake in bed with your children and expecting it to sleep nicely. We all knew it was only a matter of time before the communists struck. We did get to see joyful reunions of POWs with their families when they came home, some of them, like John McCain, after many years of captivity in North Vietnam. To me, those reunions made the deal worth it.

It all came undone in a few days in late April of 1975. The communists launched attacks against the Army of the Republic of South Vietnam, and they simply retreated and melted away. President Ford asked Congress for money for military assistance to the South Vietnamese, but Congress refused; anyway, it would be too little, too late. On April 30, the North Vietnamese arrived in Saigon driving Russian-made tanks, as the last remaining Americans, and as many South Vietnamese as they could take, helicoptered out of the city to ships stationed off the coast. Despite their desperation to get out of the country, many South Vietnamese were left behind to their fate. Their fate might mean imprisonment for the crime of cooperating with the Americans or being sent to reeducation camps to get their minds straight. No wonder many South Vietnamese escaped the country jammed into tiny boats and made their way to the United States via Thailand or some other friendly country.

Gerald Ford ran for president in 1976, but his pardon of Richard Nixon proved a little too much for him to overcome. His Democratic opponent was the governor of Georgia, Jimmy Carter, who had a very down-home folksy style. He promised, "I will never lie to you." In the post-Watergate stench, that sounded refreshing, and the voters gave Carter the presidency. The margin was actually surprisingly small. In spite of Watergate and the pardon, a shift of ten thousand voters in Ohio would have given Ford the presidency.

Right away, Carter tried to set a new tone for his administration. He was going to be more open and informal, and he was going to be straightforward and honest. To set the tone, he broke with tradition on Inauguration Day and got out of the presidential limousine during the trip from the Capitol Building to the White House and walked with his wife, Rosalynn, and daughter Amy down Pennsylvania Avenue. He wanted to show that the people would have more access to this president.

The late 1970s were not a very good time to be president, as Carter soon discovered. The economy was not in good shape, inflation was a constant worry, and gasoline prices were constantly going up, as OPEC (the Organization of Petroleum Exporting Countries) kept jerking us around with their production policies. Most of those countries were Arab nations who hated our support for Israel, so they made the most of the fact that we depended on them for forty percent of our oil supply.

A personal rant: The fashions people were wearing in the seventies were ridiculous. The garish clothing—bell bottoms pants, tie-dye shirts, platform shoes, and leisure suits—made everything bad that was happening seem even worse.

In the midst of the discouraging economic troubles, Carter produced a major foreign policy achievement. He got Egyptian President Anwar Sadat and Israeli Prime Minister Menachem Begin to come to Washington to negotiate a peace treaty between their two countries. Israel and Egypt, intense rivals since biblical times and sworn enemies since the Six-Day War of 1967, when Israel seized Egypt's Sinai Peninsula, were as likely to make peace with each other as a snake and a mongoose. And yet Carter kept the two leaders engaged at Camp David for twelve days, met with each of them separately and together, and finally got them to reach a peace accord. They agreed to the terms in September 1978, and signed a formal treaty on the White House lawn in March 1979. In the agreement, Israel returned the Sinai Peninsula to Egypt and Egypt recognized Israel as a state, something no Arab country had ever done before.

I thought Carter's negotiation of this treaty was a spectacular achievement, but I don't think many Americans appreciated the magnitude of it. The public was in a funk in the summer of 1979, and President Carter sensed it. To address the situation, he decided to give a special talk to the people. To prepare himself, he retreated to Camp David for several days. On the night of July 15, 1979, Carter looked into the camera and spoke as if he were talking to the people personally. He never smiled, and he almost appeared to be chastising the people for their bad behavior when he said things such as "… too many of us now tend to worship self-indulgence and consumption. Human identity is no longer defined by what one does, but by what one owns." He asked the people to tackle the energy problem by conserving more. He also said there was a "crisis of confidence" in the country that we had to overcome. By the end of his talk, which lasted almost an hour, many people, if they were still listening, were depressed. It was a total downer. I thought he had made some very good points about our excessive materialism and energy piggishness, but I knew it would hurt him in the long run, because people don't want a leader who blames them for the problems that exist and offers no vision for a brighter future.

People got even more disheartened a few months later when a radical Shiite cleric, the Ayatolla Khomeini, overthrew the Shah of Iran and seized power. When Carter gave the Shah permission to come to the United States for treatment of his cancer condition, enraged college students in Tehran seized the American Embassy and took fifty-two Americans hostage. Carter responded by freezing Iranian assets in our country. After five months, he tried a surprise raid to liberate the hostages, but the mission failed when the aircraft crashed in the desert. By the time of the presidential election of 1980, the hostages had been held captive for almost a year, and Carter appeared to be totally ineffective. In 1980, Americans were in a mood to look for new leadership.

For most liberals in the country, Ronald Reagan was anathema. He was a conservative who was once a movie actor and who had gotten his political start by giving a well-received speech for the ultra-conservative Barry Goldwater in 1964. As governor of California, he had sent the National Guard to crack down on student protests at the University of California, Berkeley.

Conservatives, on the other hand, thought he was the answer to the country's problems: a man who would not be pushed around by the ayatollahs of the world, who would build up the military, cut welfare rolls, and restore patriotism and pride to the people. He was a gun totin', horse ridin', tall-in-the-saddle cowboy with a quick wit and an easy smile. What was not to like if you were a conservative?

In the debates between Carter and Reagan, the president seemed humorless and stiff. At one point, he tried to prove that Reagan didn't care about people's health because he had once opposed Medicare. Reagan smiled, tilted his head, and said, "There you go again, trying to portray me as a heartless man who doesn't care about people's health." (The "There you go again" line is still quoted today.) He then went on to explain that he had only opposed the health care bill Carter was referring to because he favored a different one. His easy jocularity made many people realize he was not the redneck, rock-ribbed conservative they might have thought he was. In the last debate, Reagan closed the deal in his final statement when he asked, "Are you better off now than you were four years ago? If the answer is yes," he went on, "then you should vote to return the president to office. If your answer is no, then you should vote for me." With the on-going hostage crisis and the troubled economy in mind, many voters thought they were clearly worse off—hadn't Carter himself told them so?—and they decided to vote for Reagan.

Reagan won the election in 1980 handily, and he was reelected in 1984, when he won every state in the Union except Minnesota. His presidency defined the eighties, and for me it was a great decade, so I look back fondly on Ronald Reagan. He was the president when my kids were little, and we had great family times, so my view of his presidency is probably colored by that.

Reagan paradoxically got his presidency off to a good start by getting shot. He had just delivered a speech at a Washington hotel when a deranged young man fired several bullets at him. One of the slugs bounced off the limousine Reagan was about to step into and hit him in the chest. It was a tense time at the hospital since the doctors had to remove the bullet from near his heart and drain out the large amounts of blood that were collecting in his lungs. But we heard stories, apparently true, of how he joked with the doctors who were about to operate on him, saying, "I hope you're all Republicans." How very brave, we thought, and how Ronald Reagan! Within two weeks, he was back at the White House, and within a month, he was speaking to a joint session of Congress. Those of us who had lived through several major assassinations already—John F. Kennedy, Malcolm X, Martin Luther King, Jr., Robert F. Kennedy—loved Reagan just for surviving and sparing us one more round of intense grief.

Conservatives loved Reagan for his tax cuts and defense buildup, two basic conservative goals. The economy did respond to the cuts, and we entered a decade of prosperity, and the military did get stronger, which gave us more clout in our dealings with the Soviet Union. But a third major conservative goal, balancing the federal budget, was totally destroyed by what it took to achieve the other two. The federal budget deficits were in the hundreds of billions of dollars in the last years of the Reagan presidency.

At the beginning of his presidency, Reagan did not even try to disguise his hatred for communism, the Soviet Union, China, Cuba, North Korea, and Vietnam. He told jokes about the failures of communism and predicted that communism would eventually collapse of its own rot. He called the Soviet Union the Evil Empire, and he increased the defense budget to oppose it. He also proposed an anti-missile defense system capable of shooting down incoming Soviet rockets. That would give us a distinct edge in the arms race, but many Americans derisively called the proposal a "star wars" plan that would never work. Nevertheless, all this talk about a major missile build-up unnerved the Russians, who knew their system could not keep pace with what Reagan seemed to be doing. This certainly played a part in what happened next.

In 1985, a new Communist Party chairman took power in the Soviet Union. Mikhail Gorbachev was clearly a different kind of man from the dour, scowling dictators who had preceded him. He had a kindly look, a ready smile, and a friendly demeanor that said, "I'm sure we can work this out." He and Reagan were a perfect match, and even though they had a few spats, they worked steadily toward reducing tensions between the two super powers. The most famous photo of the two shows them leaning in to talk with each other from upholstered chairs in front of a warm fire. Their talks resulted in the Intermediate-Range Nuclear Forces Treaty (INF). More significantly, real democratic reforms were occurring within the Soviet Union. This was more than the détente of the Nixon years—a relaxation of tensions between two still very hostile superpowers. This was a genuine meeting of the minds, as Gorbachev worked for more openness in Soviet Society (Glasnost) and a restructuring of the Soviet system to allow for more democracy and capitalism (Perestroika).

As the Reagan years drew to a close, those of us who had been around for all of the Cold War years were daring to hope that a real thaw was happening and that we might actually see the end of it in our lifetimes. In 1987, Reagan went to Berlin. Standing at the Brandenburg Gate near the Berlin Wall, Reagan said, "General Secretary Gorbachev, if you seek peace, if you seek prosperity in the Soviet Union and Eastern Europe, if you seek liberalization, come here to this gate. Mr. Gorbachev, open this gate. Mr. Gorbachev, tear down this wall!" When I saw this on the news that evening, I thought, "Oh, right! Like he's ever going to do that! That wall will be there forever." It turned out that "forever" would be two years and five months away.

Those who would like to put Reagan right up there with Lincoln and FDR as a leader have to deal with one major blot on his record. While he was apparently not paying close attention—which was the flip side of his management style of laying out the major plan and leaving it to competent appointees to carry out the details—a few of his top national security people sold weapons to Iran to secure return of some hostages, and then used the money from those sales to support the anti-communist group in Nicaragua known as the Contras. Aiding the Contras violated a law that banned aid to the group. The Iran-Contra scandal was the kind of offense that would have brought down a president such as Richard Nixon, who was not well liked by many members of Congress. Reagan, on the other hand, was liked by almost everyone, and so he was never impeached. I saw this as yet another example of the truism that most people don't lose their jobs for incompetence or laziness; they lose them because the people they work with simply don't like them.

When Reagan left office in 1989, he was succeeded by his vice president, George H.W. Bush. I had always liked Bush and, in fact, had worked for his campaign in 1980 when he ran for the Republican nomination against Reagan. (Yes, I worked for George McGovern, a liberal Democrat, in 1972, and George Bush, a conservative Republican, in

1980. If your name is George, you have my vote! Seriously, though, I look for character first, and both of those men had it, with plenty to spare.) Bush had been a congressman from Texas, ambassador to China, chairman of the national Republican Party, head of the CIA, and ambassador to the UN. I thought he was far more qualified than Reagan; I was very disappointed when Reagan got the nomination, but I was pleased when Reagan chose Bush to be his running mate. I will discuss Bush's qualities more in the chapter on role models. He is one of my *few* role models from recent American history.

Bush excelled in handling foreign affairs, as one might expect from a man with his background. In his first year in office, communism collapsed in all of the countries of Eastern Europe, and the Berlin Wall came down. It was truly an amazing sight in November 1989 to see Berliners on top of the wall hammering the concrete into millions of pieces. A year later, the Soviet Union collapsed and broke into the fifteen separate republics. Communism in Europe was as dead as Karl Marx. Bush deserved credit only insofar as the Reagan Administration's military buildup and Reagan's relationship with Mikhail Gorbachev created the conditions for it to happen. What Bush does deserve credit for is how he handled it as it was occurring. He was very careful not to gloat or do any sort of victory celebration. There were people who wanted him to go to Berlin and declare the triumph of capitalism and democracy, but he refused, saying he would not do a victory dance on the wall. He knew that kind of display would encourage the hardliners in Russia and the other former communist countries to attempt a counter-revolution to overthrow the new democracies. Instead, he had one last phone call with Gorbachev, who no longer had an empire to govern, and wished him well.

The summer after the Berlin Wall fell, a new crisis unfolded that was to test President's Bush's leadership and serve as a harbinger of much that was to come. Saddam Hussein, the evil dictator of Iraq, sent his armies into Kuwait, took over the country, and declared it annexed to Iraq as the nineteenth province. Declaring "This will not stand," Bush immediately began to take action. He organized a coalition of nations to drive Saddam out of Kuwait and assembled a force of more than five hundred thousand soldiers in Saudi Arabia to protect the country from an Iraqi invasion and to liberate Kuwait. On January 17, 1991 (my birthday), the Gulf War began when coalition planes began bombing Iraqi positions in Kuwait. Four weeks later, on February 24, a ground invasion began, and within five days, the Iraqi Army was defeated and driven from Kuwait.

In February 1991, there were many people who wanted President Bush to send our armies all the way to Baghdad and remove the evil Saddam Hussein from power. Bush demurred, saying he was not authorized by the congressional resolution to do so and that the Arab countries in the coalition would oppose it. Besides, he said, once that mission was accomplished, we would then have to govern Iraq until a new, stable government could be set up. How would that go? His words were to prove prophetic for none other than his own son twelve years later.

After the Gulf War, Bush's popularity ratings were up around eighty percent. He seemed to be a sure thing for reelection the next year, but then the economy went sour, unemployment began to rise, inflation took off again, and, suddenly, people didn't feel positive about the future. The Democrats nominated the young and very appealing governor of Arkansas, Bill Clinton, who kept his campaign focused on the economy. Then, the final blow to Bush's chances came by way of Texas billionaire Ross Perot entering the race. As a wealthy businessman capable of financing his own campaign, and as a simple man who talked common sense about reducing government waste and balancing the federal budget, his fresh ideas were likely to draw votes from many of the Bush supporters. The result was a Clinton victory and the end of twelve years of conservative Republican rule. It was a bitter pill to swallow for those of us who liked George Bush and thought he was a fine, moral, and upright man. Now we were going to have a president who had dodged the draft and a number of scandals, including sex scandals, and whom his detractors called Slick Willy.

Clinton and his wife, Hillary, promised a dynamic administration that would change the country, starting with the health care system. Bill put Hillary in charge of a committee to develop a nationwide health program, and she came up with a proposal that sounded simple and effective at first: Every employer would be required to provide health insurance, and everyone would get a card, similar to the Medicare cards, that entitled them to medical services. But her plan exceeded one thousand pages, was far too complex, and was dead on arrival in Congress. That was the end of health care reform for another two decades.

After this rocky start, what Bill Clinton gave the country was a moderate approach to most problems. When the issue of gays serving in the military came up, he engineered a compromise known as "don't ask, don't tell," under which men would not be asked to state their sexual orientation before induction. If they never said or did anything that gave them away as gay, they could remain in the service. The gay community was never satisfied with this solution because over the next seventeen years, thousands of gay men were denied the right to serve or were discharged. The law was repealed under Barack Obama in 2011, and gays were allowed to serve openly in the military.

In 1993, an explosion occurred in the parking garage underneath the World Trade Center. Six people died in the blast and the entire building was evacuated. Investigations by the FBI revealed that a truck bomb had exploded, and it was surmised that the bomb was supposed to topple the North Tower into the South Tower, bringing them both to the ground. Ultimately, six Islamic terrorists were convicted of carrying out the attack. Security at the World Trade center was increased, and most of us believed the buildings were safe from a future attempt to bring them down with a bomb planted in the basement. In the nineties, it was unimaginable that anyone could attack the World Trade Center from the air.

During the Clinton years, the United States tended to stay out of events abroad, but Clinton did play a major role in bringing an end to an ugly civil war in Bosnia. Clinton also intervened in the civil war in Somalia, an intervention that resulted in the Battle of Mogadishu, in which two Black Hawk helicopters were shot down and eighteen Army rangers were killed. In 2002, Hollywood memorialized the heroism of the soldiers involved in the film *Black Hawk Down*. Another civil war in Rwanda pitted two rival groups, the Tutsis and the Hutus, in a bloody civil war that resulted in thousands of people being massacred. The United States did not get involved in this war, but after he left office, Clinton admitted that this was one intervention he wished he had made, because the slaughter in Rwanda was so horrific.

In 1994, the Republicans won control of Congress and Clinton now had to deal with the newly energized Republican Speaker of the House, Newt Gingrich. The speaker was the originator of a new concept, the Contract with America, in which Republicans would demand a balanced federal budget. They would never vote for an unbalanced budget, even if it meant shutting down the government because there was no budget at all. The result was a government shutdown in late 1995, when Clinton vetoed a Republican sponsored budget that did not have the level of funding for Medicare and other federal programs he wanted. The public tended to blame the Republicans (Gingrich) for the shutdown, but the long-term result was a bipartisan deal and four federal budgets in a row that were balanced. There had not been a balanced budget since 1969, and never four in a row since the 1920s.

Clinton actually was able to work with Newt Gingrich in a civilized way, a fact that has been noted in recent years when we observe the acrimonious relations between the Democratic president and the Republican Congress. In 1996, they produced a welfare reform act that required welfare recipients to seek employment and turned more of the management of welfare over to the states. There was a lot in this reform that conservatives had been demanding for years, so some Democrats were a bit miffed that their party leader, the president, had "sold out" to conservative Republicans.

On balance, the nineties seemed like a pretty placid decade, and Bill Clinton could have left office in 2001 with a solid record of good management. He could have if he had managed his libido; instead, he had an affair with a twenty-four year old White House intern named Monica Lewinsky. Most of 1998 was occupied with some story or another about exactly what transpired in the Oval Office between the two of them, and some of what turned out to be the truth was so gross that I wondered if Clinton would ever be able to show his face in public again. To my surprise, but apparently not to the surprise of many others, he not only made his usual presidential appearances, he even gained in popularity. It seems that the image of the president having sex in the Oval Office with a young intern was not a problem for the majority of the people in the United States. It was also not a problem in Europe, especially France, where it was expected.

The special prosecutor did have a problem with Clinton lying under oath, and so did the Republicans in the House of Representatives. Articles of impeachment passed the House in December 1998, charging Clinton with perjury and obstruction of justice. He may have lied to a grand jury about his Lewinsky affair during investigations of other sexual assault cases pending against him. The trial in the Senate resulted in a total partisan outcome: fifty Republicans voted guilty (no Democrats did), and that was far short of the sixty-seven needed to remove Clinton from office. Thus, just like Andrew Johnson in 1868, Bill Clinton was impeached but not convicted and remained in office until the end of his term. He left office more popular than when he entered the White House.

In the 2000 election, Clinton's vice president, Al Gore, won the Democratic nomination. The Republicans nominated George W. Bush, governor of Texas and the son of George Bush, the forty-first president. Gore won the popular vote by two hundred fifty thousand votes (point five percent of the total), but the vote in Florida was extremely close, and whoever won that state's electors would win the majority in the Electoral College, the only result that counts. For weeks, election officials in Florida tried to sort out the votes. The problem was that the new electronic system being used produced computer cards that sometimes were not read properly by the machines because the holes next to a candidate's name were not punched through. Consequently, thousands of votes had to be counted by hand. Finally, in the case of *Bush v. Gore*, the United States Supreme Court ruled that the last count that had Bush the winner in Florida must be allowed to stand: Bush had two hundred seventy-one electoral votes to Gore's two hundred sixty-six. Democrats screamed they'd been robbed, and the usual calls went up to ditch the Electoral College, but George W. Bush became the forty-third president on January 20, 2001.

President Bush hoped to be the man who reformed the education system in the country just as he had upgraded the public schools in Texas. Ironically, he was reading a story to a group of first graders in Florida when he got the news that would mean he would be a war president instead. Two passenger jets had crashed into the Twin Towers at the World Trade Center in what quickly became clear was a terrorist attack. Also, a plane had crashed into the Pentagon, and another had gone down in a field in Western Pennsylvania. There was no doubt that the country was under attack!

Everyone who was old enough to know what was happening remembers how he or she heard the news that day. I was teaching a class in Tewksbury High School, in Tewksbury, Massachusetts, when a girl came into the room and told us a plane had crashed into the World Trade Center. Naturally, I assumed it was some errant pilot of a small plane who had screwed up, until I got down to the main office after the period was over. On the television, I saw smoke billowing out from a big hole in each tower, and just as I arrived in the room, one of the towers began cascading down, collapsing into itself like a house of cards. For the rest of the day, everyone in the country, including me, and probably everyone in the world, watched replays of the planes flying into the buildings and the collapsing towers. It was such a nightmare; we could hardly believe our eyes.

President Bush handled the crisis very well. He went on television that night to reassure Americans and to make it clear that justice would be served. "These acts shatter steel," he said, "but they cannot dent the steel of American resolve." He also made it clear that the United States would "make no distinction between the terrorists who committed these acts and those who harbor them."

Within a day, we knew that the terrorists were members of Al Qaeda, an Islamic terrorist group whose leader was Osama bin Laden, and that the Taliban government in Afghanistan was harboring them. On October 7, 2001, the United States, along with our ally Great Britain, launched Operation Enduring Freedom, an invasion of Afghanistan to drive the Taliban from power and to capture Osama bin Laden and other Al Qaeda leaders. The mission was later joined by other NATO allies, and it quickly succeeded in driving the Taliban out of Kabul and installing a new government. Osama bin Laden, however, eluded capture and was not cornered and killed in Pakistan until 2011.

All seemed to be going tolerably well in Afghanistan in 2002, but President Bush began telling us we faced an equally ominous threat from Saddam Hussein in Iraq. There was evidence he had weapons of mass destruction (WMDs) and that he was even developing nuclear weapons. This all sounded very plausible; after all, Hussein had used chemical weapons in a war against Iran in the 1980s, he had invaded Kuwait in 1990, and he had refused to cooperate with UN weapons inspectors while Clinton was president. In March 2003, Bush ordered an invasion of Iraq, and within weeks, our forces occupied Baghdad, took over Hussein's palaces, and began setting up a more agreeable Iraqi government. No WMDs were found, however, and, ominously, the removal of Hussein sparked feuding and sectarian warfare between Shiite and Sunni factions in Iraq. By the end of 2003, the United States had lost control of the situation. We succeeded in capturing Saddam, and he was tried and executed by the Iraqi government. The Iraqis managed to hold elections, but every day it seemed there was some form of roadside bombing or an attack on American soldiers by one group or another.

As the wars in Iraq and Afghanistan dragged on through 2004, Bush's approval ratings dropped to Nixonesque levels. He managed to get reelected in 2004, before the bottom fell out, but by 2007, even some of his top advisors were telling him to withdraw our forces from Iraq and cut our loses. Such a move would have left him limping through the last two years of his presidency as a failure and would have left the country demoralized from losing thousands of soldiers in a forlorn cause.

Instead, Bush decided to try to pull victory from the jaws of defeat by sending twenty thousand additional troops to Iraq and adopting a new strategy of enlisting the help of Sunni tribal leaders. Under the capable guidance of General David Petraeus, American forces stationed themselves in Baghdad, rather than in bases far outside the city, and began working with the local leaders and building relationships. The goal was to act as partners in nation building, rather than as an occupying force. By 2008, the level of violence in Iraq was considerably reduced. Bush's critics attributed this to other factors, but his supporters argued that the gutsy *surge* had worked. Either way, Iraq was a functioning democracy, even if a fragile one, as George W. Bush prepared to leave office.

Lost in the deluge of criticism of his Iraq policies were some achievements Bush made that I felt should have gotten more attention. He got an educational reform bill passed through Congress. Working with Senator Edward Kennedy, he produced No Child Left Behind, a reform to increase federal funding to local schools who met educational standards as determined by standardized tests. Of course, the law has met with considerable criticism, as every attempt to reform schools does, but I believe it has opened the way for more rigorous standards and has helped students in minority districts a great deal. President Obama and Congress updated the concept and made some needed changes to revert more of the testing procedures back to the states in a new law called the Every Student Succeeds Act.

Bush also got Congress to fund major programs for the battles against AIDS and malaria in Africa. The President's Emergency Plan for AIDS

Relief guaranteed fifteen billion dollars in relief funds. Over five billion dollars was budgeted for the fight against malaria. Since leaving office, Bush has expanded his role by taking on cancer in Africa as well. He was only partially joking recently when he said he could be elected president of Ghana today much more easily than president of the United States.

Just as Bush was starting his last year in office, the economy went into a major tailspin. First, the housing market collapsed, as home prices fell; then, many of the banks collapsed because they had written many questionable mortgages. Fortunately, the president and Congress, as well as the Federal Reserve Board, had the lessons of 1930 to guide them, and they did not make the same mistakes. Instead of trying to balance the federal budget, expensive jobs stimulus programs in construction blossomed. Instead of tightening the money supply, the Federal Reserve Board reduced interest rates to almost zero, and then actually to zero, so banks could lend out money more readily. And instead of restricting trade as Congress did in 1932 with the Hawley-Smoot Tariff, trade was left with no additional restrictions. Unemployment topped ten percent, and there were some pretty scary months in early 2009, but the recession gradually came to an end, and it was statistically over by the end of 2009.

Meanwhile, one of the most significant presidential elections in American history was about to take place. After a hard fought battle in the primaries, Barack Obama, a one-term senator from Illinois, won the Democratic nomination. For most of us, even if we didn't support his policies, it was pretty exciting to see a major political party finally nominate an African-American for president. If you were aware of the history of slavery and racial discrimination in this country at all, you had to be impressed with how significant this was.

The Republicans nominated John McCain, a senator from Arizona and a war hero from the Vietnam era. As a prisoner in North Vietnam, he had endured six years of torture and deprivation, but had not broken. He was a true hero, but he was up against a formidable opponent in the charismatic Obama. To try to give his own campaign a new cache,

McCain chose Sarah Palin, Governor of Alaska, to be his running mate. Pretty and personable, she made a good impression at the Republican National Convention with her acceptance speech, but over time, her lack of experience and ignorance in foreign affairs made her more of an anchor than an asset to the McCain ticket. Obama won easily, and he became the first black president in American history when he was inaugurated on January 20, 2009.

Obama's signature achievement as president was the passage of the Affordable Care Act, often referred to as Obamacare, in March 2010. This act represented the culmination of over seventy years of dreaming by Democrats that a federal law could make health care available to everyone. Franklin Roosevelt had dreamed of it, Harry Truman had proposed it, Lyndon Johnson had pushed through Medicare to provide health insurance for the elderly under the Social security system and Medicaid to help states provide medical care for the poor, and, of course, Bill Clinton had set his wife, Hillary, to craft a national health insurance system in 1993. The Republicans are practically catatonic in their hatred for the law, and they vow they will repeal it if they win the White House in 2016.

Most of what Obama has done domestically fits the profile of a liberal. He appointed liberal justices to the Supreme Court; he repealed Don't Ask, Don't Tell; and he applauded the decision by the Supreme Court that requires all states to permit gay marriage. To show his support for the decision, he ordered the White House to be bathed in the rainbow colors of the gay movement on the day the decision was announced. He has come out strongly for gun control and, with Congress reluctant to pass any legislation, has tried by executive order to require background checks at private gun sales.

Obama also tried to confront the ongoing problem of illegal immigration into the United States. By 2010, it was estimated that there were eleven million people living in the country who had outstayed their visas or had come into the country illegally. Conservatives were proclaiming that these people were stealing American jobs and that many of them were committing crimes. If the critics on the right were correct, the very fabric of the nation was being torn and hordes of terrorists were coming into the country every day with bombs in their knapsacks and mayhem on their minds. On the other side were people who were ready to overlook the crimes of the parents who had immigrated illegally in order to offer a future for their children who, after all, were not responsible for anything their parents did. One point of contention was the Fourteenth Amendment, which gives citizenship to all persons born in the United States. Originally intended to ensure citizenship for the newly freed African-Americans in 1868, this provision irked conservatives who were convinced that millions of people were crossing the border just to give birth to babies who would immediately be citizens and entitled to all the benefits this would entail. The arguments over these issues were frequent and furious.

Obama was naturally inclined to be sympathetic to the new immigrants; after all, his father was from Kenya, and it was only his American mother, who gave birth to him in Hawaii (a fact his enemies repeatedly tried to dispute), who made him eligible to become president of the United States. Unable to get a comprehensive bill for immigration reform through Congress, Obama issued an executive order that protected approximately five million people from being deported, by allowing them to acquire work permits. The Republicans, who controlled both houses of Congress, were appalled at what they considered Obama's overreach of executive authority. In the fall of 2015, the Supreme Court agreed to hear a case, *United States v. Texas*, to decide on the constitutionality of Obama's action. Regardless of how the court decides, the issue of illegal immigration will be a prominent issue in the presidential election of 2016 and in political debates for years to come. The controversies over immigration go back to the Alien and Sedition Acts of 1798, and they are not likely to be resolved any time soon, if ever.

On the global scene, Obama came into office very critical of George Bush's wars, especially the war in Iraq, which he had opposed right from the start, when he was a state senator in Illinois. In 2011, he withdrew our last combat troops from that country. He increased our military presence in Afghanistan by thirty thousand troops in 2010, but set a date certain for their removal. By 2013, it was clear that Obama's primary goal was to remove our troops from the Middle East entirely. Unfortunately, new dangers have arisen in the region. The Islamic State of Iraq and Syria (ISIS), an extremist Muslim group even more fanatical than Al Qaeda, has taken over a large swath of territory encompassing Northern Syria and Western Iraq. They have launched terrorist attacks in Paris, San Bernardino, California, Brussels, and elsewhere. They have taken hostages and executed them with brutal beheadings. As the United States heads into another election year, Republicans are portraying the scary events in the Middle East as the natural result of Obama's "wimpy" policies. Obama counters by saying that many of the radical groups have formed or have grown because of the American presence in the region. He believes that if the United States had never gone into Iraq, ISIS would not exist, and if we act with a heavy hand militarily in the Middle East, ISIS will grow.

This chapter, which covers what has happened during my lifetime, is a little longer than the others because in this time of instant communication and high speed travel, much more happens in a shorter period of time. One of my grandchildren could end up writing about the next century, and I can't even imagine how crowded with Earth-shaking events it will be. I won't even guess at what our country will be like in 2080, when my grandson would be seventy-one and my daughter one hundred one.

THE WAY WE WERE

Old Sturbridge Village in Massachusetts recreates life as it was in small town America in the early 1800s. Visitors to the village, mostly old people and a few school children who have been bused in, are fascinated by the slow pace of life and the way almost everything people needed had to be made by hand. Whenever I have been there, I have always been interested in the comments people make as they watch the village reenactors ply their trades. While the blacksmith hammers a piece of iron into a horseshoe, the older people will ask, "How many nails do you use to put the shoe on the horse?" Or "How many horseshoes could a blacksmith make in one day?" They seem to almost yearn to live at a time when the village smithy stood beneath the spreading chestnut tree and worked his hammer with sinewy arms and hands. The students cannot wait to leave the smelly, sweaty shop and get back to their iPhones.

I can understand the old people's point of view. I think I would prefer to hang around talking politics with the smithy while he shod my horse. That would beat driving my car to the dealership and then sitting in a stuffy waiting room watching daytime TV while the mechanics worked on my car. On the other hand, I'm sure there were many smithies who were surly men who were not very agreeable conversationalists. I guess keeping your transportation operational can be a disagreeable task no matter which era you live in.

Traveling by horseback or carriage involved endless hours of tedious buckling and strapping, rubbing the horses down, feeding them, cleaning up their waste, tending to them when they got sick, and shooting them when they broke their legs. Perhaps the young people are right: It is so much better now, and the old ways were boring and sometimes a bit disgusting!

What good does it do us to know how people *used* to live? Do we have to know how great-grandpa had to walk ten miles to school through snowdrifts up to his waist? Do we even believe it? Probably not. So what good does it do us now to know about the old ways? Maybe this is a part of American history that truly is useless crap we learned in high school! Is this an area of history that doesn't have a utilitarian aspect no matter how hard I may try to give it one?

I could make the argument that understanding the technology that was available in the old days helps us to understand our parents and grandparents better. If we have any interest at all in picturing how they lived and want to feel closer to them because we have an understanding of what their life was like, then this aspect of history does have some value. When my father told me that his first car was a Model T Ford, it was helpful to me to be able to picture that car and him driving it, bumping along the cobblestone streets of Boston. When he tells me about his life as an accountant, making spreadsheets by hand because computers didn't exist, I can appreciate what a tedious job he had to do. I feel closer to my mother when I picture her as a teenager making most of her own clothes on an electric sewing machine, rather than ordering them online.

Besides these familiar things, I have benefitted from knowing the lifestyles and patterns of life in the olden days, because that knowledge helps me fully understand how technology, inventions, and changing ways of life affect many aspects of our lives, and not just the obvious ones. More specifically, I have observed how the changes in our homes, our clothing, our schools, our workplaces, our travel, and our entertainment have affected our values, our relationships, and our families. The typical American family of 2016 is certainly not the same as the typical American family of 1776. What have those two hundred forty years done to us?

Shortly before he died at the age of ninety, in 1989, I remember my grandfather marveling to me how much had changed in the country in the years he had been around. He was born in the age of the horse and buggy, and he lived to see men land on the moon and cars routinely going seventy miles per hour on the highways. If we take the years since the Declaration of Independence, 1776 to 2016, and divide them into three lifetimes of approximately what my grandfather lived (eighty years), we can get a good idea of how the *way we were* changed for us. So let's do that.

THE FIRST LIFETIME: 1776-1856
OVERVIEW

You are born the year the Continental Congress declared independence, and you grow up hearing old people tell stories about the American Revolution and about the heroes of that era: George Washington, Ben Franklin, Thomas Jefferson, and others. As a young man, you may choose a military career (there is no military draft), and you might see action in the War of 1812, but most likely you are not involved in the fighting and read in a newspaper about the burning of the president's house and the Battle of New Orleans. You most certainly experience the growth of patriotic spirit that follows the war. By the 1830s, as you approach old age, you have definite opinions about the major people and issues of the day: Andrew Jackson, the National Bank, slavery, abolitionism, the women's rights movement, the Mexican War, and the Compromise of 1850. As your life draws to a close, if you still have your marbles, you are concerned about the growing dispute over slavery between the North and the South.

Ninety percent of the people live in rural communities and grow and raise all or nearly all of the food they eat. The houses are mostly wooden frame of the Cape Cod or colonial style, many with kitchen additions on the back, which make them look like saltboxes: large wooden boxes with sloped lids used for storing salt. These houses are called saltbox colonials. In the 1830s, a Greek revival style of architecture catches on because of the revolution in Greece. These homes look like little Parthenons, with faux pillars and Greek temple rooflines.

The largest city in the country is New York, which has a population of 500,000 people by 1850, but the next largest, Baltimore, has only 169,000, and the third largest, Boston, has only 136,000. In the cities, there are no buildings taller than four stories, and there are no apartment buildings. Many people live in boarding houses, where they have a room, but share dining facilities with all the other boarders. Meals are served family style, so it's possible that the food a person wants is several people away, so he or she might half stand and reach across the table to get it. This was known as a boarding house reach, and this phrase was commonly used to describe the rude manners of the typical boarding house resident.

Most cities in the early part of this lifetime are along the Atlantic Coast and are seaports. Many people have occupations that have to do with fishing or foreign trade, such as shipbuilders, sailors, and merchants. By the 1850s, cities are springing up around factories. Lowell, Massachusetts, is the home of several textile weaving mills and dormitories housing the hundreds of mill girls (teenage girls straight off the farms) who operate them. The Merrimack River Valley becomes a hub of textile cities and farms that raise sheep to provide wool for the mills. Elsewhere, towns or small cities spring up around factories that produce iron, hats, shoes, clothing, farm implements, and countless other products ranging from pins to muskets.

All of what I've just described is north of the Potomac and Ohio Rivers. The South remains entirely agricultural through the entire period. The few southern cities, such as Charleston and New Orleans, are devoted to commerce, chiefly exportation of tobacco, rice, indigo, cotton and, of course, slaves. Only a small percentage of white Southerners own any slaves at all—not much more than thirty percent of the people own even one slave—and only about one percent of Southerners own large plantations with fifty or more slaves. The majority of Southerners live as Northerners do. They tend their farms themselves and hope for favorable weather. In some sections of the South, such as the Ozark section of Arkansas, the condition of the poor white farmers is deplorable. The land is so rocky and piney that it is almost impossible to produce a crop of anything.

Students often ask why so many poor whites and other Southerners who had no slaves were willing to fight and die in the Civil War to save the slave system. The answer partly lies in the fact that the poor whites in the South had no one to look down on but the slaves, and they wanted to keep it that way. "I don't live any better than a slave does," a poor white from the piney woods of Arkansas would say, "but I'm a free white man, and he's a black slave. That makes all the difference." The irony is that many of the slaves who either work in the big houses or are field hands identify with the plantation on which they live and the wealthy family for whom they work, and they look down on the "poor white trash."

The insides of most houses are cramped and uncomfortable by today's standards. Only the well-to-do have upholstered furniture; everyone else has chairs made of wood. The walls of every house, even those of the wealthy, are often smudged with carbon, collected from years of smoking candles that provide light. The more well off people use oil lamps for light, and they produce much less smoke. At least until 1860, most oil lamps use whale oil, which is extracted from the blubber of giant sperm whales. Whaling is the energy industry of your time. Whaling ships leave from New Bedford and other seacoast towns to hunt and harpoon the giant beasts. In 1851, Herman Melville writes the definitive account of the dangers and brutality of whaling in his novel *Moby Dick*.

Very few homes, until at least 1850, have central heat; most houses have a fireplace in each room; if not, people gather around one fireplace to get warm. You can easily see that daily living requires a lot of work. In the cold months, you have to keep tending to the fire, and in the warm months, you have to cut up the wood to store for the winter. There is no air conditioning in the summertime. Everyone simply sweats, takes an occasional bath, and goes around emitting his or her own distinctive odor.

Until 1850, very few houses, including those of the wealthy, have any indoor plumbing. The Executive Mansion in Washington (what we call the White House) doesn't get indoor plumbing until the 1830s, and even then, there is no indoor toilet. Every president and first lady up to the 1870s, including Lincoln, has to defecate into a bedpan that, ultimately, a servant will take away, or they go outside to the privy, a facility similar to a Porta-Potty, only made out of wood. I always wonder where Lincoln did so much profound thinking without the use of a nice bathroom.

Most families have four to six children, but many have more. It is quite common for children to die at an early age, so it is important to provide for your old age by having several children to be workers and caregivers. Lincoln has two children die before they reach adulthood, Garrison has two, the Adams families have several, and so it goes. After 1840, it is a macabre practice to lay out a deceased child on a bed or a sofa. It's also not unusual to have a photographer take a picture of the child dressed in his or her best outfit.

Children are raised with very strict discipline; "spare the rod and spoil the child," is the operative philosophy along with, "children should be seen but not heard." Wealthy families usually hire a tutor and then send their smart children off to college at about age sixteen. A poor rural community might set up a schoolhouse and hire a teacher to instruct the children of all ages who attend. It is only in Massachusetts, starting around 1845, that public schools become standard and compulsory. Until the 1850s, there are no Roman Catholic parochial schools in the country because there are not enough Roman Catholics to support them. There are some private Jesuit schools in places where there are Catholics, mostly Maryland and Louisiana. Regardless of the circumstances, every tutor or school teacher emphasizes fundamental reading and writing skills, instruction in strict moral discipline, and practice in speaking correct English. Increasingly, after 1836, the standard textbook for teaching reading skills, and morals, is the McGuffey Reader series. Progressing in difficulty through six grades, these beautiful little books give students a solid grounding in spelling, vocabulary, grammar, and public speaking. Every story has a moral and many of them are biblically based.

Work for most people is agricultural, but there are craftsmen in nearly every town, people who make shoes (cobblers), barrels (coopers), horseshoes (blacksmiths,) and many other items, such as wagon wheels (wheelwrights). Besides cooking, cleaning, and raising the children, most women make the clothes for the family. Increasingly, after 1820, they do not have to spin the threads and make the cloth themselves; they buy it from a store and then sew the garments together by hand. A mother of six children can take pride as she sits with them for a family picture, knowing that she made every article of clothing the family is wearing. Until 1840, though, the picture will be an oil painting, and only the wealthy few can commission an artist to do the job.

Most cities of any size have at least one newspaper. Boston has several, and on New Year's Day in 1831, a new one hits the streets: William Lloyd Garrison's *Liberator*. Every newspaper at this time espouses a particular political party or a cause. The way newspapers are produced is very tedious, and being aware of the process makes me even more respectful of the commitment to their causes many publishers had.

Each page of the paper has to be set in type one letter at a time. The printer has a large box, or case, with twenty-six compartments for capital letters and twenty-six compartments for small letters. The capital letter boxes are at the top of the case and the small letter boxes are at the bottom of the case; hence, they are upper case and lower case. There are also boxes for punctuation marks, lines, and blank spaces. Each of these letters, punctuation marks, and spaces is a flat piece of metal with the letter or symbol embossed on the top. The printer stands before his case with a composing stick in his hand. The composing stick is a metal box, open at the top, and attached to a short handle. In this metal box, he sets the pieces of type, one at a time, as he selects them from the case, and slowly forms a line of type. The composing stick will hold about seven lines of type at a time. When the printer has it filled, he places it in a large frame and then begins another set of lines. As he does this, he is working from a handwritten document, unless he is composing as he goes, which is a real skill! When he has the entire frame filled with blocks of type, he locks it together and lightly hammers down the typefaces with a wooden mallet to make sure they are all set evenly; then he runs an ink roller over the faces of all the type and places the frame in the printing press. He then places each piece of paper in the press, pulls a large handle to lower the paper down onto the inked type, pushes the handle back to lift the paper off, and peels the printed sheet off the press. He hangs this on a line to dry the ink. All of this produces one page of the newspaper. After the printing of the paper is completed, the printer must clean all the type with an alcohol solution; it must be thoroughly cleaned or the next paper will have blotted letters. When clean, all the pieces of type are placed, one by one, back into the correct boxes in the case. Garrison puts out his first *Liberator* using borrowed type.

When I was in junior high school, I took printing as one of the shop classes we were required to take, and I went through all of the type setting I just described. It was very tedious, especially for a twelve-year-old, and it was easy to make a mistake. A "u" at the top of a piece of type looks very much like an "n," for example. Why we had to learn this process in 1957 baffles me, but later in life, it did give me an appreciation for what publishers had to go through to put out their papers.

Printing is just one example of how almost all work in your lifetime is very labor intensive. Except for the spinning and weaving machines in the textile mills, almost every job is done by hand. A bookkeeper in a shop has to write all his accounts with a pen that he dips into an ink well; a farmer harvesting wheat has to swing a scythe in large sweeps all day long in the hot sun; canal diggers working on the Erie Canal have to dig the dirt out with shovels and throw it into baskets that will be hoisted up by horses with a pulley system to the bank above. There are, however, machines being invented in the 1840s and 1850s, such as the reaper for harvesting wheat and the sewing machine, that will make work easier in the future.

Travel is also very tedious in your lifetime. As Carl Sandburg said in his biography of Lincoln, it is a very *horsey* time, because almost every mode of transportation depends on horses. You ride a horse, hitch a horse to a carriage or a wagon, or watch a horse pull your flatboat down the canal. Steamboats are common by 1830 along the major rivers, but most people in most places have to use horses. Of course, horses are great, and they are pretty to look at, but they have to be taken care of, and when you have to hitch one up to a carriage or wagon, you have to manage a whole series of straps and buckles, all the while being careful that the adorable horse doesn't kick you in the knee ... or higher! We have the nostalgic image of a horse pulling a sleigh as the family rides across the fields to Grandma's house, but the reality is that someone in the house, probably the father, has to go out in the cold and dark and, with freezing hands, hitch up the horse to the bulky sleigh. Then everyone has to pile into the sleigh, cover their legs with heavy blankets, and freeze their butts off as they feel the icy winds nip at their faces. When they get to Grandma's, Father has to unhitch the sleigh, put the horse into the barn, put a blanket over him, give him a feedbag, and rub him down. No one complains about this kind of work because they don't know anything different, and whining is not allowed in the early nineteenth century.

By the late 1830s, it is becoming increasingly possible to take a train to some destinations, especially in the northeast. By the last years of your life, railroads are forming a web across the country, at least in the north. Early rail travel is very uncomfortable and not particularly fast (15 mph), but by the end of your life in the mid-1850s, trains are moving along at an incredible forty miles per hour, and if you have the money, they are the only way to go from Boston to New York or from New York to Chicago. Of course, they scare the farm animals as they roar through the countryside belching smoke and sparks. Occasionally, a wood burning boiler on a locomotive explodes and kills all on board, but that is becoming increasingly rare and most people are willing to take their chances. The same is true of the steamboats on the Ohio or Mississippi rivers. In one year, one in five steamboats suffers a boiler explosion, but that means you have an eighty percent chance of getting to where you are going, so it's "all aboard!"

For entertainment in your day, there are theater productions in the cities and a few primitive theaters for stage plays in the towns. For most people, social life revolves around the church: church services, church socials, church picnics, and church dances. On the frontier, religious revival meetings, sometimes drawing thousands of people for three- or four-day events, are the highlight of the year. Great preachers such as Charles Grandison Finney in Ohio, hold audiences spellbound for hours as they summon the Holy Spirit. Many towns have lyceums, groups who hold meetings to hear lectures on various topics. In 1837, Abraham Lincoln famously gives a talk to the Young Men's Lyceum of Springfield, in which he exhorts his listeners to pay strict obedience to the law.

The only music available is what you can hear at a minstrel show or what you might play on your harpsichord in your own home. A minstrel show is what would later be called a variety show, with songs, dances, and comedy skits. They feature white performers in blackface, mocking the speech and antics of blacks as the whites like to think of them: dimwitted, but with a great sense of rhythm. One of the popular songs of the day is "Old Folks at Home," by Stephen Foster. Sometimes called "Swanee River," this song depicts plantation life in the South from a slave's point of view. The problem for our modern ears is that the song has the slave still longing for "de ole plantation" and for "de ole folks at home," as if his life there was idyllic. Other songs people listen to are old folk ballads and, of course, religious hymns.

Communication is slow and unpredictable. The only way to get a message to someone in a distant town is to write a letter, post it at the U.S. Post Office in town, wait three days to two weeks for it to get there, and then the same amount of time for an answer to come back. Because so much time will transpire before you hear from that person again, you tend to write long, newsy letters, and when a letter comes to you, you read it over and over and carry it around in your pocket. In 1830, if you take mail out of your pocket to read, it was probably written a month ago, not a minute ago, and you're not certain the person who wrote it is still alive.

Overall, your eighty years on the planet have been pleasant and you have seen some positive changes. The country is growing and has reached the Pacific Ocean by the time you are in your seventies. Daily life for you is really not too much different from what it was like for the generations before you, except there are some clear symptoms of drastic changes to come as you enter old age. The railroad and the new factories presage an industrial nation that will be very different from what you have experienced in your lifetime. There also seems to be some nasty bickering and a lot of talk about a civil war that, if it comes, could change things a whole lot. But all of that will be for your great-grandson, born in 1856, to experience.

THE SECOND LIFETIME: 1856–1936
OVERVIEW

You are fortunate enough to be too young to take a military role in the Civil War, but certainly by the time you are nine years old, you are very aware of the high price in human suffering the war took on people from every city, town, and village in the country, North and South. After the war, you are aware of the great questions of how the emancipated slaves should be treated. Depending on whether you are from the North or the

South, you have quite different ideas on this, but maybe less so as the years go by. Sadly, by 1900, almost every American is a racist who wants to keep the Negroes *in their place*. As a young adult, you may have the opportunity, or the misfortune, to find work in one of the many factories and railroads that are springing up. If you're lucky, your parents are part of the upper crust of society, the golden gild in what Mark Twain calls the Gilded Age. If you're unlucky, you are part of the lower class and live in a slum or in a sod hut out on the prairie. In 1898, you marvel that Teddy Roosevelt, a man almost your age, goes to fight in the Spanish-American War and comes home a hero. By the time you are in your fifties, automobiles are making their appearance, and before long, you *own* one, probably a Ford Model T. You hear about the Wright brothers' first flight in 1903, and by the time you are seventy-one, a man named Charles Lindbergh is flying an airplane across the ocean to Paris! At the age of sixty, if you have a grandson, you may see him go off to fight in the Great World War. In the 1920s, you probably do not approve of the fashions, dances, and fast lifestyle of the young generation. At the end of your life, the country slides into a great economic depression. By the time of your death, you have a definite opinion about Franklin Roosevelt and his expensive New Deal. You are probably only dimly aware of the new war that is brewing in Europe and Asia. It will soon lead to another world war. Some of the people your age, who were nine when the Civil War ended, will actually live to see the beginning of a second world war.

Your home could still be a cape or a colonial or a Greek revival, around since your grandfather's time, but it could very well be the popular new gothic style that will soon be called Victorian, after the queen of England, whose name will be given to the era. These are large, elaborate houses with several gables, towers, or peaks. They often have large porches, and they always have elaborate trim, along the eaves, around the windows and doors, and even along the porch railings. They also have elaborate color schemes, often involving three or four colors, such that the window frames are one color, the siding is another color, the trim is yet a third color, and there may even be an accent stripe between the two stories of the house that is a fourth color. (As an impoverished teacher, I used to paint houses during the summer to make ends meet, and I can say without hesitation that one hundred-year-old Victorian houses were a nightmare: tall structures with detailed color matchups, where one color met another and I had to paint the line perfectly while clinging to a forty-foot ladder.)

By the turn of the century (1900), you probably live in a house with indoor plumbing, but not necessarily. Houses in rural areas still often have outdoor pumps for water and, of course, outhouses (or privies) for personal necessities. It is possible you could live your entire life without indoor plumbing, because some areas don't get it until the 1950s.

If you live in the city, you have oil lamps that increasingly use kerosene rather than whale oil. Gas lighting is available after 1870, and by 1890, you might very well switch to the new electric lighting made possible by Edison's incandescent light bulb and the electric power plants being built in most of the larger cities. If you live in the country, it's gas lighting for you, until at least 1920, and maybe not until FDR's New Deal creates the Rural Electrification Administration in 1936, the last year of your life.

Your house is probably equipped with central heating provided by a coal-burning furnace, unless you live far from a city and still have to depend on a wood stove or fireplace. The coal furnaces, and the factories that also burn coal, are filling the air with black soot. In some cities, the air is so polluted that you can barely breathe, except on those rare occasions when the wind blows fresh and clear from the northwest and blows the smoke away.

Boarding houses become increasingly scarce as millions of city dwellers take residence in apartments, living units that have their own utilities, which means the owners do not provide meals or other services. The problem is, these buildings are often poorly built, are dirty, and are crowded. By 1880, the age of the tenement slum is in full force, and you're lucky if your parents are not residents in one.

Until the turn of the century, and even beyond in many cities, horses still dominate the transportation system. Horses pull carriages, wagons, and the new trolleys that run up and down city streets. Many cities still do not have very good sanitation systems or water supplies in 1900, so between the smog in the air and the horse poop and garbage on the streets, a city is not a very pretty place. Gradually, in your later years, as automobiles become common and the cities build sewer systems, urban life improves, but even in the 1920s and '30s, you might still walk down an alley and encounter a dead horse.

Many families still have multiple children, for the same reasons they always did. Child mortality is still very high; how could it not be with all the vermin and filth around? During some hot, fetid summers, the number of children (and adults, for that matter) dying from typhoid, tuberculosis, and other diseases carried by contaminated water, is almost as bad as it was in Europe during the plague years. My grandparents on my father's side had six children between 1915 and 1925. Three of them died before they were twelve.

Almost all children now go to public schools that are managed pretty much like factories. The children sit at desks that are bolted to the floor in straight rows. The teachers are almost always strict disciplinarians who are not constrained from using physical punishment on misbehaving urchins. Since the "new immigrants" from Eastern Europe began arriving, there are a lot more Roman Catholics in cities such as Boston and New York, so Catholic parochial schools are starting to spring up. It is becoming fairly common for most teenagers to at least attend high school. College is still for the very wealthy or the very high achieving. By 1935, only about four percent of Americans have college degrees.

For children and young adults in the late 1800s, the clothing styles are very elaborate and bulky. Women's dresses cover everything from the neck to the floor and are often multi-layered. Corsets are required to form the hourglass figure. A bustle on the backside—a wire framework—holds the fabric of the dress up and keeps it from dragging on the ground. It also has the effect of giving a woman a large rear end, a *look* that many men of your time find attractive.

Fortunately, the bustle is gone by the early 1900s, but the head-to-toe dresses continue until the end of the First World War. By then, you are getting on in years and are not as able to appreciate the new styles that come in during the post-war 1920s. Almost overnight, off come the corsets and other restrictive paraphernalia women wore before the war and in come the short skirts, the bobbed hair, and the dangling beads. Out goes the waltz and in come the Charleston and other fast dances accompanied by jazz music and a new morality that embraces freedom. You are in your seventies by now and are most likely scandalized by the whole scene, or mad as hell that it didn't happen when you were young and could enjoy it. Either way, you are a cranky old person.

Entertainment and communication have improved immensely during your lifetime. Since the 1915 movie *Birth of a Nation*, a three-hour film that glorified the rise of the Ku Klux Klan, full-length feature films have become common. In 1927, with *The Jazz Singer*, films have become "talkies," and by the end of your life, people are going to the movies every weekend. For music, you no longer have to rely on having a piano or a harmonica in the house; there are recordings that you can play on your phonograph. Also, as the 1920s move along, radio becomes a standard piece of equipment in almost every home. Millions of people tune in every night to their favorite radio programs, such as *Amos and Andy*, a sitcom about two black men from Georgia who try to find a better life as owners of a taxi cab in Chicago. The voices are done by two white men, and the situations often reflect on the racial stereotypes about black people: Amos and Andy and their friends, such as George "The Kingfish" Stevens, all speak with heavy Negro accents and are always trying to concoct ridiculous "get rich quick" schemes. *Your Hit Parade*, an American radio and television music program, offers the most popular and bestselling songs of the week each Saturday night. By the last decade of your life, you could sit and listen to the radio all day, and many people your age do just that.

Getting around becomes much easier during your lifetime. All of the cities and most of the towns are paving their roads by the 1920s, and the automobile has become a fixture on American streets. By the late 1920s, it is possible to drive coast-to-coast on pavement. The model T Ford is on the way out by your seventieth birthday in 1926, and there are now dozens of other choices: Henry Ford's new Model A, Chevrolet, Buick, Cadillac, and the luxurious Packard, to name a few.

By the 1930s, it is possible to fly coast-to-coast in an airplane. The Democratic presidential candidate in 1932, Franklin Roosevelt, flies from New York to Chicago to personally accept his party's nomination. He is the first presidential candidate ever to accept in person and the first ever to fly in an airplane. The air age has arrived.

Within the cities, trolley cars have become electrified and have extended their lines out to the local suburbs. Some cities, led by Boston in 1897, have developed subway systems that have put the trolleys underground for at least some of their routes.

Gradually, the tall buildings with steel girders rise up in the middle of the cities. The age of the skyscraper arrives, complete with the new elevators that carry people up the multiple stories. In 1931, the tallest building in the world goes up in mid-town Manhattan. In spite of the deepening depression, the Empire State Building soars one hundred two stories and provides thousands of people with steady work. My grandfather, Carmon Elliott, is one of them. He works to install the elevators in the Empire State Building and stays on as elevator maintenance manager.

In your lifetime you have seen the United States come of age and become a world class industrial power. Many Americans are not quite prepared to accept the responsibilities of that status by the time you pass on, but they will soon have to. When you were a child, it was still possible to live on a farm and think the rest of the world was very far away. Most people did. As you lived through your decades, the world closed in upon you. The country fought a terrible civil war within itself; immigrants from strange places arrived; cities that gobbled up the land and covered it with smoke-belching factories spread into the countryside; and railroads and automobiles appeared and made it increasingly unlikely that you and the people around you would stay in one place for very long. In your last years you might be among the very first people ever to yearn for the old days, when life was simpler and change didn't come so fast.

THE THIRD LIFETIME: 1936-2016
OVERVIEW

When you start first grade, the world is fighting yet another world war. You are nine years old when it ends and are very focused on the war—the tanks, the airplanes, the parachutes, the battle ships—and you spend much of your young years hearing the veterans talk about their experiences in the Pacific, in Italy, in Belgium, and in all kinds of places with strange names all over the globe. This lifetime approximates my lifetime (1944-?), and I grew up hearing about New Guinea. My father would often say, "When I was in New Guinea ..." In the fifties, you are afraid of atomic bombs, but on a lighter note, you are also infatuated with the new cars that come out every year. The sixties bring the Vietnam War and the Civil Rights Movement, and you are likely to be emotionally involved in either the liberal dove side of those issues or the conservative hawk side. People in the middle, where I tended to be, were often very torn. In your middle age years, you see the incredible Watergate scandal unfold. After that, a decade of Ronald Reagan either excites you if you are a conservative, or appalls you and you call the president Ronald "Raygun." But by the 1990s, it seems the country has solved many of its problems. The cold war comes to an end, the economy glides along prosperously, and all seems fine except for a few bumps in the road, such as the first bombing of the World Trade Center. But then comes the real attack on the World Trade Center, the horrific events of 9/11, and as you reach old age, the whole world seems to be entering a very dark period of terrorism, moral confusion, and increasing complexity

The early years of your life might be a little difficult for you and your parents. Your father is very likely off to war (fifteen million American men were) and your mother is left at home, possibly holding a job at a war materials factory. You and your family have to deal with rationing of meat, dairy products, and such exotic items as pineapple and coffee. As a young child during the war, you might help with the war effort by collecting old metal pots and pans and buying war bond stamps at school.

The post-war era starting in 1945 brings new prosperity to many Americans. If you are white, your father might get a well-paying job and your family buys a house in one of the newly emerging suburbs. In 1947, Arthur Levitt starts a planned suburb of six thousand small but efficient cape-style homes on Long Island. The houses go up quickly (thirty houses a day in 1948), and families, many of them returning G.I.s, are able to afford them and move in. By 1951, over 40,000 people live in Levittown. Symptomatic of the times, all of them are white because the sales agents will accept no applications from potential black buyers. (So much for the idea that only Southerners are racists!) Other suburbs across the country spring up quickly and nearly all of them are white.

In 1951, my family moves into a new suburb in Melrose, Massachusetts, near Boston. All of the houses are small colonials or capes and every one of them is owned by a white family. If a black family ever tries to buy there, I'm sure there will be a huge uproar, but as far as I know, the issue hasn't come up.

By the 1950s, almost all houses and apartment buildings have indoor plumbing and electricity. Coal furnaces are on their way out, even in large factories and schools. Oil burning furnaces, and later gas furnaces, take their place, yet, even as late as 1960, there are coal trucks dumping coal down chutes into the cellars of houses that have coal furnaces. If your family still has such a furnace, you might be the lucky young man who gets to shovel the coal into the furnace every morning and bank the coal fire every evening.

The late 1940s and early 1950s are a great time to be a white kid in America. The baby boom is in full swing, the economy is more prosperous than ever, and the future really looks bright. It seems like your only concerns are what the new cars will look like this year, what great westerns or war movies are out, and what players will be in your next pack of baseball cards. By 1952, your family probably has a television set with a huge antenna on the roof to pick up the signals. There are three networks, so every night you have three choices of what to watch every half hour. Sunday night at eight is always the *Ed Sullivan Show*, which features many famous singers and comedians. If you are a suburban white fourteen-year-old in 1950, you will never have it so good again. But the country is about to experience dramatic changes.

The sixties start out like a continuation of the fifties. Rock and roll music, which first appeared in 1955 with Bill Haley's "Rock Around the Clock," has really taken hold. Ed Sullivan had Elvis Presley on his show in 1957 and wouldn't allow the cameras to focus below Elvis' waist so the audience couldn't see the hip gyrations, but we're getting past that kind of squeamishness in the sixties. Other rock and roll singers are not only playing the hard beating rhythm, they are moving all over the stage, even playing the piano standing up and hitting some of the keys with their feet. The older generation that grooved to the Big Band Sounds of Glen Miller and Tommy Dorsey, who expected their singers like Frank Sinatra to stand still at the microphone and simply sing, are uncomfortable with the new brand of showmanship. Still, the performers wear nice dresses or jackets and ties, and they have nice haircuts. The offenses to the senses are mild compared with what is to come.

After the Kennedy assassination in 1963, a confluence of forces comes together to produce a social revolution of greater proportions than the country has seen in decades. The millions of babies born during the boom of the late forties and early fifties reach college age in the sixties.

The natural rebellion that people in their late teens and twenties feel toward their parents and their parents' generation starts to kick in. Add to that the Vietnam War with the older people supporting it out of habit and the younger people despising it because they are the ones who are fighting and dying for elusive reasons, and you have a recipe for a great youth rebellion. The struggles of the black population add energy to the mix because young people blame their parents for creating the racism that has caused all of the problems. By the late sixties, you see a counter culture all around you: hippies wearing outrageous clothing and smoking pot, rebellious rock music screaming at you about sex, drugs, and revolution, and rioting in the streets over the war, racism, and other issues.

Born in 1936, you reach your thirties when the counter culture is in full swing, and it is very disconcerting. You are getting to an age when you might want to settle down with a permanent job, get married, have children—the whole American Dream. But the rebels are screaming at you that you are selling out to the establishment. By your thirtieth birthday in 1966, even getting a haircut seems like a sellout to the bourgeois values and the military industrial complex.

As the seventies begin, the outrageous clothing and music continue; in fact, they peak. Everyone starts to look like they are part of the cover of the Beatles' *Sergeant Pepper's Lonely Hearts Club Band*. Bell-bottom pants and wildly designed psychedelic shirts are in. A shopping trip for men's clothing is fruitless if you are looking for traditional jackets and ties; only the staid top-of-the-line stores, such as Brooks Brothers, have anything close to that. Bring a fat wallet when you shop in those places. Sears and other stores with moderate prices carry clothing you think only a clown should wear, so you go an entire decade without buying a single set of new threads.

The music, movies, and television shows through the last decades of the twentieth century become increasingly sophisticated and complex. By the end of the century, you are watching films that have special effects undreamed of when movie making first started. Probably the epitome of movie making is the epic film *Titanic*, which employs millions of gallons of water on the set, a giant mockup of the ill-fated ship, computer generated people falling to their deaths off of the stern of the broken ship, and film editing so carefully done that audiences feel like they are right in the middle of the tragic sinking.

During the eighties and nineties, as you go through your middle aged years, life seems to have returned to the way it was before the wild disruptions of the sixties and early seventies. Whether Reagan's election brought it in can't be known, but there is a return to more conservative clothing, and the older generation is not as reviled as they were.

One aspect of life around you that changes dramatically as you go through your forties and fifties is the way women see themselves and the role they play in society. Your mother may have worked in a factory during the war as a Rosie the Riveter, but after the war, she was supposed to give up her job to a man (presumably a returning vet) and go back to having babies and being a housewife. Most women did just that, and the fifties TV shows always depict them in their aprons, staying at home and watching the kids. June Cleaver, from the TV show *Leave It to Beaver*, becomes the icon of the 1950's mom. But the 1964 Civil Rights Act that includes gender in the list of factors employers cannot use in determining employment and Betty Friedan's book *The Feminine Mystique*, a bestseller through the last seven years of the sixties, begin to change that. By the 1970s, women are demanding to be set free from their stereotypes. They want the Mrs. and Miss prefixes to be replaced by a simple Ms., so that a woman's identity is no longer determined by whether or not she has a husband. They want to be seen on television and in the movies as leaders and action heroes. There have always been the Joan of Arc and Amazon anomalies, but now women want those types of women to replace June Cleaver as the role models for young girls.

In the last years of the twentieth century, one thing that is becoming increasingly important is the advent of the personal computer and the cellular phone. Word processing and desktop publishing become possible. When you were in college, you literally had to cut and paste to edit a manuscript you were writing, and you had to erase a mistake or cover it with Wite-Out. Now you can make an entire page letter-perfect before you print it out. Even more amazing, by the late nineties, you can send a letter—an email—to someone through the internet! No more waiting for days for a return letter from your lover, your brother, your mother, or your best friend. If you don't get a response in a few minutes, you start to worry.

To make the new age even more amazing, you no longer have to go to the library to look something up. The new internet makes it possible to research a topic on your computer and read several sources about it without having to take a step. The only problem is that you no longer have an editor between you and a misguided or uninformed writer, so you might get information that is flat out wrong. One day you look up Theodore Roosevelt and one site tells you he said, "We have nothing to fear but fear itself." Wrong on two counts: It was Franklin Roosevelt who said that, and his actual words were, "The only thing we have to fear is fear itself." The website was probably the work of some geek holed up in his bedroom with nothing much to do except send out misinformation.

You soon realize that wrong research is not the only problem caused by the new personal computers. All kinds of computer games become available, starting with Pac-Man in the eighties and advancing to very sophisticated video games by the early twenty-first century. Now the player can slam dunk a basketball on his screen and actually feel like he's doing it, even though he never leaves his chair. The result of all this inactive action by so many players becomes evident as the twenty-first century dawns: many people are getting no real exercise and are getting fatter and fatter. By the year 2016, the obesity epidemic is a serious concern, and you are very likely to become part of it if you let your screens rule your life.

In the second decade of the twenty-first century, the technology problem becomes compounded by the advent of iPads, iPhones, and social media sites such as Facebook. Now people can send and receive text messages, watch music videos online, and do all sorts of other things while they are sitting in a restaurant or even walking down the street. The result is a whole generation of people who are totally self-absorbed and disconnected from what is happening around them, even from their own friends and families. Paradoxically, they are also *too* connected, constantly able to see what everyone else is doing and becoming dissatisfied with how *their* lives compare with all the others.

In 1900, Mark Twain said that the twentieth century was not his century, even though he was still alive. In a farewell that was a few years early (he died in 1910), he wished the new century well, but he knew it would be very different from the one that he had inhabited. You feel a bit like Twain. The twenty-first century is not yours, and you are finding it increasingly difficult to comprehend the changes, let alone adjust to them. In June 2015, when the Supreme Court rules that the Fourteenth Amendment requirement that states must give "equal protection of the laws" to all people means that states must permit gay couples to marry, you are rattled. Some of your contemporaries have no trouble (presumably) accepting a change in the definition of marriage that has been accepted for ten thousand years. You, and many others your age, are at least, to some degree, troubled by it, whether you admit it or not. As you think about it, however, one thing comes into focus: In the fifties and sixties, when you were young and the idea that two men could get married was absolutely and totally unthinkable, you knew some young men and women who were very likely gay, although they never would have admitted it, even if they were tortured. Instead, they had to suffer in silence as they watched the *normal* people go on dates, fall in love, get married, and have children. You now realize that must have been hard for them; in fact, their lives may have been a living hell, and your view softens a bit, if not a lot.

Also, sometime during the fifties or sixties, you remember reading George Orwell's book *1984*. Published in 1949, the novel described life in the future (1984), when the government has become totalitarian and keeps total control over the citizens. Big Brother, the master of all, keeps watch over all the people by means of video screens in their homes. There is no escaping the eyes of Big Brother in this totalitarian dictatorship. The actual 1984 comes and goes, and even though a few people see Ronald Reagan's reelection that year as another step toward dictatorship, most people are rather complacent about the possibility of total government control of their lives. But after the attacks on September 11, 2001, and the passage of the Patriot Act the following year, government surveillance becomes increasingly common. By 2015, almost any activity that takes place outside of private homes is caught on camera by monitors that are posted almost everywhere. Often this is a good thing, as criminals are caught in the act, police brutality is exposed, and those falsely accused of crimes are able to prove where they were at the time. For these reasons, most of the younger people are perfectly fine with the all-pervasive cameras. "We have nothing to hide," they say when asked about it, and they have to be asked about it for them to even think about it. You, by contrast, conjure up images of *1984*, of government control, and Big Brother monitoring your every act to make sure you are conforming to the views of the state. You wish the younger folks weren't quite so calm about it all, but then, when terrorist attacks occur, you are glad, along with everyone else, that cameras filmed the bad guy wearing the white baseball hat as he brought the bomb into the Boston Marathon finish line area.

As you near the end of your days in 2016, you are completing the third lifetime that has been lived since the United States became a nation. The people who lived the first lifetime (1776-1856) saw relatively few changes in their entire time on Earth. The only really significant differences in those eighty years were the beginnings of railroads and factories and the invention of the telegraph. Everything else was pretty much the same for most people in 1856, as it had been eighty years before. Those whose lives spanned the second period (1856-1936) saw much more change, as the country went through an industrial revolution and fought in a world war. Not only was the railroad system completed, automobiles made their appearance and became ubiquitous, and airplanes took to the skies. Cities grew huge and skyscrapers made the streets of the big cities into canyons. As you looked around you in 1936, you saw a much different world than you did when you were a child in the late 1850s.

The lifetime that spanned the years 1936 to 2016, however, saw the greatest changes of all. The population of the country more than doubled; it went from one hundred thirty million in 1936 to three hundred twenty million by 2016. The airplane became a rocket to the moon and the jet plane was flying six hundred miles per hour; roads became superhighways traversing the country up and down; radio gave way to television, and television gave way to the internet and many forms of instant communication.

A person coming back to life from the first lifespan in 1936 would be startled at the changes, but would probably be able to adjust fairly quickly. The airplane would probably be the biggest shock for this time traveler, but that same person coming back eighty years later, in 2016, would be totally bewildered. Everywhere he looked he would see things that disoriented him: jet planes, television, the internet, people walking down streets and talking on the telephone as they walked, blacks not only voting but getting elected president, women not only voting but running for president, and two men getting married to each other. The changes each lifetime has witnessed have been increasingly fast and profound.

This overview of the way we were in the three lifespans that have occurred since the Declaration of Independence has been quick and superficial. A thousand-page book would be required to tell the full story of how life was in each of those periods: the names of the songs that were sung, the actors and other performers who got peoples' attention, the brand names of the products that people used, and so much more would help you experience life as it really was for the people who lived those lives. Yet even with just what I've presented here, I hope you can get an appreciation for how different it was for the people who lived each era. If you try to relate to history and see it as something that your ancestors—your great grandparents, your grandparents, your parents, and, yes, even you—have lived, you realize it is not irrelevant; it is the substance of your life.

Think of how different your life would be if you were born into one of the other eras, how differently you would think about things and how differently you would relate to your family and friends. Is it not likely that the very same *you* living in the first lifetime (1776-1856) would have been more limited in your view of the world, more racially prejudiced, more religious, more physically fit, more devoted to your family, and more likely to get married and stay married to the same person?

I always have my students do a project called "History and Me." The project requires them to interview the older people in their families and then write a paper and create a poster detailing something interesting about the life of that person. For example, express how he served in Vietnam, how she immigrated to the United States, how she worked in a factory making bullets during World War II, etc. The stories students bring in to share with the class are always very interesting. Through this assignment, I hope to show the students that history has a lot to tell them about their families, about their ancestors, and about their own lives … if they will let it. That last point is key; you have to let history into your life and not just view it as "crap we have to learn."

If you don't know what came before you, or where you fit in the march of time, then you are living in a vacuum, you are floating around in a void, you have no bearings. At the end of your life you may think you will disappear into the nothingness, when in fact you won't. *You* will become part of history, and some people in the future will know who you were or at least what you and your generation did.

ROLE MODELS

JOHN QUINCY ADAMS.

As a Christian, I believe that the Bible is the best source for role models, and we certainly need to look no further than Jesus for life instruction. The question "What would Jesus do?" has certainly guided me, at least in the years since I became a believer. There are numerous people in American history who have led exemplary lives, and it is no accident that many of them were devout Christians. There is a very long list of men and women from whom I have learned the secrets of leading a useful and productive life, but the ones who top my list include John Adams, his wife, Abigail, and their son, John Quincy Adams, William Lloyd Garrison, Angelina and Sarah Grimke, Dorothea Dix, Henry Clay, Abraham Lincoln, Booker T. Washington, John Marshall Harlan, Theodore Roosevelt, Eleanor Roosevelt, Dr. Martin Luther King, Jr., Ronald Reagan, and George H.W. Bush. None of these people were without flaws, as I will be sure to point out, but they all embodied at least one personal characteristic or devoted their lives to an ideal that I admire and have tried to incorporate into my own life. You might find their stories inspirational, or you may have or develop your own list. At the end of the chapter, I will suggest other possible role models you might want to adopt, even though they didn't make the cut for me.

THE ADAMS FAMILY,
MODELS OF HARD WORK AND INTEGRITY

I have an uncommon interest in the family of John Adams because I was born in Quincy, Massachusetts, just a short distance away from the Adams family homestead. My family moved away before I was five, so I don't remember the town from those days very well, but since I moved back to Boston, I have visited the Adams houses several times and have walked through them with considerable interest.

The Adams family ranks high in my esteem in spite of the one serious personality flaw that bedeviled at least the men among them. John Adams and his son, John Quincy, were both decidedly vain and could not get their egos out of the way of their relationships with other people, even though they were acutely aware of the problem. John was repeatedly writing to Abigail during his long absences from home about how his vanity was making it difficult for him to form alliances with the other members of the Continental Congress in 1776. Later, as vice president and then president, he had the same problem with the Congress of the United States. The musical *1776* has Adams admitting to Jefferson that he is "obnoxious and disliked," and that was actually true. That line was not just thrown into the show for humor. John Quincy, likewise, was so pompous that the Jacksonians had no trouble lampooning him in political campaigns. This flaw was so serious that the Adamses almost made it into Chapter VII of this book: cautionary tales of how *not* to behave.

Despite this, all of the members of the Adams family, John, Abigail, and John Quincy, led lives based on such high principles of morality, industriousness, and devotion to duty that they are on my list of role models. During the buildup to the American Revolution, John Adams was one of the leading advocates for American rights as Englishmen in the British Empire, and by 1770, he had become convinced that a complete separation from Britain was the only solution to the difficulties. In Boston, he was an ally of his more radical cousin, Sam Adams, and was well regarded in revolutionary circles. However, when British soldiers fired into an unruly crowd in front of the old state house on March 5, 1770, and the outraged people of Boston began referring to the incident in which five men died as a massacre, John Adams declared that the soldiers deserved their rights as Englishmen, just like everyone else. He decided to defend them in court to make sure they received a fair trial. Adams was a very capable lawyer, and he was able to show at trial that the soldiers were indeed threatened by the mob and had some justification for using their weapons. The trial ended with the acquittal of six of the eight soldiers who were charged, and a finding of guilty of manslaughter for the other two. Adams was not disowned by his fellow revolutionaries for taking the soldiers' case, but it did take courage to defend Redcoats who were so thoroughly hated in that inflamed city.

In the thirty years that followed the Boston Massacre, John Adams sacrificed time with his family, personal comforts, and the chance to acquire great wealth as an attorney, in order to serve his country. As a delegate from Massachusetts to the Continental Congress, he skillfully maneuvered the vote for independence that occurred on July 2, 1776. During the ensuing revolutionary war, he traveled to Europe to work with Benjamin Franklin to enlist the help of the French. He also went to Holland to acquire Dutch financial assistance. Back home, in 1780, he authored the constitution for the state of Massachusetts that is still in use today and that served as a model for the United States Constitution seven years later. When George Washington was elected president in 1788, John Adams was elected vice president and served for eight years in the hero's shadow.

Finally, in 1796, Adams won the presidency himself. It was as president that he performed his last great service to the country. As was so often the case with Adams, he was hated for it. In 1798, the country was screaming for war with France because the French Navy was attacking U.S. ships and the French government had insulted our ambassadors by demanding bribes. John Adams could have easily gotten a war declaration from Congress at that time, and he would have been very popular if he had done so. He would have easily been reelected in 1800 as the leader of a nation that was at war. Instead, Adams refused to satisfy the warmongers. He knew the country was not ready for a war with France and that the result might very well be defeat and a considerable loss of prestige, if not actual territory. Instead of a war message to Congress, he sent a peace delegation to Paris, and the result was an agreement with the new government in France, headed by a man named Napoleon Bonaparte. Adams was sure that he had done the right thing, and history bears him out: Napoleon was about to conquer most of Europe, and it doesn't stretch the imagination much to see how he would have done the same to us. With a touch of irony, which was as close as Adams ever came to humor, he suggested that his tombstone should say, "Here lies John Adams, who took upon himself the responsibility of peace with France in the year 1800."

From John Adams, then, I get a sense of how important it is in life to do your duty and to dedicate yourself to what is right, regardless of the difficulties involved or the opposition you encounter. His partner in this, his stalwart wife, Abigail, is also admirable. I admired this woman so much that Abigail was on our short list of names for our daughter. She held the fort in their little home in Braintree while John was away serving his country. During the Revolutionary War, the British Army was constantly threatening her home, and she, alone with the children, was prepared to defend it. She endured smallpox epidemics and kept the farm producing so that her family was not without food. She raised four children, educated them herself, to a large degree, and molded their character. A faithful person, she began their moral education and set them all on a path of regular Bible reading, study, and prayer.

When John was away at the Continental Congress in Philadelphia, she wrote to him often and offered advice. Her most famous letter admonished him to "remember the ladies" in the deliberations and make sure their rights were protected. "All men would be tyrants, if they could," she reminded him. There is little doubt that much of John Adams' wisdom at the congress was the product of his exchanges with his enlightened soulmate, Abigail.

One of their children, John Quincy Adams, entered public life as a teenager by accompanying his father on his diplomatic mission to Paris.

He eventually served as secretary of state and president. Carrying on the strict discipline and sense of duty that he inherited from his parents, John Quincy Adams set the most admirable example of them all. After leaving the presidency, he chose to reenter politics as a member of the United States House of Representatives, representing the Quincy and Braintree districts of Massachusetts. He was the only ex-president ever to reenter the government as a member of the House. Serving for seventeen years, he gained a reputation as the most eloquent opponent of slavery in Congress. He tirelessly presented abolitionist petitions on the floor of the House in spite of the fact that the southern congressmen had passed a gag resolution banning such speech. Adams served his country and the abolitionist cause until the very end of his life. He collapsed in his House seat on February 21, 1848, and died two days later.

John Quincy Adams' son, Charles Francis Adams, also served in Congress and was United States ambassador to Great Britain during the Civil War. His service there was crucial in keeping Britain from supporting the Confederate States of America and possibly helping the South achieve its goal of a slave-holding republic.

For almost one hundred years, then, the Adams family played critical roles in American history. Besides admiring their accomplishments, I admire the way they lived their lives. They were dedicated to public service, they were serious scholars, and they were faithful people who tried to do God's will. They set the bar pretty high, but that's what we should look for in role models. Many modern day role models have looked spectacular for a while, and then it turns out they have feet of clay; they were not at all what they seemed. Lance Armstrong and Bill Cosby come to mind. But John Adams, Abigail Adams, and John Quincy Adams never had any drug problems, any cheating scandals, any extramarital affairs, or sex crimes in their lives. They never let me down.

WILLIAM LLOYD GARRISON
CHAMPION OF THE OPPRESSED

In Boston, on the Commonwealth Avenue mall between Dartmouth and Exeter Streets, sits a large statue of William Lloyd Garrison. The irony behind this impressive tribute to one of the city's most famous citizens is that when Garrison was a young man in 1835, the most wealthy and influential men of the city dragged him through the streets with a rope around his neck, intent on hanging him from a tree on Boston Common. Only the intervention of the mayor and the police saved Garrison. His offense was that he disrupted the profitable economic relationship between the North and the South by speaking out against slavery and publishing a radical anti-slavery newspaper, *The Liberator*. In the end, of course, Garrison proved to be on the right side of history (as we say these days) and, thus, earned himself a statue. The pigeons poop on it and most people walk past it without a glance, because they have no idea who he was.

I became aware of Garrison in high school and was immediately impressed by him. It wasn't his glasses, although that was a definite plus for me, and it wasn't because our history book praised him; it did not. In fact, it passed him off as a crank who was far too radical to have much influence, even in the North. I admired him because, as a very young man, he took on a cause that he passionately believed in, fought for it against overwhelming odds, withstood verbal and even physical attacks, lived a life of almost abject poverty for more than thirty years, and ultimately saw his goal achieved. I wondered if I would have the physical and emotional strength to endure what he did for an oppressed people.

After I began teaching, I learned more about Garrison's career and became inspired enough to write a book about him and another man I admired, Abraham Lincoln. *The Agitator and the Politician* tells the story of how Garrison was drawn to the cause of freeing the slaves. He then published *The Liberator* every week, calling for the slaves' immediate emancipation. So uncompromising were his demands for immediate abolition of slavery—with no compensation to slave owners for their loss of property—that even politicians such as Abraham Lincoln, who disliked slavery, would have nothing to do with him. But Garrison set a standard; he created a moral magnet toward which political leaders with some anti-slavery feelings would be gradually drawn. The slave owners themselves would hasten this process by overreacting to Garrison's provocations. They physically attacked him, they silenced abolitionist talk in Congress with a gag rule, they confiscated abolitionist mail, and they ultimately argued that slavery was a good thing and should be expanded into the newly acquired western territories. This growth of slavery was something even a moderate politician like Lincoln could not tolerate, and the battle was joined between the pro-slavery and anti-slavery forces in the country.

Garrison was a keen observer of the process that was occurring. When he first established the New England Anti-Slavery Society with only twelve members, he said, "… our numbers are few and our influence limited; but mark my prediction, Faneuil Hall will ere long echo with the principles we have set forth. We shall shake the nation by their mighty power." On another occasion, he told a fellow abolitionist, "Your cause will not prosper … until it excites popular tumult and brings down upon it a shower of brickbats and rotten eggs and is threatened with a coat of tar and feathers." Garrison knew that his extreme moral stance was a provocation that the southern slaveholders and their northern allies would react to so outrageously that even moderate politicians, such as Lincoln, would have to take sides, and they would side with what was morally right.

For me, this has always been a great example of a person being courageous enough to take a strong moral stand, and aware enough to realize that if he held fast, other people of less stern stuff would gravitate to his position.

When I was a senior in high school, I had a chance for a Garrisonian moment. My school was in Birmingham, an upper middle class suburb of Detroit. The city of Detroit was considering imposing a one percent income tax on people who worked in the city, regardless of where they lived. Since many of the people in my government class had parents who worked in the city, as did I, they all parroted their parents' outrage at this high-handed attempt to impose "taxation without representation." One day, in class, the city income tax issue came up. I decided I agreed with the tax, despite the fact that my father was horrified at the proposal—and at my attitude. The argument for the tax was that those who had jobs in Detroit benefitted from the roads, water system, and police protection that the city provided and that they should help pay the costs. There was also a racial component to the debate, because it seemed to the Birminghamites, all of them white, that they were being hit up for extra money for the mostly black inner city, when their businesses were already paying property taxes to Detroit for services.

I quickly realized I was the only person in the room who supported the tax. The teacher, Mr. Miller, told me later how impressed he was that I did not back down. I argued that since the people who worked in the city benefitted from city services, they should be willing to help pay for them. That was the standard argument. But then most people in the room really thought I had lost my mind when I said that those of us who were white and very well-off should be willing to sacrifice a little bit to help the black people of the inner city. Even Mr. Miller flinched when I said that. Several of my classmates got visibly angry at me even though I tried to express my radical views in as friendly a manner as possible.

I began to understand how Garrison must have felt when the Boston mob threatened to hang him. In the end, I won no one to my point of view, but it felt good to stand firm for a moral principle against virulent opposition. William Lloyd Garrison would approve, I thought.

Since high school, there have been a few occasions when I summoned my "inner Garrison" to take an unpopular moral position. I hasten to add that I say this at the risk of sounding like a self-righteous prig, which I try very hard not to be. One incident stands out. In 1987, I was part of a group of history teachers participating in a summer institute on the U.S. Constitution at Phillips Andover Academy. One day, the twelve of us got into a discussion about the Supreme Court's abortion rights decision, *Roe v. Wade*. I spoke rather forcefully against the ruling and soon found myself confronting a dozen angry faces, demanding to know how I could oppose a woman's right to decide what to do with her own body. Again, another lynch mob. Of course, I was in no danger of being strung up—I don't think—but the angry looks, particularly from the women, made me pretty uncomfortable. But I had to be Garrisonian; I had to stand by my moral view and not amend it just to assuage their anger.

I looked at a young man who had become the most vocal of the pro *Roe* group. "Do you think the state should allow a woman to abort her baby in the ninth month of her pregnancy?" I asked.

"No, of course not," he replied, "but *Roe* allows states to prohibit abortions after the sixth month."

"Okay," I went on, "so at day one hundred eighty (the end of the sixth month), the fetus is a person, but at day one hundred seventy-nine, it is not. Is that what you're saying? And just how is it that it is a life deserving of protection on one day but not on the day before?"

I thought I had skewered the pro-abortion argument pretty well. My point was that there is another person involved besides the pregnant woman, and the Supreme Court is arbitrarily deciding on a day when that person is entitled to enjoy the right to have his/her life protected by law.

The man and most of the others in the room tried to ignore my question, and several repeated the same argument: the woman should be the one to decide whether or not to continue her pregnancy. But then a startling thing happened. One man, uncomfortable with the question I had posed, said that he thought a woman should have the right to choose to abort right up to the day the baby is born. Only at birth, he said, does a fetus become a person entitled to the protection of the law.

A gasp of horror went up across the room, but for me it was a true Garrisonian moment. I had provoked an extreme reaction, and for a moment, at least, several people in the room rethought their pro-abortion position. After the session, one of the women told me she agreed with me but didn't want to confront the whole class. I agreed with her that being accosted by angry looks and loud voices was very uncomfortable. As fellow history teachers, we discussed how William Lloyd Garrison was never happier than when he was in that very situation. The day the mob dragged him through the streets of Boston with a rope around his neck was one of the best days of his life! I told her that Garrison had been a role model for me ever since high school and that Garrison's life offered one of the practical lessons we as history teachers can offer our students: In moral disputes, stand strong for what you believe in the face of all opposition!

I haven't always been a true Garrisonian, of course. There were times when I knuckled under, but there were also times when I made an issue of something when I probably shouldn't have. There were times when Garrison himself probably should have backed off a bit. In fact he *did* become more accommodating when the Civil War came and he supported Lincoln's gradual approach to emancipation, much to the annoyance of some of his abolitionist friends. One of the dilemmas in my life has been to know when to model William Lloyd Garrison's *radical agitator* side and when to model his accommodating side. Knowing his story enriches my decision-making process.

ANGELINA AND SARAH GRIMKE OF SOUTH CAROLINA, INDEPENDENT WOMEN

The Grimke sisters grew up in Charleston, South Carolina. Their parents owned slaves and were part of the elite slave-owning class in that city. Sarah was the sixth of fourteen children and Angelina was the youngest. By the time they were teenagers, both of them had rebelled against the restrictions of the society around them. They believed that women should play an equal role with men and that slaves deserved to be set free. Their parents, as might be expected, were appalled at their attitude.

By the time they were in their twenties, they had broken with their family, moved north to Philadelphia, joined the Quaker faith, and had become full-throated abolitionists. By the late 1830s, they were members of William Lloyd Garrison's American Anti-Slavery Society. They spoke at public rallies against slavery and were much reviled for stepping outside the bounds of proper behavior for women. They lived to see slavery abolished in 1865, but both died in the 1870s, long before women got the right to vote.

I admire all of the abolitionists and women's rights crusaders, as I've made clear by now, but the Grimke sisters have always held a special fascination for me. Other abolitionists were Northerners whose families and religious backgrounds led them very naturally to the abolitionist cause. The Grimkes broke with their family and the society in which they grew up. Despite tremendous pressure to conform, and despite the physical dangers involved in speaking to scorning men, they bravely stepped up and fought for African-Americans and for women.

When I was in college, the Grimkes' story inspired me to realize that I might not agree with my parents' values in all cases, and that it was possible to break away from what they believed and even oppose their beliefs. I did not become a rebel, and I did not break from my family as the Grimke sisters did, but I did oppose my parents on several issues: the war in Vietnam, the Civil Rights Movement, the importance of protecting the environment through the regulation of business, and other issues that were important to all of us in the sixties.

DOROTHEA DIX
COMPASSIONATE REFORMER

In the 1830s, mentally ill people in Massachusetts who could not care for themselves and had no family to provide for them existed in deplorable conditions. In many towns, those people were placed in private homes, where they were poorly fed, caged, and beaten, because the owner of the home only wanted to collect the small fee from the town. The few state mental hospitals were grossly underfunded and the inmates were locked up in cells as if they were criminals.

In the early 1840s, Dorothea Dix investigated the treatment of mentally ill people in Massachusetts and was appalled at what she found. Having spent time in Great Britain with people who thought the government should take responsibility for helping the poor and the ill, Dix went before the Massachusetts state legislature to present a report on what she had found. Her *Memorial* to the lawmakers said, in part, "I proceed, gentlemen, briefly to call your attention to the present state of insane persons confined within this Commonwealth, in cages, stalls, pens! Chained, naked, beaten with rods, and lashed into obedience...." Her report had an impact. The legislature passed a bill to expand the state mental hospital in Worcester.

Following her success in making some progress for the mentally ill in Massachusetts, Dix went to other states, including New Jersey, North Carolina, Louisiana, and Pennsylvania, where she was a driving force in the creation of the state's first public mental hospital at Harrisburg. By the 1850s, she was working at the federal level and got Congress to pass legislation to set aside more than twelve million acres of federal land for the care of the insane; the government would sell the land and distribute the money to the states for the construction of insane asylums. President Franklin Pierce vetoed the bill on the grounds that social welfare was the responsibility of the states, so it never happened.

Learning about Dix's career made me much more aware of the problem of mental illness and people with other kinds of disabilities. When I drove past the Tewksbury State Hospital every day on my way to and from work, I felt sympathy for the poor souls I saw walking the grounds or sitting on the stone wall. After the state shut down the mental hospitals, I felt more needed to be done to care for the homeless people, many of whom were mentally ill and were now out on the streets. I have never begrudged a penny of what the government spends to help these people, and I often believe the government needs to do more. At the same time, I have tried to do my part privately to help those who are mentally ill or disabled.

Dorothea Dix devoted her entire life to the care of the mentally ill and the disabled. I believe we should all, in some small way, try to be a little bit like her.

HENRY CLAY OF KENTUCKY, THE "GREAT COMPROMISER"

It probably seems strange that I would have a compromiser as a role model when most of my other picks are people who took strong stands and hated compromising. The fact is, the advocates I've picked were strong in their positions until the moment when compromise was necessary or else nothing would happen. John Adams was all in for independence from Britain, but he undertook the defense of the British soldiers in the Boston Massacre. Even William Lloyd Garrison pulled back a bit during the Civil War when he saw that Lincoln had to sail the abolition ship carefully into port. So, compromisers have an important role to play. When the alternative to compromise is terrible bloody war, the country should be grateful when a person like Henry Clay is available to find the common ground.

Henry Clay's career had several incarnations. Early on, as a member of the House of Representatives from Kentucky, he was a war hawk, screaming for war with England. During the War of 1812, he was a negotiator at Ghent, Belgium, working on the treaty that ended the fighting. When the war ended, he began his thirty-year quest for the presidency by proposing his American System, a plan for developing the roads and waterways of the nation with money collected from tariffs. The tariffs would protect American industry, enabling it to grow. The South could develop its own industry and sell its cotton to textile mills in America instead of in Britain and France. Meanwhile, the internal improvements would open the West to trade. A national bank was an essential part of the system because it would collect taxes, store federal revenue, and provide a stable currency; thus, all the sections would benefit as the country became laced together in a great web of commerce. Clay was convinced his plan would be appealing in all sections and that it would propel him to the presidency. I am a big advocate for investing in infrastructure, so I think Clay's plan was not only brilliant, it was essential for the country to grow. It was also an implied compromise, as each section would have to accept a policy it opposed in order to benefit the whole country.

The sad part of Clay's story was that there was always one section or another that would detest his plan. No section was willing to give a little for the benefit of the whole. The South did not develop its own industry and began to see the tariff as nothing but a wet blanket that suffocated its sales of cotton to Europe. The West saw the bank as a tool of the wealthy businessmen in the East and a monster that stifled the free flow of money.

And then there was Andrew Jackson. Jackson was from the West, just like Clay was, but he was a military hero who captured the public imagination as Clay never could. He was the hero of the common man, and he was able to portray Clay, with his tariff and national bank, as a wealthy snob. In his war hawk days, Clay was a fun-loving, card-playing, convivial playboy. He was Harry of the West. He stayed that way his whole life, but the Jackson forces were able to portray him as a rich, arrogant aristocrat, not Harry of the West, but Prince Hal. It was very unfair.

Through all of his struggles to get his American System accepted, Clay maintained still another persona. He was an enlightened slave owner, one of the few people in the country who could be reasonable about slavery. Kentucky was right in the middle of the country, a border state, right on the line between North and South. Clay owned slaves, but he was very conscious of the evils of slavery, and he believed the system would one day have to be done away with, preferably by sending the entire black race to Africa. He was one of the founders of the American Colonization Society that set up the colony of Liberia in West Africa.

This was a racist scheme and certainly not the answer to the slavery question, but Clay's support for it shows how tortured he was about the institution.

With his balanced view on slavery and sectional interests, Clay was the ideal man to compromise the feuds that threatened to break up the Union. In 1820, he got the sections to agree to bring Missouri into the Union as a slave state, while Maine came in as a free state, thus maintaining the balance of slave states and free states in the Senate. The 36°30' line established the boundary between slave territory and free territory in Louisiana, and both the North and the South seemed satisfied. In 1833, he got the North to accept a revision of the tariff so that rates would gradually go down over a ten-year period. This got South Carolina to back away from nullification, and the Union was saved. Finally, in 1850, he devised his most intricate compromise yet. In return for California's admission to the Union as a free state, he gave the South the federal Fugitive Slave Law and the chance for the Mexican Cession to have slavery under the concept of popular sovereignty: letting the people who lived in the territory decide whether to have slavery.

In all of these compromises, Clay showed political genius in devising the terms in a way that gave something to everyone. He also showed great tactical skills in getting them passed. Especially in 1850, when civil war truly did seem possible, he worked hard to line up effective speakers and to offer enough to each congressman that they were all able to go back home to their constituents and honestly say they had gotten all they could for their state or district.

Henry Clay died in 1852, so when the next great threat of secession came in 1860, he was not in Congress to douse the flames. His successor as senator from Kentucky, John J. Crittenden, tried to "pull a Henry Clay" by offering a plan to keep southern states from leaving the Union after Lincoln was elected, but the plan failed. Southern congressmen said they would support his proposal to extend the 36°30' line to the Pacific and place a thirteenth amendment in the constitution guaranteeing the permanence of slavery as long as any state wished to have it, but Lincoln, the president-elect, told all his Republican friends in congress to vote "no." He had been elected on a platform of no extension of slavery, and he would stand by it; he would not back away from it before he even took office. The southern states, thereupon, seceded.

Henry Clay had always been Lincoln's political hero. Lincoln totally supported the American System, he worked hard in the failed effort to get Clay elected president in 1844, and he supported Clay's compromise plan of 1850. If it had been *Clay* who had proposed compromise in 1860, would Lincoln have agreed to it? Probably not. But here is why I regard Clay as a role model. In 1850, he knew the great Massachusetts senator, Daniel Webster, would probably oppose his compromise plan, especially because the people of Massachusetts were totally against a federal fugitive slave law. So, on a snowy January night, Clay went to Webster's home and spent the night with him sipping bourbon before a warm fire and convincing him to support the plan and avoid thousands of deaths in a terrible civil war. It can't be known, of course, but I think if he were still living in 1860, Clay would have paid a visit to Lincoln in Illinois, where he was waiting to take office, and convinced him to support compromise.

John Crittenden was no Henry Clay. Lincoln had said in a letter to a friend, "Stand firm (against compromise) as a chain of steel." Yet perhaps he would have listened to the man who now held his role model's old Senate seat. But Crittenden never paid such a visit, and that is why no one today knows who he was; he is not even known as the mediocre compromiser. It is a fitting ironic twist to Crittenden's failure to get his compromise passed that one of his sons served as an officer in the Confederate Army and the other served as an officer in the Union Army. He couldn't prevent the split in the Union or in his own family.

Compromise is an art, and Clay was a master. I truly admire people who stand by their principles, and I hate to see anyone back away from a stand, especially when morality is involved. But, there are times when compromise is not just possible, it is mandatory if disaster is to be avoided. Henry Clay served his country well by crafting compromises and holding off civil war for forty years.

There are people in politics today who apparently do not know history very well and seem to think compromise is a dirty word. I often wish such people would read a little about the sectional disputes before the Civil War and the work Henry Clay did to postpone what proved to be the bloodiest war in American history.

ABRAHAM LINCOLN, **THE GREATEST AMERICAN**

Lincoln is such a great role model in so many ways that he would be my choice for the greatest American who ever lived. He will figure prominently in the chapter on the power of words and the chapter on the principles of great leadership. Here, I would like to discuss the aspects of the way he lived his life that have had a profound effect on the way I have tried to live mine.

One of the first things I ever knew about Lincoln was that he was a voracious reader who would walk miles to borrow a book and would stay up late into the night to read by the fireside. He would practice writing by using a piece of charcoal on a plank or a wooden shovel. He only went to a formal school for a total of six weeks in his entire boyhood. Almost everything he knew he taught himself. This studious boy became the man who produced some of the greatest speeches and state papers of all time!

The school Lincoln went to for a short time was called a *blab* school. Students would all read from their books aloud so their instructor would know they were doing their lessons. From this experience, Lincoln developed a life-long habit of reading everything aloud; that way, he said, "I get the information into my brain through two senses, sight and sound." Ever since I read this about Lincoln, I have tried to do the same thing in my own reading whenever possible. I have found it to be very effective. It certainly helps me to stay focused on what I am reading, which is a huge problem for me, and almost everyone, I'll bet.

In his young adult life, Lincoln became skilled at two professions, strictly through his own study. He became a surveyor and later a lawyer, solely from reading the classic books in those fields. Lincoln was also an athletic, active young man who enjoyed wrestling and other vigorous activities. He was not just a stodgy scholar. His example of being an athlete and a scholar at the same time modeled for me the kind of man I wanted to be.

One of the things that most impressed me about Lincoln's eagerness to learn was his decision to teach himself geometry and algebra as a way of developing his reasoning skills. He became one of the most logical thinkers of all time, and his ability to develop an argument by proceeding logically from one point to another made him one of the greatest debaters who ever lived. Knowing this about Lincoln motivated me to try a little harder in the mathematics courses I had to take. This was very helpful, because math was difficult for me and it helped to be motivated.

Lincoln had a unique ability to tell funny stories and to make his point by using humor. Some of the people who knew him, most notably Secretary of War Edwin Stanton, were not amused by his stories and were critical of his habit of launching into a yarn at a moment of great tension. Lincoln's response to complaints about his propensity to use levity in solemn moments was that he had to use humor to break the tension, otherwise he would break down; thus, when he gathered his cabinet to discuss his momentous decision to finally make emancipation of the slaves a war objective, he took ten minutes to read an excerpt from the story *A High-Handed Outrage at Utica*, by the humorist Artemus Ward, before getting down to the business at hand.

When I learned this about Lincoln, I found that using humor in tough situations, even if it's a thought in my head that I don't express, helps me keep my composure and get through the situation with less drama.

Lincoln is probably the foremost example in American history of a person who had to persevere through incredible trauma, setbacks, and horrific tragedy. In his personal life, he lost two sons to ghastly illnesses. His wife, Mary, increasingly showed signs of mental illness and deep depression. He suffered from depression severe enough that in today's world, he would probably need medication. As president, he had to lead the country through the most horrific war any nation had ever experienced. His armies suffered constant defeats and thousands of casualties. In his second inaugural address, after four years of fighting, Lincoln revealed that he believed God was putting the nation through the horrible war to atone for the sin of slavery.

In the Bible, we have the story of Job; in American history, we have Lincoln. Fortunately, in my life, I have not had to endure anything close to the trials Lincoln endured. If, or when, I do, I hope to be able to persevere as he did, always aware that what is happening is God's will, and always hopeful that tomorrow will be better.

At the time he was assassinated, many Americans compared Lincoln to Jesus Christ. He was the savior of the nation and of the African-American race; he was martyred on Good Friday, April 14, 1865. He was a man capable of Christ-like forgiveness. He forgave soldiers who fell asleep on guard duty and spared them a firing squad. He forgave politicians who said vile things about him and even appointed some of them to his cabinet. And, just a month before his murder, he forgave all the people of the South who were willing to repent and declare their loyalty to the Union. In one of the most magnanimous gestures of all time, he said, "With malice toward none, with charity for all, with firmness in the right as God gives us to see the right, let us strive on to finish the work we are in, to bind up the nation's wounds, to care for him who shall have borne the battle, and for his widow and his orphan, to do all which may achieve a just and lasting peace among ourselves and with all nations." When I was in college I thought John F. Kennedy was pretty cool when he said, "Don't get mad, get even." Since then, as I've matured, I've preferred to be like Lincoln and do the Christ-like thing: "forgive those who trespass against us."

Lincoln did not forgive everyone indiscriminately. There were certain offenses that were so heinous that he felt there should be no clemency. A notable example was the slave merchant Nathaniel Gordon, who was arrested and convicted for violating federal law by attempting to import eight hundred slaves into the country. In Lincoln's view, Gordon's actions were offensive by every conceivable moral standard. He ordered Gordon's death sentence to be carried out, granting only a two-week stay of execution for the condemned man to prepare his soul.

As a parent and as a teacher, I have thought about Lincoln many times when making decisions about forgiveness. It is important to teach children the consequences of their actions and to hold them accountable, but it is also important to show them love and forbearance. Lincoln drew the line when a moral issue was involved or when the offending person refused to acknowledge wrongdoing and repent. I have tried to draw the same line.

Lincoln's friends offered mixed accounts about his religious faith, and few would have said he attended church regularly. Nevertheless, in almost every major matter during Lincoln's career I can recall, what Jesus would have done and what Lincoln did were probably pretty close. When I think of Lincoln as my second most significant role model after Jesus, I don't usually face a dilemma, as their advice would be very much the same.

BOOKER T. WASHINGTON, EDUCATOR

My inclusion of Booker T. Washington as a role model will cause many people to cringe and question how I could choose a man who accepted segregation and second-class status for his race. So far, I have admired men who stood tall against injustice, so how could I admire Washington, who appears to have been an "Uncle Tom" who sold out his race? The answer is that I admit his personal faults and the shortcomings of his leadership, but I admire his personal qualities, I admire what he did to become successful, and I think his leadership *did* provide a solid foundation for thousands of African-Americans at a time when their future was very uncertain. His autobiography, *Up From Slavery*, was one of the first complete books I ever read; the book and the life it described made a huge impression on me.

Washington was born a slave on a Virginia plantation in 1858. One of his first memories was the day his master called the slaves together and announced they were all free. At first there was wild celebration, he tells us, but then anxiety set in as the *freedmen* wondered what they would do with their lives. When I read these pages as a ten-year-old, I was surprised when Washington said that he and his fellow slaves felt no bitterness toward their master or his wife and children. In fact, they felt some sadness that their long-standing relationship would have to end. For the rest of his life, Booker T. Washington forgave the white race for slavery and all the transgressions white people committed against him and his "less favored" race. His primary motivation was not revenge; his primary feeling was not hostility. He was totally focused on the future: improvement for himself and for as many of his fellow African-Americans as he could reach.

In recent years, the world has very justly acclaimed Nelson Mandela as a hero. In 1990, after twenty-seven years of torture and deprivation at the hands of the apartheid government of South Africa, Mandela emerged from prison with no bitterness in his heart. He was elected president of South Africa four years later and immediately instituted a policy of reconciliation. Even though he could easily, and very popularly, have initiated a policy of retribution (seizure of lands and businesses, etc.), he urged his people to forgive, put the past behind them, and move their country forward. Because of the leadership he provided for South Africa after his release and his election, Nelson Mandela was, in my opinion, one of the greatest leaders of the twentieth century.

Similarly, I admire Booker T. Washington's lack of vindictiveness and focus on the future. In my view, he was the Nelson Mandela of the nineteenth century. Although it could be argued that Mandela had a seventy percent black majority in South Africa behind him, so his act of forgiveness was more genuine, I believe Booker T. Washington was not simply bowing to reality. To be sure, if he had urged his race to exact retribution, they would have been annihilated by the white population, but he truly was a Christian man with no vindictiveness in his heart. That is a model I have always tried to emulate.

I also admire Washington's focus on learning for self-advancement. Like Abraham Lincoln, Booker T. Washington went to extraordinary lengths to achieve an education. After freedom came, Booker T., his mother, and an adopted brother had to find work wherever they could. He found himself working in a coal mine, walking a mile each day into the mine to get to the face of the coal, where he would swing a pick all day long. In the mine, he heard other workers talk about a wonderful school called Hampton, where a black boy could work for tuition and learn a trade. Booker decided to get to that school any way he could, and so he set out with hardly any money and only a vague idea of where the school was. He arrived in Richmond, Virginia, without a penny and no place to stay, so he found a spot along the wooden sidewalk where it was possible to crawl underneath, and he spent several nights there until he found work. It impressed me a lot as a ten-year-old that he would be willing to sleep under a wooden sidewalk in his quest to find work and go to school!

When he finally found Hampton, he was thrilled beyond words at the beautiful brick building. With no money to pay tuition, he nevertheless went in to ask the head teacher for admission to the institute. Despite his ragged appearance, she gave him a chance to prove himself and told him to sweep one of the classrooms. Booker swept the room three times and even took a rag and dusted all of the furniture, railings, and walls. The woman was so impressed with his diligence that she accepted him into Hampton with the understanding that he would do custodial work in the building to pay for his tuition. Booker worked nights cleaning rooms and spent his days in class studying. When I read Booker T. Washington's account of this, I was very impressed and thought of his example every time I had to do a job. Shoveling the driveway, for example, became my chance to produce excellent results through hard work. I found that kind of achievement very satisfying, just as Booker T. did. He said he was as thrilled with passing that *test* as he would have been at passing an entrance exam into Harvard or Yale.

Hampton was a school dedicated to the teaching of industrial arts and the training of teachers. The superintendent of the school was General Samuel Chapman Armstrong, a white man who had led "colored troops" during the recent Civil War. Armstrong believed that the newly freed African-Americans would be best served by an education that taught them literacy and trade skills. That kind of training would enable them to become respectable, hard-working, financially independent citizens. He took the young Booker T. under his wing and became his guiding spirit for the next twenty years. Washington idolized his mentor and said of him in *Up from Slavery*, "I never met any man who, in my estimation, was the equal of General Armstrong." With the general's encouragement and guidance, Washington established the Tuskegee Institute in Alabama, a school modeled after Hampton and dedicated to teaching African-Americans useful trades.

Washington's story of how his school attracted young black Americans from all over the country who wanted to better themselves is inspiring. The students knew that learning to read and learning a trade was their only way forward from slavery. In the early years, the students built all of the buildings themselves, even manufacturing their own bricks.

To support his school, Washington approached wealthy white people, such as Andrew Carnegie, for philanthropic donations. He was very successful, partly because he was not demanding social or economic equality for his race. At that time, that kind of demand would have turned many potential donors away. He articulated his approach most dramatically in a speech he gave in Atlanta in 1895. That city was hosting a southern exposition—a fair of many displays illustrating the advances the South had made in the thirty years since the Civil War. Washington spoke in a lecture hall to a large audience that included many white dignitaries from across the South. What he said was reported all across the country and was hailed by many as the Atlanta Compromise. The concept was simple: if white businessmen and political leaders would financially support schools such as Tuskegee and hire black tradespeople, the African-American race would be loyal and law-abiding, as they had always been, and accept racial segregation as the natural order of things. "In all things that are purely social, we can be as separate as the fingers, yet one as the hand in all things essential to mutual progress," he proclaimed. At the conclusion of his address, the white audience gave him a loud ovation and many flocked onto the stage to shake his hand.

Some black people at the time, and many historians since, have condemned Washington's accommodating approach. Washington's critics point out that the United States Supreme Court may have been responding to him when it upheld the constitutionality of segregation the following year in its *Plessy v. Ferguson* decision. The African-American people, as a result of that ruling, suffered the baneful effects of Jim Crow laws for at least the next seventy years. Booker T. Washington, critics say, should have stood tall against segregation in his Atlanta speech and in everything he did. Instead, he accepted the gross injustices being perpetrated by white people just so he could get money for a school that guided black students into menial occupations.

I agree with those criticisms, up to a point, but I believe that in the climate of the times (the late 1890s and the early twentieth century), Washington would have gotten nowhere fighting for integration and his school would have suffered. Emblematic of the racism of the day was the firestorm that erupted when President Theodore Roosevelt invited Booker T. Washington to the White House for dinner in 1901. So fierce was the condemnation in the press and in letters from his political supporters that the usually intrepid TR had to apologize for his indiscretion—allowing a black man to eat off White House china in the White House dining room—and promise never to do such a thing again. Booker T. Washington was a realist who believed that for the time being, black people in the United States should accept *less favored* status (as he put it) and quietly build a solid foundation of economic stability and law-abiding citizenship.

In the meantime, Tuskegee was a wonderful place. Under Washington's leadership, buildings were continually added to provide training in a wide variety of skills, ranging from cooking and sewing to carpentry, plumbing, and auto mechanics. A young African-American man or woman who wanted to become self-sufficient and provide for his or her family could get everything necessary at Tuskegee. The school was a forerunner of the technical high schools and the community colleges that today play such a large part in our educational system. There has recently been a renewed interest in preparing students for specific skills at these schools. Some educators even believe that the government should provide a free community college education for all who desire it. Recently, when I spent a few years teaching at a community college, I became a believer in the value of the education these institutions provide. Many of the students in my history class were getting their associate's degrees in nursing or some other medical career. After graduation, they would be prepared for lifetime occupations. Washington's approach had merit!

A final word on Booker T. Washington: I think reading his autobiography was the first experience I had that motivated me to become a teacher. When I read what he wrote on page sixty-six of *Up from Slavery*, I began to think that if I wasn't good enough at baseball to make the Red Sox, I would teach! Washington said, "(at Hampton) … I began learning that those who are happiest are those who do the most for others." Wouldn't it be more useful, valuable, and satisfying to teach young people how to improve their minds than to hit home runs at Fenway Park? I thought. Of course, the decision on a career path was made much easier when it turned out I stunk at baseball!

JOHN MARSHALL HARLAN, A MAN FOR JUSTICE

I always have a special spot on the wall of my personal hall of fame for those who stood alone battling for what was right. The *alone* part is what makes it heroic. In the section of the hall devoted to stand-up people, John Marshall Harlan deserves a special shrine, because he took his stand in one of the most important Supreme Court cases of all time, and did so in a radical departure from his background.

Harlan grew up in a slaveholding family in Kentucky and was surrounded by slavery through all of his formative years, yet when freedom came for the black population in 1865, he realized that the country needed a new model for race relations. When he was elevated to the United States Supreme Court, he stood alone against the other justices in favor of equality for blacks on several different occasions. His most significant stand occurred in 1896 in the case of *Plessy v. Ferguson.* In that famous case, Homer Plessy contended that the Louisiana law that required him to travel in a separate railroad car designated solely for blacks was unconstitutional because of the "equal protection" clause of the Fourteenth Amendment. Eight of the justices disagreed, saying his car was "separate but equal" and, therefore, did not violate the Fourteenth Amendment. In a scathing dissent, Justice Harlan wrote, "We boast of the freedom enjoyed by our people above all other peoples, but it is difficult to reconcile that boast with a state of the law which, practically, puts the brand of servitude and degradation upon a large class of our fellow citizens, our equals before the law. The thin disguise of "equal" accommodations for passengers in railroad coaches will not mislead anyone, nor atone for the wrong this day done."

Harlan was a lone voice in the wilderness in 1896, and segregation, with its legal foundation of "separate but equal," remained in place for seventy years. However, in 1954, in *Brown v. Board of Education,* the Supreme Court voted nine to zero to strike down "separate but equal" in public schools, and declared that segregated schools were "inherently unequal." Harlan, dead since 1911, was finally vindicated.

I like people who grow and change and discard old thought patterns when those ideas become untenable. John Marshall Harlan was no abolitionist in the 1850s, and he was not enthusiastic about emancipation in 1863 (he voted for George McClellan over Lincoln in 1864), but when freedom came, Harlan changed, and even though he had to stand alone on the court, he spoke strongly for equality. I admire that.

THEODORE ROOSEVELT,
PARAGON OF ENERGY AND ENTHUSIASM

While Theodore Roosevelt is an excellent role model for life in many ways, and while he will be a major part of the chapters on leadership and the power of words, he does have some negatives that exclude him from my list of people I would want to emulate entirely. His negatives follow:

1. Despite the fact that he invited Booker T. Washington to the White House for dinner in 1901, he was decidedly racist in his outlook. After a racial incident in Brownsville, Texas, he ordered an entire regiment of black soldiers dishonorably discharged even though there was very little evidence against any of them for causing the trouble.

2. During the negotiations for the Panama Canal Zone, he referred to the Colombians as a bunch of *dagoes*. His policies toward Latin America, particularly the so-called "Roosevelt Corollary to the Monroe Doctrine," which effectively told the Latin American people they were the children of the United States, caused one hundred years of bad relations between the United States and the countries in the Caribbean, Central America, and South America.

3. He was far too enamored with war for my taste. As Assistant Secretary of the Navy, he pushed hard for a war with Spain, and when it came, he left his family of five children, including newborn Quentin, to go seek glory in Cuba. He was thirty-nine years old. There is no disputing his courage in the fighting in Cuba, but I think he was a little less interested in the men who died or suffered terrible wounds than he should have been. His love for battle, his pride in how the "wolf rose in his heart" at San Juan Hill came to haunt him in a tragically ironic way. That very same baby Quentin, whom he left behind when he went to fight in Cuba, became an Army pilot twenty years later in World War I and was shot down and killed in France in 1918. Roosevelt was so grief stricken that he never really

recovered and died himself four months later. I must say, receiving the news of Quentin's death was the first time he really understood the heavy price people pay in war.

4. He killed animals in a way that makes me uncomfortable. As a young boy, he dreamed of being a natural scientist, and he drew excellent pictures of birds and small animals. I admire his studiousness in that area, but he also killed numerous animals to stuff for his natural history museum, and when he became a man, he went on numerous hunting trips and bagged hundreds of trophies. When I visited his home on Long Island (Sagamore Hill), I noticed the huge number of animal body parts with which he surrounded himself. There was a rhino leg carved out to be an ash bin for cigarettes at the front door; there were numerous heads and skins hanging from the walls; there were hides on which to walk and vacant eyes looking at you from everywhere. It is true he got kudos from the public for sparing a young bear on a hunting trip, an incident that led directly to the "teddy bear," but that cub was the only animal that survived an encounter with the trigger happy TR.

Yet there are several good lessons I have learned from studying the life of Theodore Roosevelt. Foremost is the way he overcame asthma and became a robust, energetic man. He was a very sickly child, but his father encouraged him to take charge of his body and build himself up, and that is what he did. He lifted barbells, went for long hikes, rowed boats, wrestled, and boxed. By the time he went to Harvard at sixteen, he had left his sickly childhood behind. One of his favorite activities, one that he led his children to do and even corralled visitors to the White House into, was his point-to-point races. These were cross-country races in which participants had to run from point A to point B, in a straight line, never going around any obstacle, be it rock, ledge, stream, or river. I have always resonated with this activity and I have taken some point-to-point runs myself. One of my most memorable was a run I took up a long hill near Oakland, California. I kept going up, over rocks, through brambles that scratched me from head to ankle, and up some ledges that I had to scramble up on all fours. After almost an hour, I reached the top: a parking lot from which I could see the entire San Francisco Bay Area. It was a truly spectacular sight, definitely worth the torturous climb. I took the road down and thoroughly enjoyed a nice, easy downhill run that afforded gorgeous panoramic views of the Bay Area at every turn. I owe that experience to Theodore Roosevelt, because I never would have started up that hill without having read about his point-to-points.

Complementary to his drive for fitness was TR's tremendous enthusiasm for everything life had to offer. His favorite word was *bully*, meaning *wonderful* or *great!* Unless it is really overdone or totally out of place, this kind of enthusiasm inspires everyone around you and makes them feel good. I'm not always successful, but I always try to incorporate a little TR into my outlook on life; I try to get up each morning, as I'm sure he did, excited about what the day has to offer. I always want to do things instead of just mope about saying, "I'm bored." I think very often people think they're sick when their real problem is they don't try to get out and *do* something.

I also admire TR's concern for the poor and disadvantaged in American life. His beloved father taught him to take action and do whatever he could to help people and to correct the wrongs of society. As a state legislator in New York and later as police commissioner in New York City, he was one of the very few political leaders who ventured into the slum areas. Sometimes he was accompanied on these visits by Jacob Riis, author of *How the Other Half Lives.* He wanted to see just how people below the poverty line existed. He was one of the first political figures of any consequence to believe government had a role in improving the lives of the people. He introduced legislation to protect cigar workers and to require health and safety standards in tenements. It was a time of laissez-faire capitalism, so few of his proposals passed, and those that *were* passed got struck down by the courts as violations of employers' property rights; however, when he became president, he was able to accomplish more. He gave striking coal miners a fair hearing and helped them win concessions from the mine operators, and he got legislation passed to clean up the food processing industry and to regulate the abuses of the railroads. Roosevelt was a Republican, and I sometimes use him as an example to my Republican friends that even a Republican can support worthy government activity in the economy.

Finally, I really like TR's interest in protecting the natural resources of the country and in expanding the national park system. During his presidency, millions of additional acres of land were placed under the protection of the federal government. Whenever I enter a national park, I'm always happy to see the rangers in their tan and green uniforms, rather than an amusement park operator or a luxury hotel mogul. For that we are all indebted to Theodore Roosevelt.

ELEANOR ROOSEVELT, COMPASSIONATE WOMAN

In her youth, Eleanor Roosevelt would not have imagined in her craziest dreams that she would ever play a major part in the history of her time. Her mother called her an ugly duckling, and she always assumed she would never be in the public eye, and she didn't want to be. But distant cousin Franklin Roosevelt did find her attractive—as much for her mind as her appearance—and they got married. He was a rising star in the New York political firmament, hoping to follow in the footsteps of his cousin Theodore (Eleanor's uncle), and Eleanor assumed her role would be simply to support him.

After they had five children and Franklin had risen to the position of assistant Secretary of the Navy (a post Theodore had once held on *his* way to the top), Eleanor discovered that Franklin was having an adulterous affair with another woman. Her decision to stay in the marriage and support his political ambitions is not why I admire her. I might admire her more if she had said "Now you've done it! Be gone!" I do admire her for what she did in the years that followed.

Three years after their marriage almost ended, Franklin came down with infantile paralysis (polio) and permanently lost the ability to walk. Eleanor insisted this was not the end for him, and for six years during the 1920s, she encouraged his efforts to regain his strength and devise ways to appear to be standing on his own. In one of the most astounding political comebacks of all time, FDR was elected governor of New York in 1928 and then president of the United States in 1932. For these achievements, he owed much to his wife for her encouragement, her willingness to overcome her shyness and break out of her shell, and for going out and campaigning for him.

Through Franklin's twelve years as president, Eleanor was his eyes and ears. She traveled all over the country to see how his New Deal programs were working and to report back to him what she thought still needed to be done. One area she thought was being terribly neglected was African-American civil rights. She became a scold (a woman who nags or grumbles constantly) to her husband about how he wasn't doing enough to battle the racist laws in the southern states or even the racist policies of the United States government, such as segregation in the military. A particularly courageous act was her refusal to allow the Daughters of the American Revolution to stop the black singer Marian Anderson from performing in Washington, D.C. When they would not allow her to perform in Constitution Hall, Eleanor Roosevelt arranged to have her concert at the Lincoln Memorial. A quarter of a century before Dr. Martin Luther King spoke there, Ms. Anderson sang "My Country Tis of Thee" to an integrated audience beneath Lincoln's benign gaze.

After Franklin died in 1945, Eleanor became a leading figure on the world stage. President Truman appointed her to be the special U.S. representative to the United Nations to lead a committee to write a declaration of human rights. The Universal Declaration of Human Rights, adopted by the UN in 1948, holds up to the world the same humanitarian principles that Eleanor fought for all of her years in the White House. Although most people today have probably never heard of it, this document has been the foundation of many international agreements and treaties.

Eleanor Roosevelt's struggle to overcome her own insecurities and her devoted concern for the disadvantaged people all over the world always inspires me. When I'm thinking that it's such a chore to go serve a meal at a soup kitchen or to help a handicapped person maneuver his wheelchair into a building, I am instantly ashamed of myself and I think of what Eleanor Roosevelt would say to me. She was very eloquent in her own right, and I'm sure she would let me have it with some strong words!

DR. MARTIN LUTHER KING, JR., A DREAMER AND A DOER

Doctor King will figure prominently in the chapter on the power of words, but I have to mention him here because his modeling of the nonviolent approach to civil disobedience has always earned my respect. Drawing on the strategies used by Mahatma Gandhi and on the teachings of Jesus Christ, Dr. King never wavered and achieved more for civil rights than anyone could have imagined when he began his leadership during the Montgomery Bus Boycott of 1956. In the nearly fifty years since Dr. King's assassination, it has become fashionable in some circles to disparage the things he accomplished and to pass him off as a bit of an Uncle Tom for exhorting his followers not to fight back against white tormentors. The fact is, though, he never accepted racial injustice, fought effectively against it, and made the country a much better place for African-Americans than it was when he started his fight. Very few people thought we would ever see the end of segregation, but the 1964 Civil Rights Act made it a federal crime to deny people equal treatment because of their race. The United States became a much more hospitable place for African-Americans because of Dr. King's law.

Personally, I have a tendency to fight back violently when I feel I am being abused or bullied. My family has heard several times of the incident in junior high when I punched a bully in the face and knocked him right off his chair because he had been pushing me around for weeks and had stuck his nose into the ice cream I was eating. I can't say I'm not just a little bit proud of how I gave Lenny his due that day, but

I also feel quite a bit of shame for that and the other times when I used violence to make my point. In the years after that incident, I witnessed Dr. King's nonviolent protests and I read about it and described it for my students. As I've matured, I have become increasingly impressed with his approach and the way he was able to *stay* with it despite considerable provocation.

Knowing what I know now, if I could go back into my chair in that junior high cafeteria where Lenny stuck his nose into my ice cream … I have to admit, I think I still would punch him in his punky face! Role models can only do so much!

RONALD REAGAN, GENIAL CONSERVATIVE

There was one aspect of Ronald Reagan's personality that I have used as a role model ever since he was president in the 1980s: his skill at deflecting confrontation. As a conservative, he had many disagreements with people in government, in the press, and out in public. People were frequently attacking him for his views on cutting taxes, increasing military spending, trimming welfare, opposing abortion rights, firing all of the air traffic controllers for going on strike, and many other things. I always admired the way he would respond to the sometimes vicious attacks. He would look his assailant in the eye, dip his head a bit and say, "Well, I see your point" and then, with a genuine, benign smile, make his own point in a very clear and non-threatening way. He usually would not get his attacker to change his or her mind, but he would get people who were watching the encounter to consider his point of view, and he made it clear to the whole world that a person with conservative views was not necessarily a raging maniac or a Hitleresque fascist. Reagan's ability to get along with the Democratic leadership in Congress, particularly Speaker of the House Tip O'Neill, was legendary.

In my younger days, I was constantly firing off letters to the editor in true William Lloyd Garrison style. I still want to be like Garrison in standing by my position, especially when there is a moral principle involved. Now that I'm in my older years, I have added Ronald Reagan to the mix and have tried to be "all on fire" like Garrison was, but nice like Reagan was.

GEORGE H.W. BUSH,
A MAN OF IMPECCABLE INTEGRITY

In 1980, I read an article in *Time* magazine about George Bush and became interested in him as a possible candidate for president. Since I always think character is more important than anything else in a candidate, I looked for that first, and in him, I found it in abundance. Here was a man who, right out of high school (Phillips Academy, two miles up the road from my house), enlisted in the United States Navy to serve in World War II. He signed up on his eighteenth birthday and went off to basic training and flight school. During the war he flew several combat missions, but what impresses me the most is that when one of his friends went missing in action, he wrote a letter to the man's parents to console them and tell them how much their son was loved by his companions. This was just one of the thousands of letters and notes George Bush wrote to people to support them, to cheer them up, to congratulate them, or to just let them know he was thinking about them. I'm not talking about emails or text messages; these were real letters, written by hand, placed in envelopes, addressed and stamped, and taken to the post office. I always admire a man, especially a *man*, who is very aware of the feelings and needs of other people and tries to address them. This comes naturally to most women, but it is rare to find it in a man. (If you are giving me a dirty look right now for saying such a politically incorrect thing, you're wasting your time. I can't see you.)

Bush's loving personality did not mean he was in any way a wimp. There was a brief time during the election campaign of 1988 when his opponents tried to portray him as a wimp, but anyone who knew anything about him at all knew the charge was absurd. He was one of the most courageous men who ever lived. On one of his last missions in the war, his plane was hit by enemy antiaircraft fire and was going down in flames. With smoke filling the cockpit, he completed his bombing run before parachuting into the Pacific Ocean. His radioman and his gunner died in the crash, something that still devastates him. He always wondered if he could have done more in those final seconds to save them. Of course, he wrote letters to their families and stayed in touch with them for many years.

Bush was rescued in the ocean by an American submarine. Rather than go home on leave with the rest of the submarine crew, he returned to duty on his aircraft carrier. When he eventually did get home, he married the girl he had fallen in love with before the war, Barbara Pierce, and they began a marriage that has lasted for seventy-one years. (I am writing this on January 6, 2016, the Bushes' seventy-first anniversary.) During those seventy-one years, there never has been even a hint of an extramarital affair or any other kind of scandal. These days, that alone qualifies George H.W. Bush to be a role model.

When the war ended, Bush was twenty-one years old and married, and it was then that he went to Yale University. Typically, when Thanksgiving came and he realized that several fellow students couldn't get home for the holiday, he invited them all to his house, and he and Barbara shared their first Thanksgiving turkey sitting on the floor surrounded by ten of his friends. As his son George W. Bush said in his adoring biography of his father, "Once you were a friend of George Bush's, you had that status for life."

At Yale, Bush was a star first baseman on the baseball team, an outstanding student, and after a year, father of a baby son. When George W. Bush was born in 1946, his father was a war veteran, a sophomore in college, and barely twenty-two years old.

After graduating from Yale, Bush decided not to go into finance like the rest of his family; instead, he took a chance and entered the complete unknown. He headed out to Midland, Texas, to try his hand in the oil business. Midland was a hot, flat, dry, dusty place. Going there from New England was tantamount to going to the moon. Nevertheless, through sheer hard work and a bit of risk taking, such as getting into the new and unproven off-shore oil drilling, he was successful. Along the way, he and Barbara had five more children: two daughters and three sons. His youngest daughter, Robin, died of leukemia in 1953. It was a heartbreaking loss that he and Barbara never really got over.

All these experiences revealed the character of George Bush. By the 1960s, he was a man of substance. He had a family with five children; he had a very competent and devoted wife; he had a successful business he had built himself; and he had a broad network of friends and contacts not only across Texas, but around the country. He also had a politically successful father. Prescott Bush was a senator from Connecticut who was building a reputation for being a stern moralist.

In the 1960s, George H.W. Bush decided to get into politics himself. He ran for the U.S. Senate in 1964 and campaigned vigorously, traveling across the huge state of Texas dozens of times and attending any gathering he could put together. But 1964 was not a good year to be a Republican in Texas. Texan Lyndon Johnson was on his way to a landslide victory for president, carrying the state by more than seven hundred thousand votes. Bush did well to lose to his Democratic opponent by only three hundred thousand.

In 1966, Bush was finally successful when he won a seat in the House of Representatives from Texas; however, in 1970, he tried once again for the Senate and lost. It seemed like his political career was over, but it was actually just about to take off. President Nixon appointed him to be ambassador to the United Nations; then, after Nixon opened diplomatic relations with China, Bush became the American ambassador to Beijing. After that he was the chairman of the Republican National Committee, and, finally, he was the director of the Central Intelligence Agency (CIA).

So it was in 1980, I had my candidate. George Bush now had international credentials to go with his other attributes. He had a sparklingly clean record, totally untouched by scandal. I was so impressed that I decided to sign up and work for his campaign. I made hundreds of phone calls to potential supporters, and Diane and I went to one of his rallies before the Massachusetts Republican primary at the Danversport Yacht Club. There was an overflow crowd at the rally, so we were among the group that had to be shuttled into a downstairs room to watch the speech on closed circuit TV. We'll always remember a smiling, white-haired lady coming over to us and thanking us for coming. "George is so glad you're here," she said. At most anyone else's rally, I would have thought, "Yeah, right, he doesn't give a damn that we're here," but from the way she said it and from what I knew about George Bush, I believed her. We did a double take when we realized it was Barbara Bush.

Bush won the primary in Massachusetts but, of course, Reagan got the Republican nomination and we had to settle for Bush as the running mate. During the eight years of the Reagan presidency, Bush was a loyal right-hand man to the president and did a huge amount of global travel. He met leaders and key people in countries all over the world and developed friendships that were going to be very helpful when he became president. By 1988, as Reagan prepared to leave office, George Bush was even more qualified to be president than he had been in 1980.

It really surprised me during the early part of the fall that year that the democratic candidate, Governor Michael Dukakis of Massachusetts, had a lead over Bush in the polls. Dukakis, or "the Duke," as he was known here in Massachusetts, had been a decent governor, who ran a clean administration and worked hard for improvements in several areas I approve, such as public transportation, but I never thought he had the stature to be the leader of the free world. For one thing, he would have to be introduced to Mikhail Gorbachev, Margaret Thatcher, Francois Mitterand, and the other world leaders. Bush already knew them all and had built good relations with every one of them. Dukakis would also have to get up to speed on military matters. Bush, of course, had fought in World War II as an eighteen-year-old and was very well acquainted with all things having to do with national defense. Fortunately, the voters got to appreciate the difference in this area when Dukakis made the mistake of taking a ride in a tank while the cameras rolled. His helmet was too big for him and he looked ridiculous. Nothing could have highlighted the difference between the two men on national defense better than that photo opp. By Election Day, the voters had come to their senses, and Bush was elected by a comfortable margin.

I've described the major events of Bush's presidency in Chapter IV of this book, but I would like to add that it was his genial personality that enabled him to put together the coalition that won the Gulf War and drove Saddam Hussein out of Kuwait and that kept our relations with Russia on a smooth path during the collapse of communism in Europe. In all of his dealings with foreign leaders and the military, George Bush set a great example of being firm, yet flexible, when he needed to be, courageous, yet not foolhardy, and intelligent without being pedantic. In essence, he was a very nice man who could be tough when necessary. He was the embodiment of everything I would like to be, if I could.

I was very sad to see George Bush lose to Bill Clinton when he ran for reelection in 1992. I realized Clinton was brilliant and a great campaigner, but his moral core was far inferior to Bush's, and that was to become quite evident in his second term. It bothered me that many of the baby boomers, the people born right after World War II, were thinking it was time to throw out the old generation and bring in the new. It was even more irritating that young people in their twenties were voting for Clinton because they thought he was cool playing the saxophone on *The Arsenio Hall Show*.

In the quarter of a century since he was president, George Bush has continued to impress me. After his son George W. became president, he agreed to "W's" proposal that he and none other than Bill Clinton work together to raise funds for relief for the victims of the tsunami in Southeast Asia. He and Clinton worked well together, and they got together again to raise money for the victims of Hurricane Katrina in 2005 and the victims of Hurricane Ike in 2008. Nicknamed *the odd couple* by reporters, Bush and Clinton became good friends. Their relationship was a display of the "we can oppose each other but we can still be friends" attitude that Bush had exemplified his entire life. To be fair, Clinton had that outlook as well. It was heartwarming to see them touring disaster areas together, and it also makes me a bit angry that today's politicians can't show a little bit of that same attitude.

In 2010, George Bush began having trouble walking and has since relied on using a wheelchair to get around. During his presidency, he signed the Americans with Disabilities Act, so he now gets to take advantage of the ramps and other conveniences that law requires. Because his socks are on prominent display as he sits in the chair, he has made it his new trademark to wear colorful socks for all to see—whimsically, a different color on each leg.

A photo that George W. Bush included in his book *41, A Portrait of My Father*, shows George H.W. Bush sitting in his chair holding the two-year-old son of one of his secret service agents. The boy has leukemia and is bald from chemotherapy; the former president is bald because he shaved his head to show solidarity with him. It is a very touching photo that brings tears to my eyes. It tells me all I need to know about George H.W. Bush.

In this chapter I have described several people in American history whose lives have inspired me and who have served as role models for my own behavior and thinking. There are a few more I could have mentioned, but I think I have described the major ones who have influenced my life. Maybe these people inspire you as well. There may be others whose lives and thoughts resonate more with you, like Andrew Carnegie, who came to the United States as a penniless Scottish immigrant, developed a fortune of over four hundred million dollars in the steel business, and became one of the country's foremost philanthropists, donating millions to libraries and schools across the country; or John D. Rockefeller, who outperformed all the other oil refiners in the country, garnered ninety percent of the oil refining business, and became the world's first billionaire; or Thomas Edison, who devoted his life to invention, and through sheer hard work, developed the lightbulb, the phonograph, the motion picture, and many other inventions; or Malcolm Little, who left behind a life of petty crime, converted to Islam, adopted the name Malcolm X, and introduced the concept of "black power" to the African-American community. There are countless others who march across history's pages. The point is that the study of American history introduces you to these people and their stories help you formulate your own lifestyle and belief system. Why stagger through life blindly when there have been so many interesting people who can show you the way?

CHAPTER VII

ROGUES AND CAUTIONARY TALES

AARON BURR.

As I said before about role models, the Bible is the best source of life instruction, and that is true for tales of wrongdoing and downright evil as well. One need look no further than Cain and Abel or the story of David and Bathsheba to find stories that put you on your guard against making similar choices in your own life. American history is rich with stories of people warning us to avoid making the mistakes that some of our ancestors made. Most of the people discussed in this chapter are famous and were usually well meaning. Some are renowned to the point that they might make other people's lists of role models. In this chapter, I will be discussing the questionable morality and/or the bad decisions of Benedict Arnold, Aaron Burr, Andrew Jackson, William Tweed, Joseph McCarthy, Richard Nixon, John C. Calhoun, Jefferson Davis, Robert E. Lee, and Andrew Johnson. Some of these choices have certainly raised one or both of your eyebrows and had you thinking, "Why is *he* on *this* list; I thought he was *great*?" A few of them you may never have heard of, but all of them have done something that has put them in my personal hall of shame and has put me on high alert to avoid doing something similar in my own life.

BENEDICT ARNOLD,
TRAITOR

If Benedict Arnold had suddenly dropped dead of a heart attack in 1779, his name would be among those who were heroes in the American Revolution and not a name synonymous with traitor. In the early years of the struggle for independence, Arnold performed some remarkable deeds on behalf of his country. In the fall of 1775, he led an expedition of eleven hundred men on a strenuous trek through Maine in an attempt to capture Quebec City. In the ensuing battle that ended in failure, Arnold suffered a severe leg wound, but soldiered on, much to the admiration of his troops. Forced to retreat by the advancing British, Arnold withdrew to Lake Champlain and prepared to stop the British before they could reach Fort Ticonderoga.

What Arnold did on Lake Champlain during the fall of 1776 is little known, but truly spectacular. With incredible energy he mobilized his soldiers to construct a small fleet of warships to augment the flotilla the Americans had been building during the summer. Hewing planks out of freshly cut trees with axes, the soldiers worked night and day to construct boats that were barely seaworthy. When the great British armada came down the lake in early October, Arnold had taken positions concealed behind Valcour Island on the western side of the lake. After the British warships passed the island, Arnold's fleet engaged them in a fight between the island and the New York shoreline. Most of Arnold's fleet was destroyed, but he kept fighting on until darkness settled in. During the night, he led his few remaining ships on a daring run past the British fleet and was able to escape. The next day, the British fleet caught up to Arnold again and he was eventually forced to burn his remaining ships. During all of this fighting, Arnold was constantly running about, staying visible to the British gunners, and encouraging his men. Although the result of this fighting was defeat, the battle so damaged the British fleet that General Carlton, the British commander, stopped his advance down Lake Champlain, went into "winter quarters," and did not resume his campaign toward the Hudson River until the following spring.

Because he had delayed the British, Arnold gave the Americans in the area time to prepare an adequate defense. The following year, in upstate New York, the American forces inflicted a monumental defeat on the British Army at the key battle of Saratoga. The victory proved decisive in securing French help for the American Revolution. Arnold played an important role in that battle, was again severely wounded in the leg, and really should have been acclaimed as a major war hero.

This is when Benedict Arnold's story begins to sour. He walked with an extreme limp as a result of his wounds, he was acclaimed by all of the men who had served under him at Valcour and at Saratoga, and yet he was not satisfied with being a war hero, and he certainly was not content to have made a major contribution to American independence. He wanted financial gain and he wanted to be on the winning side. In 1779, he began to think the British would win the war and he began dealing secretly with them. By 1780 he had contrived a plot to turn over the American fort at West Point to the British for a sum of twenty thousand pounds. Arnold's plot was only uncovered at the last minute. Indeed, Arnold had to escape by boat down the Hudson River just before General Washington arrived at West Point.

Benedict Arnold made it into the British camp and served the remainder of the war wearing a red coat and leading British troops. When the war was lost, he went to England, then to Canada, and finally back to England. He died in 1801 a lonely figure, unpopular even in Britain and demonized as a traitor in the United States.

There was a time when I would defend Arnold. I would describe his exploits in the early years of the Revolution and acclaim his energy and leadership skills; I would make the case that he should have been given more credit for his accomplishments and more promotions; I would argue that if he had been treated fairly, the Revolutionary War would have been won sooner and we might even, at some point, have had a President Benedict Arnold. As an American history teacher, I thought it was fun to present the other side of Benedict Arnold's story, to describe his considerable skills and to justify his dissatisfaction.

I'm over that now. I see him as a self-centered, egotistical, power hungry, greedy villain who betrayed his country's cause for personal gain. He inspired the men under his command to work as a team, but he himself was not a team player. He was just what people have always said he was, a traitor. I believe in staying loyal to the cause you have taken up and doing whatever is needed to make it succeed. I believe in working for the success of the enterprise you are part of and not being concerned at all for personal gain or fame. I believe in these things because I do not want to be like Benedict Arnold.

AARON BURR, ULTIMATE ROGUE

The tragedy of Aaron Burr is that he could have been one of the greatest of the founding fathers. He was certainly right up there in intelligence with Jefferson and the others, and he was, as all the women at the time would attest, the best looking. He also had some very good personal qualities. He was one of the few men in his time who believed women were as intelligent as men and deserved equal political rights. In fact, he was probably more democratic in his philosophy than any of the other founders.

The problem was that he had a streak of cynicism in him that ran very deep, and he could not imagine that every other politically active man of his time was not equally as cynical. In his great novel called *Burr*, Gore Vidal has Aaron Burr as a reminiscing old man contemptuously describing Washington as a vain man with a face scarred by smallpox. The great general, Burr recounts, had a butt so large he created a hilarious spectacle every time he mounted his unfortunate horse. Jefferson gets branded as a hypocrite when Burr describes the author of the Declaration of Independence presiding over a plantation populated by slaves, several of whom sport red hair very similar to their master's. Going through life constantly thinking the worst of everyone, as Burr did, must have been poisonous. Furthermore, this outlook caused him to justify his own nefarious deeds with the self-deluding justification that illegal or immoral behavior was necessary for success in this corrupt world.

Vidal has great fun lampooning the founding fathers through Burr, but what was it that Burr actually *did* in his lifetime that is a cautionary tale for me? There were three times in his life when I believe he acted dishonorably. The first was when he attempted to steal the presidency; the second was when he killed Alexander Hamilton in a duel; and the third was when he committed treason by attempting to create an empire for himself in the West. For each of these acts, he offered self-righteous justification, but I believe his deeds were the product of greed and pride.

In 1800, Thomas Jefferson was the Republican candidate for president and Aaron Burr was the party's candidate for vice president. They were running against the sitting president, John Adams, and Charles Pinckney. When the electors voted, the Republicans carried the election seventy-three to sixty-five, and one would think that Jefferson would take office as the new president and Burr would assume the vice-presidency. But wait. There was a problem. Since the electors did not designate their ballots for president or vice president—they simply wrote the names of their two choices on their ballots—Aaron Burr technically tied Jefferson with seventy-three votes! The choice between Jefferson and Burr would now have to be made in the House of Representatives, where the Federalists had the majority.

Had Burr been an honorable man, and had he considered the needs of the country above his own ambition, he would have made it clear to the members of the House that Jefferson was the choice of the electors for president and the House should simply follow their wishes and vote for him. Instead, Burr saw his chance and used every political device he could to win votes from the Federalist members of the House of Representatives. Many Federalists, seeing Jefferson as their main enemy, were inclined to vote for Burr, and they did so in enough numbers that after thirty-five ballots, neither candidate had received a majority. Alexander Hamilton, whom many Federalists considered to be the leader of their party, even though he was not in congress, finally weighed into the contest in a major way. He told Federalist members that Burr was a dangerous man, that Jefferson at least had *some* principles, even if they didn't agree with them, and that they should cast their votes for Jefferson. On the thirty-sixth ballot, the House gave Jefferson the majority and Burr had to settle for the vice-presidency.

Aaron Burr never forgave Hamilton for the role he played in that election. Then, in 1804, when Burr tried to run for governor of New York, Hamilton again stood in his way. Reiterating his charge that Burr was a dangerous man not to be trusted, Hamilton yet again helped bring about Burr's defeat. This was too much for Burr, who was still vice president, by the way, and he challenged Hamilton to a duel. Hamilton foolishly accepted the challenge (he would argue he had no choice or he would be branded a coward), and the two met on the morning of July 11, 1804, at Weehawken Heights, New Jersey, above the Hudson River. Accounts differ as to what actually happened that morning: Did Hamilton purposely fire his pistol over Burr's head assuming Burr would do the same? Did Hamilton's shot go astray after Burr had already shot him? The end result, however, was indisputable: Burr shot Hamilton in the stomach and Hamilton died a day later. Burr fled the scene to avoid prosecution in New York or New Jersey, where dueling was illegal, and he went to Washington and resumed his role as vice president, presiding over meetings of the Senate.

While Hamilton's role in this tragic event is not clean—after all, he foolishly put his life on the line and left his wife and five children—Burr's behavior is despicable. He killed one of the leading men in America and then went about his business with no more remorse than if he had shot a squirrel.

Two years later, Burr, no longer vice president, formed a volunteer army in the West, floated his rag-tag group of heavily armed frontiersmen down the Mississippi on rafts, and appeared to be on a mission to create an empire for himself in the West. It is not clear what he was up to. Was he trying to break Louisiana away from the United States and create a new country with himself as emperor? Was he trying to invade Texas and take it away from Spain? Whatever his scheme, it was solely to benefit only Aaron Burr with money and power. He was arrested for treason against the United States and tried in a federal court in Virginia. Since conviction for treason requires two witnesses, and two could not be found, Burr was acquitted. Soon afterward he left for a self-imposed exile in Europe.

It is amusing to see Burr, as Gore Vidal does, as an intriguing rogue, and I can do that. I enjoyed Vidal's book very much, and I am amused, on one level, by Burr's cynical outlook and constant scheming. (Near the end of his life, as a seventy-seven-year old man, Burr married a wealthy widow for her money!) I would never want to have a reputation as sullied as his, however. He is my talisman for bad behavior, and I am always alert for whiffs of Aaron Burr in any decision I am about to make.

My adorable grandson is named Aaron. My daughter assures me he is named after the brother of Moses, not Aaron Burr. Thank goodness! I'm sure he will bring great honor to the name.

ANDREW JACKSON,
A RACIST, RECKLESS MAN

With his flowing hair and sturdy gaze, Andrew Jackson graces the front of the American twenty-dollar bill. At least he does at the moment; he's about to be replaced in 2020 by Harriet Tubman, an African-American woman who escaped from slavery and then returned to the South many times to help other captives find their way north to freedom. This decision by the Treasury Department removes one irony and creates another. It *is* ironic that Jackson's face would appear on any paper currency issued by a national bank because he hated paper money and opposed the national bank of his own time with reckless abandon. It *will* be ironic when his face is replaced by a runaway slave because he was a slave owner himself and did everything he could while he was president to protect slavery, including ordering the postal authorities to destroy abolitionist literature and newspapers sent through the mail.

Dumping Jackson and replacing him with an abolitionist former slave is a great way to demonstrate how far our country has come.

Another American woman who was considered for Jackson's spot was the Native-American who guided Lewis and Clark on their expedition to explore the Louisiana Purchase, Sacajawea. Selecting her also would have had a nice touch of irony because Jackson probably did more than any other American political leader to drive the Native-Americans from their lands.

In the years before he was elected president in 1828, Jackson gained a reputation as an Indian fighter. Once in office, he pursued a policy of ejecting the Native Americans from any lands they controlled east of the Mississippi. In 1830, he signed the Indian Removal Act that he had proposed in his State of the Union speech. This law authorized him to "negotiate" with the Indian tribes in the southern United States and secure their expulsion to an area west of the Mississippi, which is today Oklahoma. Defying members of Congress who supported the rights of the Indians to remain, and even the United States Supreme Court, which ruled in their favor, Jackson ordered the United States Army to evict the Cherokees from Georgia, the Creeks from Alabama, the Choctaws and the Chickasaws from Mississippi, and the Seminoles from Florida.

Jackson said he believed that removal was the only way to save the tribes involved from the complete annihilation they would suffer as white civilization expanded. Transporting their cultures to Indian Territory was the only way to give them a chance to maintain their way of life. What Jackson failed to mention was that, as president, he could have protected them where they were. Instead, thousands of Indians died during the horrendous one-thousand-mile journey west in the dead of winter, known as the infamous Trail of Tears, and once settled on the barren prairies, they were no more able to reproduce their culture than if they had been sent to the moon. Furthermore, the advancing whites would eventually overtake them in the West and simply push them off their lands again. They had legal status in the states from which they had come—the Supreme Court had upheld that status—and Jackson should have allowed them to keep it and stay where they were.

There are many white men who belong in the hall of shame for their treatment of the American Indians, namely Colonel John Chivington, who, in 1864, ordered his men to massacre all the Cheyenne Indians in a village near Sand Creek, Colorado. His orders were to kill and scalp all Indians, even the children, because "nits make lice." There are many others like him, but Jackson stands out because, as president, he had the authority to establish a different policy toward the Native Americans. He could have protected their rights, but he saw them as having no rights. He saw them as inferior creatures, just as he saw his African-American slaves.

Some people would say that it is not fair to judge a man by the standards of our own times, that Jackson was very much a product of nineteenth century thinking on race and that he shouldn't be singled out for criticism. My response to that is that there were people in his time who were fully sympathetic to the Indians and wanted them to stay on their lands. Henry Clay and John Quincy Adams in Congress, and John Marshall, Chief Justice of the Supreme Court, all supported the Indians' rights to their homes. Jackson simply gave full rein to his racism and perpetrated a horrible crime against thousands of virtually defenseless people. This is not what a person with power should do.

Besides racist behavior, Andrew Jackson also displayed reckless behavior as president. In 1832, he vetoed the re-charter of the national bank because he thought the bank was a tool for the wealthy interests in the country. Furthermore, he had a personal hatred for Nicholas Biddle, the president of the bank. Then, not content to prevent the bank's re-charter, Jackson pulled all the federal government deposits from the bank and placed the money in various state banks. These acts were motivated by his hatreds and prejudices—his hatred for Biddle and his prejudice against rich people and banks—and the result was that he destroyed the economic superstructure of the country and had nothing with which to replace it. By the end of his presidency, the country was in a severe economic depression, a problem he handed off to his hapless vice president, Martin Van Buren.

Many historians rank Andrew Jackson as one of their top five presidents. They probably base most of their admiration for him on his strong stand against nullification in 1832. In that year, South Carolina nullified the tariff law and threatened to leave the Union if the president tried to enforce the obnoxious law in their state. Jackson refused to accept South Carolina's action and prepared to lead an army into the state to carry out the law and to hang every nullifier he could get his hands on. Civil war was averted when Henry Clay proposed a compromise tariff that South Carolina would accept. Jackson's strong stand for the Union and for federal law in this crisis provided the template for Lincoln's response to South Carolina's secession twenty-eight years later, in 1860. All of that is very good, and I admire Jackson's strength during that crisis.

Most of my students have admired Jackson. They love the story of how he fought a duel with Charles Dickinson, who had insulted his wife. Dickinson fired first and hit Jackson in the chest, but Jackson hung tough, stood his ground, and shot Dickinson dead. They like the way he glared at John C. Calhoun before the nullification crisis, when he told him the Union would be preserved, and when after Calhoun led South Carolina into nullification, Jackson threatened to hang Calhoun as a traitor.

In my younger days, I also admired Jackson for his toughness and willingness to "go to the wall" for the Union. In recent years, however, my esteem for Jackson has dissipated, and I no longer see a hero on the twenty-dollar bill. I see a racist and a reckless, temperamental, hotheaded man who hurt many people. Like Jackson, I have a tendency to rend my garment with rage and do rash things. Jackson's story reminds me of what can happen when a person lets his temper dictate his actions. What I have tried to do for many years, and not always successfully, is suppress my Jacksonian tendencies. For me, his story is definitely a cautionary tale.

WILLIAM TWEED,
CORRUPT BOSS

History teachers don't like teaching the years between 1865 and 1900. It seems like such a letdown after the excitement of the Civil War, and the standard view is that nothing much happened during that period. All of the presidents were boring old guys with long beards who had no memorable accomplishments, but, actually, those years *were* exciting for those who lived them. People felt the country was entering a new era of progress and invention. So many things were a marvel by the late 1800s, such as the electric light bulb, the telephone, and the motion picture. There were dramatic new structures, such as the Brooklyn Bridge. But because teachers don't particularly like this era, and because it often comes up at a dreary time of the year, usually in February, students end up disliking the era even more than they dislike any of the others.

Mark Twain called the decades after the Civil War the Gilded Age for reasons described in Chapter II, and it is easy to find villains in this period of American history. There were many men, such as the nefarious Jay Gould, who would use any means available, legal or not, to increase their wealth, and there were political leaders in Congress, such as those involved in the Crédit Mobilier scandal, who lined their pockets with money that was supposed to pay for the construction of the first transcontinental railroad. The icon of this era, though, was William Magear Tweed, the leader (the grand sachem) of the Democratic Party political club in New York City known as Tammany Hall. A study of what he did in New York in the late 1860s informs us that mankind is depraved, greedy, and selfish.

Tweed held several positions in New York during the 1850s and 1860s. He was, at various times, a representative to the U.S. Congress from New York, a member of the New York State Assembly, and a member of several different city commissions, but his real power came from his role as the "boss" of Tammany Hall. Since the Democratic Party virtually controlled the city of New York in those years, Boss Tweed ran the show. He decided who would be the Democratic candidates in each election, who would be appointed to executive positions, and, most importantly, who would get the contracts from the city for public works projects. Tweed had positively no scruples when it came to stealing money from the city. Contractors who did work for the city were told to pad their bills by two or three hundred percent; the contractor would get his money and the rest would go into the pockets of Tweed and his cronies. The scope of this corruption defies belief! The court house built during the 1860s, for example, cost the city thirteen million dollars, almost twice the amount the United States paid to Russia for all of Alaska during that same period! It has been estimated that Tweed and his men, usually referred to as the Tweed Ring, milked New York for over seventy-five million dollars in a period of less than ten years.

There is a positive side to the story of the Tweed Ring. In 1869, a brilliant and talented artist named Thomas Nast began publishing cartoon caricatures of Tweed in *Harper's Weekly* magazine. Nast depicted Tweed, accurately, as an enormous man with a scruffy beard and a diamond stickpin glittering on his vest above his ample belly. The most famous Nast cartoon showed Tweed and the rest of his Tammany Hall gang standing in a circle, each pointing a finger at the man next to him. The caption read, "Who stole the people's money?" and each man is saying, "'Twas him!" Week after week, Nast attacked the Tweed Ring with clever drawings. One showed Tweed as a Roman emperor sitting in the Coliseum, watching a tiger (the Tammany Tiger) attacking a helpless maiden who represented the people. The caption on this, as on all his cartoons, was "What are you going to do about it?"

Tweed reportedly said that he didn't care what the newspapers wrote about him because most of the people couldn't read, but they could certainly see those damn pictures!. At one point, Tweed tried to buy Nast off by sending a banker friend to offer him one hundred thousand dollars to stop attacking him. Nast asked if he could have five hundred thousand, and the banker said he could, indeed, have that much. Nast then revealed he had just been toying with him and said he had made up his mind to "put those fellows behind bars." The banker warned him that he might end up dead first, but Nast would not be cowed; he went right on drawing his cartoons. He serves as a great role model for not allowing yourself to be bought. He is also, by the way, the creator of Santa Claus as we know him today. Kris Kringle was a skinny little elf until Nast plumped him up and gave him the red suit we have come to love.

Finally, as a consequence of investigation sparked by Nast's cartoons, a grand jury indicted Tweed on one hundred twenty counts of corruption. Incredibly, after his arrest, he was able to escape and flee to Spain. More incredibly, he was recognized by Spanish authorities who were familiar with the Nast cartoons and he was returned to the United States. Back in custody, Tweed quite literally withered away (from three hundred to one hundred sixty pounds) and died in 1878. His sudden fall from power and his pathetic demise are powerful reminders of what happens to people who are activated by greed. All his millions and his diamond stickpin were of no use to the boss when the Lord came to get him.

JOE MCCARTHY, **RECKLESS BULLY**

In recent years, bullying has gotten a great deal of attention because of the ease with which a bully can intimidate his or her victims in social media, but the practice of bullying goes back to the beginning of time, and American history offers a prime example in the person of Senator Joe McCarthy.

By 1950, Americans had become very fearful that communism, which now ruled the Eurasian continent from the Elbe River in Germany to the Pacific Ocean, was infiltrating the United States. In 1948, top Hollywood figures, including actors, directors, writers, and producers, were summoned to Washington to testify before the House Un-American Activities Committee about the presence of communists in the movie industry. It was feared that there were people producing films that would cast communism in a favorable light and corrupt the minds of unsuspecting moviegoers. Ten people refused to answer the committee's questions, were suspected of being communists or communist sympathizers, and were blacklisted. Most of them were not able to get work in Hollywood for the rest of their lives. In 1949, a former State Department official named Alger Hiss was convicted of perjury for lying under oath about his activities as a Soviet spy. It seemed as though communist agents were everywhere working to overthrow the government and bring communism to our country.

In this atmosphere, Senator Joe McCarthy of Wisconsin saw an opportunity to advance his political career. Having been elected to the Senate in 1946, he was fearful that he might not get reelected in 1952 unless he found a way to enhance his popularity. In early 1950, he began making speeches in which he claimed that Alger Hiss was only the tip of the iceberg; there were many more communists working in the State Department and undermining American foreign policy. How else could we explain the failure to prevent Mao Tse Tung from defeating our ally, Chiang Kai Shek, in China and establishing a communist regime in the largest country on earth?

Joe McCarthy was a burly man with a constant five o'clock shadow. His expression was always dour and threatening. When he spoke, he often raised his voice and pounded the table with his large, hairy fist. As increasing numbers of people took notice of his accusations, he held press conferences during which he held aloft sheaves of paper and proclaimed he had documents that showed there were two hundred five "card carrying communists" employed by the State Department. When asked to reveal who those people were, he would draw back, claiming that the documents were top secret and could not be divulged at this time. By the end of the year, he was one of the most talked about politicians in the country.

I was seven years old in 1951 and just beginning to become aware of the world outside of my own little sphere. One of my first political memories is my mother saying, "Thank God we have Senator McCarthy exposing all those bad people."

As time went on, McCarthy became increasingly emboldened. The number of communists he claimed to be in the State Department kept changing, but he finally settled on the number fifty-seven. A movie that came out ten years later called *The Manchurian Candidate* featured a McCarthy-type senator who was constantly ranting about communists in the American government. At one point in the film, he is discussing with his wife how confusing it is to keep track of the number of communists he is claiming, so they agree they will settle on a permanent number. As they talk, the senator is slapping the bottom of a ketchup bottle to get ketchup onto his food. The next scene shows him at a press conference saying emphatically that there are fifty-seven communists in the state department. By 1962, when this movie was made, it was abundantly clear that McCarthy's numbers had no more validity than if they had been lifted from a Heinz® Ketchup bottle.

McCarthy's antics would have been relatively harmless—annoying and stupid, but harmless—if he had never started attacking specific individuals; however, by the end of 1950, he was putting out names and, with scant evidence to support his charges, ruining reputations and careers. When Senator Tydings of Maryland crossed him, McCarthy went after him with a vengeance and so sullied Tydings' reputation that he was defeated in his reelection bid in 1952. McCarthy even smeared George Marshall, President Truman's secretary of Defense. Marshall, as Army chief of staff, had been the architect of the Allied victory over Nazi Germany in World War II. As secretary of state, he had gone to the rescue of Western Europe with a program of financial aid that became known as the Marshall Plan. China, however, had fallen to Mao and his communists, and McCarthy accused Marshall of allowing that to happen, perhaps purposely. Was he, the famous George Marshall, a communist sympathizer? In his usual melodramatic and ham-fisted way, McCarthy accused Marshall of engaging in "a conspiracy so immense and an infamy so black as to dwarf any previous venture in the history of man." By 1952, no one dared cross McCarthy for fear of reprisal that would ruin a reputation and a career … not even General Eisenhower.

In 1952, Eisenhower ran for president as a Republican. When he brought his campaign to Wisconsin, he was advised to campaign with McCarthy and not to say anything about George Marshall. Eisenhower was a longtime friend of Marshall, had served under him during the war, and respected him deeply, but out of fear of what might happen to his chances of carrying Wisconsin (and perhaps other states), he deleted a favorable reference to Marshall that was in his speech. When a reporter found out that Eisenhower had done this, he wrote an article about it in the *New York Times*. Eisenhower was mortified. He considered his desertion of his old friend to be one of the lowest points in his whole life. The incident showed the extent to which McCarthy was able to bully even the most prestigious and honorable man in the country, the man who had led great armies in the war against Hitler and who was elected president in 1952 and again in 1956.

McCarthy's bullying tactic of accusing people of harboring communist sympathies—of being a "red" or at least "pink," meaning liberal, I guess—with scant evidence had a name: McCarthyism. Other political leaders were copying his style, and people were afraid that they, too, might be accused. The Cincinnati Reds baseball team changed its name to Redlegs to make sure no one would suspect team ownership of being communist sympathizers. A bubble gum company that included geography lessons for the kids on its gum wrappers eliminated the ones on the Soviet Union and China so the company would not be accused of poisoning the minds of children. Presumably it was okay to rot their teeth.

Finally, like most bullies, McCarthy went too far. Also, like most bullies, he was brought down when a few people had the courage to stand up to him. After McCarthy accused the United States Army of harboring communists, the Army fired back by accusing McCarthy of trying to secure special favors for one of his staff people, David Shine, who was a private in the Army. The Senate Subcommittee on Investigations held hearings on these allegations. The committee's sessions were televised in the spring of 1954 (the Army-McCarthy Hearings), and they became a major event, drawing twenty million viewers and eclipsing all other daytime TV. I remember coming home from school every day that spring and finding my mother doing her ironing and glued to the TV to watch the "show."

Many people expected to see McCarthy make minced meat of his accusers and any hapless witness who took the stand, but instead they saw a dumb bruiser with no more class than a drunken bar room brawler. A climactic moment came when a sneering McCarthy told the Army-hired Boston lawyer Joseph Welch that he should look into the background of a man named Fred Fisher, who was on his staff. The implication was, of course, that Fisher might be a communist. Welch, in total disbelief and exasperation, immediately lashed back at McCarthy. "How dare you drag that young man's name through the mud?" he asked. "Have you no sense of decency, sir, at long last?" This was an iconic moment. Viewers across the country began to see McCarthy for who he really was, a bully with no thought whatsoever for the harm he was doing to people. Within a few months, the Senate voted to censor McCarthy for his reprehensible behavior unbecoming a United States senator. His popularity in the country plummeted. By 1955, he was a hollow shell of his former self, with no influence in the Senate. In 1957, he died of liver disease brought on by alcoholism.

For me, McCarthy's story is a cautionary tale on three levels. First, it is a warning against talking about people and making accusations with little evidence. I wish I had learned the McCarthy lesson earlier, because it might have saved me from doing something for which I am very ashamed. In my younger days, I needed to be more aware of what my big mouth was capable of doing to hurt other people or drag down their reputation. In my early years of teaching, I once talked about one of the other coaches who was not present at the time. I said he was disorganized and often acted like he was "on something." Another teacher, a young woman I will always remember for this one moment, said, "I'm surprised to hear you say that. He always speaks highly of you." She might as well have stabbed me in the gut with a dagger. She was my Joseph Welch: "Have you no sense of decency, sir, at long last?" Here I was, being no better than Joe McCarthy. Years later I thanked that woman for setting me straight. She didn't remember the incident, but I'll never forget it.

Second, the McCarthy story shows how effective it is to stand up to bullies. They are usually cowards at heart. In my life, I have been fortunate to have confronted my bullies in person. I pity the poor kids today who get bullied through cyberspace and cannot retaliate very effectively.

I would like to be able to tell a few stories in which I brought down a bully with a great verbal rejoinder, such as that classic by Joseph Welch, but I don't have any. I have stood up to a few bullies, but those times were all in junior high school and they always quickly escalated into actual fistfights. I have already related the time I knocked Lenny off his chair in the cafeteria. On another occasion, one wintry day, a big guy from up the street smacked me in the back of the head with a huge ice chunk while I was delivering newspapers on my paper route. I tore into him with a barrage of fists and left him in such bad shape that he spent much of the next day at school explaining to inquiring friends how his face got so beat up. Neither of those jerks ever bothered me again, but I wish I could say I handled the job with a little of the class Joseph Welch exhibited. The Welch example became part of my maturing process and enabled me in the years to come to deal with bullies in a more sublime way.

The third lesson to be gleaned from the McCarthy story is to watch out for McCarthy-type demagogues in today's political world. It seems there are always politicians who play on people's fears to gain popularity, saying things like: Immigrants are pouring into the country illegally, and they are violent people who will wage jihad against our way of life; they will blow up our buildings and murder our children. Or, Rich people are the real enemy in the country; they buy politicians and screw the little guy.

As was true in the McCarthy era, there is often a shred of truth to the accusations, just enough to lend credibility to the rants. In the 1950s, there probably were Soviet spies and communist agents in the country; there were a few who were probably rightfully charged and convicted. But McCarthy-type hysteria is never called for. Some people who indulge themselves in it wise up years later and regret how their words and actions inflamed passions and hurt people.

RICHARD NIXON, "TRICKY DICK"

It is impossible to have a chapter on cautionary tales—stories about people who should guide us in what *not* to do—without including a section on Richard Nixon. After all, he was the only American president to be forced to resign from office for crimes he committed. Yet Nixon's story has a poignant side to it, as well, because I think he really did want to be a statesman who did good things for his country, and occasionally he succeeded. In the end, however, he was too insecure and paranoid to believe that he could get ahead on his own merits and that he did not have to utterly destroy people who opposed him. That Richard Nixon's story was so tragic makes it all the more compelling as a cautionary tale for those of us who study it.

If you visit the Richard Nixon Presidential Library and Museum in Yorba Linda, California, and tour his boyhood home, you see that Nixon grew up in near poverty and that, as a child and a young man, he never achieved success as easily as some other kids did. He wasn't as good looking and he wasn't as athletic as many of the other boys, but he was smart and he could fight harder and work harder and longer than anyone else. If anyone whacked him, he was sure to come back with an even harder punch. By the time he grew up and joined the Navy during World War II, Nixon saw himself as a smart, hard-fighting man who would scrape and claw his way to the top.

When he returned from the war, Nixon successfully ran for a seat in the U.S. House of Representatives. In Washington, as a member of the House Un-American Activities Committee, he successfully prosecuted Alger Hiss. Nixon is the man usually given the most credit for exposing

Hiss's perjury. Later, after he was elected to the Senate, Nixon became an ally of Senator McCarthy in the crusade to smoke out domestic communist subversives. In the early 1950s, he was what we might today call "McCarthy Lite," a staunch anticommunist with a somewhat less heavy-handed approach. For that reason, General Eisenhower chose Nixon to be his running mate. He wanted a man on the ticket who would be a firewall against the McCarthy forces, a man who would make it clear that the Eisenhower Administration would not be soft on communism. In the elections of 1952 and 1956, Eisenhower was free to take the high road, giving speeches about policy issues, leaving it to Nixon to do the "street fighting," calling Democratic candidate Adlai Stevenson a pinko communist sympathizer who would appease the Russians and let communists into the American government.

In 1960, after eight years as vice president, Nixon felt he was ready to take the final step up; he got the Republican nomination for president that year. His Democratic opponent was John F. Kennedy, who was the embodiment of the wealthy, good-looking, self-assured people Nixon had been battling his entire life. Emblematic of the nature of the fight Nixon had on his hands was the first television debate between the two candidates. Ten days before the debate, Nixon got the flu and lost ten pounds. On the day of the debate, he arrived at the TV studio looking pale and wearing a light colored suit. No one told him that a dark suit looks better on television. He also refused to have television makeup applied to his face. Kennedy, by contrast, was well rested and tanned. He wore a dark suit and sat patiently while the makeup people did their work. The result was that on screen (black and white in 1960), Nixon looked haggard and wan while Kennedy looked young, strong, and dynamic. People who listened to the debate on the radio thought Nixon had the best responses to the questions, but the vast majority of the people watched the debate on television, and their view was that Kennedy was the clear winner.

I remember my parents watching the debate that night on our little TV set in the basement. They were both loyal Republicans and they cheered everything Nixon said, but they were clearly disappointed with how he looked. Even they had to admit that Kennedy probably got the best of it.

Kennedy inched ahead in the polls after that night and Nixon never did catch up. The election results in November were the closest in American history. Kennedy beat Nixon with forty-nine point seven percent of the popular vote to Nixon's forty-nine point six percent. Kennedy won the electoral vote by a three hundred three to two hundred nineteen margin, but there was a chance that two states, Illinois and Texas, could be swung from Kennedy's column to Nixon's and the electors from those two would give Nixon the victory, two hundred seventy to two hundred sixty-eight. There was much talk about electoral fraud in those states, of Kennedy receiving more votes in some precincts than there were registered voters. A challenge and a recount could possibly reverse the results and put Nixon in the White House. It was a long shot, and some top Republicans wanted Nixon to go for it, but Nixon decided he did not want to put the country through a long period of uncertainty about who the next president would be, so he conceded the election without a fight.

Many people are surprised to learn that Nixon put the interests of the country ahead of his own personal quest for power, and it does seem likely that the Nixon we knew in the 1970s *would* have challenged the Texas and Illinois results to see if he could pull victory from the jaws of defeat. I think Nixon had not yet become fully jaded in 1960. His background and personal instincts fitted him to be a brawler, but he was still able to keep his impulses under control. If he had actually won legitimately in 1960, I think we would have seen a different kind of Nixon presidency than we saw in the early seventies. He would have run a relatively clean administration and put policies in place regarding the Cold War and the economy that were best for the nation from his point of view. Certainly he would have played the political game hard and used some dirty tactics, but probably not beyond what we usually accept as politics as usual.

After leaving the vice-presidency in 1961, Nixon returned to California as a private citizen, but he still had hopes of winning the White House and, in 1962, he tried to get back in the game and establish a power base by running for Governor of California. To everyone's surprise, he lost to the colorless governor, Pat Brown, who was running for reelection. At a press conference the day after the vote, Nixon ended his political career for good by announcing his retirement from politics. In a parting gesture that was quoted in newspapers and on news broadcasts all over the country, he told the reporters, most of whom he considered to be unfriendly, "Well, you won't have Nixon to kick around anymore." He appeared petulant, pouty, and a poor loser.

For the next four years, Nixon was out of politics and out of everyone's thoughts. In 1964, the Republicans nominated the ultra-conservative Barry Goldwater, and he proceeded to go down to overwhelming defeat to Lyndon Johnson by sixty to forty percent. Then, in 1966, Richard Nixon began appearing in the news again. Like a political zombie, he rose out of his grave. He made speeches for Republicans running for Congress and began getting favorable reviews, even from the press, for his work on behalf of the Republican Party. By 1968, he was back, running in the presidential primaries and a leading contender for the Republican nomination. That summer the party nominated him for a second run for president.

In the fall of 1968, I met Richard Nixon—well, I shook his hand—at a rally in a hotel only a mile from where I was teaching high school in Southfield, Michigan. Since the event was at three thirty and I would be through teaching for the day, I decided to go and be part of the crowd. I probably wasn't going to vote for the man, but I thought it might be fun to see a campaign rally; it might be something to report back to my American Government class. The ballroom at the hotel where Nixon was scheduled to speak was packed by three fifteen, and we stood there waiting for almost an hour. I was at the back of the room near the door when suddenly there was a great deal of commotion in the hallway, and before I knew it, I was standing face-to-face with Richard Nixon as he made his grand entrance. I was shocked; he was totally different from what I had seen of him on television in the Kennedy debates. First of all, he was taller than I expected, about six-foot tall. Also, having learned his lesson, he was wearing a dark navy blue suit, and he was very tan. For some reason, he focused on me, looked me in the eye, took my hand, and said, "Hi! Glad to see you!" I don't know what my response was, probably "Uh-huh." His grip was strong and he held it just long enough to make it feel sincere. Overall, I was impressed with his personal magnetism. The crowd now knew he was in the room and a huge cheer went up. He strode to the front of the room holding both hands aloft with his fingers in a "V." Little did I know that I would see that same gesture six years later, when he would leave the White House in disgrace.

I voted for Nixon in 1968, partly because he said he had a plan to end the war in Vietnam. Many people later said he had no plan at all, that his promise was just another Nixon lie, but I disagree. He had a plan; it was just that many people didn't like it. Vietnamization, gradually withdrawing American troops as the South Vietnamese Army took over the fighting, was probably the only viable way out of the war, and that was what Nixon did. By 1972, Nixon had drawn down U.S. involvement in the actual fighting in Vietnam, he had ended the military draft, and to most fair-minded people, he had resolved American involvement in Southeast Asia in the only honorable way possible. There had been some ugly bumps along the road, particularly the incursion into Cambodia that brought about the college riots and the Kent State massacre, but it all seemed to be winding down, much to everyone's relief.

Some of Nixon's other first-term accomplishments that I thought were positive included his creation of the Environmental Protection Agency and signing the Clean Air Act, which greatly increased involvement by the federal government in regulating industrial emissions into the atmosphere. Regarding foreign affairs, he pulled off the most dramatic change in American foreign relations in decades. He visited communist China and opened diplomatic relations with the government of Mao Tse-Tung (Mao Zedung). At a state dinner in Beijing with Chinese premier Zhou En Lai, Nixon provided a sight none of us ever thought we would see. For his entire political career, Nixon had been a staunch anticommunist, and here he was, opening diplomatic relations with the nation many people considered to be our biggest rival. Because Nixon had such a hard line reputation, people probably trusted him to make this opening to communist China; they believed that a man such as he would not be selling us out.

Three months later, Nixon visited the Soviet Union, our major enemy in the Cold War. Negotiating with the dower Leonid Brezhnev, the Soviet leader, Nixon produced two major arms limitation treaties: SALT I (the Strategic Arms Limitation Treaty that limited the number of long range missiles held by each side) and the ABM Treaty (Anti-Ballistic Missile Treaty that banned the development of missiles capable of shooting down incoming missiles).

By the summer of 1972, it seemed as though the long Cold War with the Soviet Union and China might be coming to an end. Nixon's Secretary of State, Henry Kissinger, had a name for the new atmosphere: détente (the easing of strained relations). Nixon was up for reelection that year and, by June, every political expert and most of the American people thought his victory would be a sure thing. His Democratic Party opponent was South Dakota Senator George McGovern, a likeable but colorless man whose major selling point was that he opposed the war in Vietnam and would pull U.S. forces out of Southeast Asia as soon as he took office. The polls showed Nixon ahead of McGovern by twenty points.

At this point, as I described in Chapter IV, Nixon's story became a tragedy and a cautionary tale of the first magnitude. On June 17, 1972, five burglars were caught breaking into the Democratic Party headquarters in the Watergate Hotel and Office Complex. As the summer wore on, it came to light that the men who were arrested had ties to the White House. On August 19, Nixon declared emphatically that no one currently employed in the White House had any connection to the Watergate break-in. In September, seven men were indicted for the break-in: the five who were arrested in the Watergate break-in and two men who had worked in the White House and were accused of ordering the break-in.

During the fall campaign, George McGovern tried to make the Watergate break-in an issue. He made a televised address in which he angrily asserted that there was much more to the scandal than was currently known and that there was rampant corruption in the Nixon Administration. I, for one, believed him. As mentioned earlier, I went to work for his campaign, spending Election Day calling registered Democrats to make sure they voted. My motivation for deserting the man I had voted for in 1968 was that for all the good he had done, Nixon was a dishonest man; he had accomplished a few good things, but now we needed to get him out of the White House.

Of course, when the votes were in, Nixon had won by a margin of sixty to forty percent and carried every state but Massachusetts and the District of Columbia. I often joke to my students that it was my work for McGovern that enabled him to carry Massachusetts. He needed me in every state!

What we didn't know on Election Day but found out later was that Nixon had ordered his top aides to cover up the extent of White House involvement in the Watergate break-in. On June 23, he had ordered Chief of Staff Bob Haldeman to see to it that "hush money" was paid to the burglars and that the FBI investigation be called off. All of this came to light when the United States Supreme Court ordered Nixon to turn over the tape recordings that he had made in the oval office to prosecutors. With this direct evidence of obstruction of justice in hand, the House of Representatives was poised to impeach Nixon—charge him with crimes—and the Senate was certain to convict him with a two-thirds vote and remove him from office. Rather than endure all of that, Nixon decided to resign.

On August 9, Nixon bade farewell to his White House staff. The moment was televised and it was painful to watch. Many people in the room were dissolved in tears, as was Nixon's family, who stood next to him.

Finally, he and his family left the room and he walked out onto the White House lawn to board a helicopter. On the top step, he turned to wave goodbye and, incredibly, gave that double "V" sign with raised arms that he had actually stolen from Winston Churchill but for which he was also famous. Most of us were baffled that he could make that gesture at such a moment.

There are so many lessons to be learned from Nixon and the Watergate Scandal. The first is that covering up wrongdoing is often worse than the wrongdoing itself. Nixon himself even said that during the summer of 1972, "The worst thing is when you try to cover it up," which, ironically, was exactly what he was doing when he made that statement. It would have been much better for Nixon if he had held a press conference shortly after the burglars were caught and said, "Some people working for my reelection have gotten overzealous in their efforts and have broken the law. Everyone involved will be dismissed from my staff and will be prosecuted to the full extent of the law. I apologize to the American people on their behalf." His popularity from the China trip and the détente policies would surely have kept him in good standing with the American people; in fact, they might have given him even more credit for making a clean breast of things.

But there are deeper lessons from the story of Richard Nixon and his fall. His biggest problem, the problem that was at the root of everything else that happened, was that he could not believe that his own abilities and accomplishments were enough to achieve success. He couldn't just win a contest by working hard and being just a little bit smarter (although he certainly tried to do that); no, he had to *destroy* his opponents. Very telling was the fact that he did not have opponents, he had enemies. When he first became president he remarked, "We are going to use the IRS (Internal Revenue Service) to screw our enemies." His advisors put together an enemies list, people marked for whatever dirt they could dig up on them. The list even included movie actors, such as Paul Newman. When the list became known, many people who were on it considered it an honor to be on Richard Nixon's enemies list.

It is easy, in the heat of competition, to start to think of your opponents as enemies rather than worthy adversaries. I remember watching a high school football coach giving a locker room pep talk to his team. He threw a folding chair against the wall and screamed, "We *hate* those guys! We don't want to just beat them, we want to HUMILIATE them!" That was the Nixon mindset, and it's a way of thinking that I can slip into if I'm not careful. Nixon provides a good model for what happens to people who do.

Nixon also models the awful results of being paranoid. He often had a furtive look on his face. His eyes would dart around the room as if he were trying to spot an assassin or a guy with a bomb. At a press conference, especially after Watergate started to heat up, he would try to uncover the hidden motive behind every reporter's question. I often said to my classes that if Nixon were in the stands at a baseball game and the catcher went out to the mound to talk to the pitcher, Nixon would think they were standing on the mound talking about how they were going to *get him*. I truly believe that if you think all people are out to get you, sooner or later they probably *will* be out to get you. If Nixon had developed a Ronald Reagan-type of self-assurance—a warm smile and a "we're all good friends here" kind of approach—life would have gone much better for him. Of course, Nixon did not have all the advantages of wealth and high society that Reagan had. His life, as I've said, was much more difficult, so our judgment of him should be somewhat sympathetic. But we have to use his cautionary lesson: Paranoia causes you to do foolish things and can actually engender the very dislike for you that you assume people have. Life is full of ironies.

The Nixon story also shows that you not only have to guard against paranoia and insecurity in yourself, you also have to be alert to signs of it in the people with whom you work or ally yourself. Several of Nixon's top people were positively demonic in their outlook. They fed into their boss's paranoia and adopted his win-at-any price philosophy. An interesting figure in the Nixon White House was Charles Colson. As Nixon's special counsel, he was the author of the original enemies list and was proud to say he was willing to be ruthless in getting things done. The White House tapes, which have been available to the public for years now, show Colson and others in the Oval Office cussing about their enemies, using racial slurs, and positively giggling about how they are going to hurt people. At times it seems that each one is trying to be tougher and more outrageous than the others, and the whole conversation spirals downward. Nixon wanted people like these men around him, but all of us should take note that we are to some degree molded by the people we have around us, so we should select those people with care.

Chuck Colson provides me with one more lesson from the Nixon story. He was one of seven men convicted of Watergate crimes and sentenced to prison. Before his sentencing, he had a religious experience and became a born again follower of Jesus Christ. At first, many people dismissed him as a phony who was only using his "conversion" for some sort of personal gain, perhaps a reduction in his prison sentence. Colson was sentenced to one to three years in federal prison (he served seven months), but he went on to prove to even the most skeptical that his conversion was real. He founded Prison Fellowship, an organization dedicated to working for prison reform and to bringing God's word to inmates. He wrote several books about his faith and worked tirelessly to spread the gospel not only in prisons, but also in various public forums. He quite literally devoted the last forty years of his life to Christ. I always remember his story when I think that any person is no damned good or totally irredeemable. Any sinner who is truly repentant can be redeemed.

These, then, are a few of the cautionary tales from American history that have been meaningful to me. You might have your own list of people whose stories are cautionary for you that are not on my list, and that's great! The point is to view all people in American history as real people worth getting to know and from who we should learn.

Following are a few other cautionary tales, more briefly told.

1

JOHN CALDWELL CALHOUN,
RACIST AGITATOR

As senator from South Carolina, and as vice president under John Quincy Adams and Andrew Jackson, Calhoun laid the groundwork for the American Civil War. He was the originator of two doctrines that were at the very root of the conflict that tore the nation apart.

In 1828, he protested against the high tariff duties passed by Congress and wrote the *South Carolina Exposition and Protest*. This document made the case that a state had the right to nullify a federal law or even leave the Union if it felt its interests were being harmed. In 1832, he resigned the vice-presidency in order to lead the fight for South Carolina's nullification of the tariff. This act could have started a civil war right then if Henry Clay had not proposed a compromise tariff that enabled the hotheads in South Carolina and the hothead in Washington (President Jackson) to back off; however, the concept of secession was still alive, and it would spring up again in 1861 to split the country.

In 1837, Calhoun gave a speech on the Senate floor in which he asserted that slavery was not a necessary evil, as the South had been saying. No! It was a positive good for both races. There has never been a society in the history of the world in which one sector of the people did not live off the work of another sector. Since the black race is inferior in every way to the white race, he continued, it is only natural that the white race should rule, and since every man will take care of his property, it is better that the white race should own the black people as slaves. The blacks, incapable of making their own way in the world, benefit by being provided for by their masters. They do much better, Calhoun smugly proclaimed, than the wage slaves who have to do the physical labor in the free societies. This idea that slavery was morally righteous motivated the South to be willing to make war rather than give it up.

Calhoun did not live to see the actual Civil War, but he was more than ready to start one in 1850, when he died during the debates over whether

California should be admitted as a slave state or a free state. He said on his deathbed, "The South, the poor South, what will become of her?" Thanks to his ideas, she was to become a smoldering ruin with her slave system destroyed. Actually, come to think of it, I should extol Calhoun as a role model, because that is exactly what *should* have happened to the Old South.

2

ROBERT E. LEE,
TRAITOR

This man is not as much a hero to me as he is to others. He may have been an honorable gentleman and a clever military leader, but he had taken an oath to serve his country, the United States of America, as an officer in its army, and he broke that oath. His priorities were wrong; he thought his first loyalty was to his state, not his country. He led Confederate armies for four years in a war against his country, and all for the cause of slavery. (No matter what states' rights sugar coating anyone tries to give it, the secession of the southern states was to protect slavery.) He should have examined his priorities a lot closer. I think it was right that his plantation was seized during the Civil War and turned into Arlington National Cemetery. *He* should have been seized as well and tried as a traitor.

In recent times there has been a movement to change the names of buildings and institutions that are named after racists. Princeton is considering eliminating the name of Woodrow Wilson from its buildings because even though he is the school's most famous alumnus (and former president of the college), he was a racist who, as president of the United States, restored segregation in the federal government. I'm not sure how I feel about the Wilson issue, but I definitely think Robert E. Lee's name should be eliminated from Washington and Lee University. Why should a slave owner who fought a war against his country be given the honor of having a university named for him, even if he did serve as president of the university for a few years after the Civil War? The change I advocate would leave just Washington's name in place and … but wait a minute, old George was a slave owning racist, too! Now what? How about going back to the school's original name, Augusta Academy?

3
JEFFERSON DAVIS
(SEE ROBERT E. LEE)

4
ANDREW JOHNSON,
STUBBORN, RACIST MAN

As the new president after Lincoln's assassination, Andrew Johnson allowed his racial and personal prejudices to interfere with his duty to guide Lincoln's program of a moderate reconstruction through to a successful conclusion. As a Southerner, he was in a perfect position to bring about a successful reunification of the country (that's why Lincoln picked him), but he hated black people, so he couldn't bring himself to do anything to help the newly freed slaves, and he hated southern aristocrats, so he botched the amnesty issue. In the end he was a complete flop as president and the country suffered. He's the perfect example of how not to be president. A good leader keeps his prejudices in check, or better yet, doesn't have any and is willing to compromise when necessary.

All of my cautionary tales are open to discussion and debate; that is why history is so interesting and worthwhile. The point to remember is that the people you meet in your study of history are not just faceless names you have to memorize; they are human beings with thoughts and feelings, who dealt with many of the same issues we do. If we accept that, we will have the luxury of seeing how their actions turned out, and we can avoid those things that turned out badly.

CHAPTER VIII
LEADERSHIP PRINCIPLES

Some of us aspire to be leaders, and most of us get to participate in choosing our leaders in the election process; thus, a good understanding of leadership is important. Fortunately, we don't have to venture forth as leaders or voters in a vacuum. We have the examples of leaders in American history, predominantly the presidents of the United States, to guide us. After studying the presidents and would-be presidents in our country's history, I have identified twelve qualities of good leaders. Some of our presidents have demonstrated all or almost all of these qualities, and some of them have fallen short in at least a few big ways. On the occasions when I have had to be a leader or when I have voted for leaders, I have applied these concepts, and I think this approach has helped me. No vacuum for me! When I am acting as a leader, I am equipped with examples of what to do and what not to do. When I vote, I know what to look for in a candidate and am not swayed by egomaniacs or incompetents.

What follows are my criteria for good leadership and a few examples of people in American politics who exemplified them, and a few who most decidedly did not.

1. A good leader is dignified and looks the part. Natural charisma helps.

A student once asked me, quite sincerely, if George Washington was a real person; did he actually exist or is he just a myth? He seems too good to be true. The capital of our country is named after him, as is a state and countless streets all over the country. There is a huge monument erected in his honor in Washington, D.C., and there are statues of him everywhere, including a gigantic one of the man on horseback in the Boston Public Garden. How could there have been a real human being worthy of such adulation?

First of all, Washington had a commanding presence. At a time when the average man was five feet, six inches tall, Washington rose to six feet, two inches. He was physically imposing and dominated any room. Moreover, he always dressed in immaculate formal attire, preferably a military uniform, and carried himself with a very erect and dignified posture. He usually arrived at places astride a huge, white horse or riding in a gilded carriage. When he spoke, he looked his listener in the eye; when someone was talking to him, he fixed his gaze on the speaker in a way that made that person feel as if what he was saying was the most profound thing Washington had ever heard.

Washington had what we have come to call charisma, the ability of a person to command attention, respect, and even adoration wherever he or she goes. No single attribute gives a person charisma; it is simply the aggregate effect of a number of factors, including dress, posture, height, and some indefinable personal qualities such as self-assurance and poise.

Most of our leaders have had dignity and some measure of charisma. The great ones have usually had a lot of charisma! There have been, however, some notable failures in this aspect of leadership.

In the 1970s, after the Watergate debacle and the collapse of Nixon's imperial presidency, Jimmy Carter believed the country wanted a more homespun, low-key leader who wore casual clothes and drove around in a compact car. To promote that image of himself, he allowed a picture to go public of his brother, Billy, and him sitting on an old, beat-up couch, drinking cans of beer, and watching TV. The picture did not go over well. The people wanted a president with more dignity. They wanted their leader to convey a sense of prestige and power. They wanted their leader to ride in a long, black limousine with American flags fluttering on each fender. They got that when they voted Carter out in 1980 and elected Ronald Reagan.

In a very different scenario, one that is almost counter-intuitive from the one I've just described, President John F. Kennedy achieved part of his charisma by playing touch football on the White House lawn with his brothers, thus showing off his youth and energy. A few years later, President Richard Nixon, a man who was humorless and stiff in public, wanted to get a little Kennedy-type charisma for himself. His aides told him he should show people he could be sporty and laid-back like the Kennedys had been. They suggested he should try going to the beach. So it was that one day his press secretary told photographers they could get a good shot of Nixon walking the beach if they went to a certain place along the waterfront. The shutterbugs did as they were told, and, sure enough, along came Nixon, strolling the beach ... wearing a suit and tie and wing-tipped shoes. They began snapping away, and the next day, a photo of a dressed up Richard Nixon, strolling along the beach, appeared in newspapers around the country. The photo didn't elicit praise; instead, he got ridiculed for his odd behavior. This incident proved to me that charisma comes from within; it's part of your natural personal style.

When I am evaluating past presidents or deciding who should get my vote in an election, I look for a person who looks presidential and who has a certain *gravitas*, and I don't think I'm being shallow in doing so. The job of president of the United States requires a person who is impressive wherever he or she goes, in our own country or around the world. He or she must command respect, indeed, a certain amount of awe. I want to feel proud of the person who leads our country; I want him or her to make a good impression.

2. A good leader demonstrates strong moral character.

A few years after George Washington died, a man named Parson Weems wrote a biography of the Father of Our Country. In his book, he told the story of George Washington, when he was young, admitting to his father that he had chopped down a favorite cherry tree, and saying the now famous line, "Father, I cannot tell a lie." Weems probably made up the story, but it stuck in Washington lore because it made the point that George was, to the core, a man of great honesty and integrity. That kind of character is what a leader should demonstrate. We should look for that character when we vote for leaders; we should exemplify that when *we* are leaders.

As a boy, Abraham Lincoln read Weems' biography of Washington, and it inspired young Abe to emulate Washington's honesty and to want to become president. Lincoln, too, earned a reputation for honesty. His signature story told of how he walked six miles—or was it ten?—to return a few pennies to a woman who had overpaid her bill at the store where Lincoln was the clerk. Lincoln earned the nickname Honest Abe, and that was one of the attributes that propelled him upward in politics.

Washington and Lincoln were not perfect. I'm sure they committed a few sins and told a few fibs, but their overall integrity is one of the major reasons they are ranked by historians as the top two of our presidents.

I have voted for candidates predominantly on the basis that they seemed to have better moral character than their opponents. A notable election in which I voted for the man with integrity over the man with whom I agreed more on policy was the election of 1972. That year, Richard Nixon was running for reelection and, as I explained in the last chapter, I thought he had done a pretty good job in his first term. He had wound down the war in Vietnam in what I thought was the only way possible, without accepting total defeat; he had achieved *détente* with the Soviet Union and opened diplomatic relations with China; and he had created the Environmental Protection Agency. However, the Watergate burglary had a smell to it that seemed to indicate the burglars were more connected to the White House than Nixon was admitting, and there seemed to be an aura about Nixon of almost Mafia-like thinking: politics is dirty business, so get them before they get you. The Democratic candidate, George McGovern, favored an immediate pullout from Vietnam and a drastic expansion of the welfare system. I didn't fully support either of those ideas, but I sensed that he was a totally honest man who had served his country as a pilot in World War II and as a senator from South Dakota. He was clearly a man of character. Nixon was shady; in fact, as events were to show, downright sinister. So, as I mentioned in Chapter IV, I worked for the McGovern campaign, and eight years later, I worked for another World War II pilot who also demonstrated great integrity: George H.W. Bush, a Republican. Clearly, for me, in terms of leadership, I believe that moral character and integrity are more important than political party or policy.

In 1992, when Bush ran for reelection, he was defeated by Bill Clinton. Besides my devotion to Bush, I was unhappy about that election because of the many rumors that were circulating and the explicit charges that were being made about Clinton's extramarital escapades. Then, in 1998, when he had to admit that he had engaged in sex with a young intern in the Oval Office, I was appalled and dropped him off my list of even better than average presidents. Had he done such a thing in any corporation in America, he would have been fired and never gotten a job elsewhere. How he remained in good favor with the American people I will never understand. The moral example he set for the American people, particularly the young people, was despicable.

I may be old-fashioned, but I believe that a good leader should set a sterling moral example for the people he or she represents. Most of our presidents have done that. Nixon and Clinton did not.

In the realm of public policy, we should expect our leaders to make good moral decisions. There has been no more controversial example of this than President Truman's decision to use the atomic bomb against Japan in 1945. Truman's detractors argue that the Japanese were about to surrender, so there was no need to continue killing their civilians, as we were already doing by firebombing Tokyo. Furthermore, Truman ushered in a whole new kind of warfare; from 1945 on, the world would tremble under the threat of nuclear annihilation. Truman's critics contend that his decision was the most immoral act ever committed by an American president.

Perhaps I am biased because my father was stationed in the Philippines in August 1945, and he was one of those who would go ashore in Japan if the war continued. The bomb spared him and thousands of other soldiers from participating in a Japanese D-Day. It allowed him to come home in September 1945.

I truly believe Truman had little choice; the Japanese had given no indication they were about to give up. To the contrary, they had fought to the last man to defend Okinawa that summer and they were sending Kamikaze pilots to make suicide runs against our ships. Surely they were prepared to defend their home islands to the death. Truman never said much on the topic—he was a very taciturn man—but he did say he would have had a very difficult time justifying any American casualties in an invasion of Japan when he had the means at his disposal to make such a horrible event unnecessary.

Having said this, however, I DO believe Truman is culpable for the deaths at Nagasaki. Only three days passed after the incineration of Hiroshima, and then we dropped the second bomb. Surely the Japanese could have been given a few weeks to evaluate the situation they were in before we hit them again. The bombing of Hiroshima was necessary; the bombing of Nagasaki possibly was not. As I will discuss elsewhere in this chapter on leadership, it is important for a good leader to delegate authority. In this case, Truman seems to have authorized the military to use the bomb, and the military leaders took it upon themselves to drop the second bomb. This may have been a case of too much delegation of authority.

3. A good leader has a servant's heart and is not focused only on power.

Every person who runs for president says that he or she wants to "serve the people." Unfortunately, very few have the kind of Christ-like attitude I admire. All of them are certainly focused on gaining power, so I guess what I'm looking for, and what I try to achieve myself when I have a chance for leadership, is a desire for power to do good, not power for its own sake.

Probably the only recent presidents who truly had a Christ-like outlook on power were Jimmy Carter and George H.W. Bush. I think Carter really did want power so he could accomplish good things, and he used it to secure peace between Egypt and Israel, an enormous accomplishment. The work he did after he left the presidency on global humanitarian projects such as Habitat for Humanity, prove that his heart was in the right place.

George H.W. Bush came from a family in which public service was a true calling. His mother instilled in him the attitude of a team player. He was a gifted athlete, but she never wanted to know how well he played in a game; she wanted him to tell her how the *team* did. He signed up for the military on his eighteenth birthday and served through World War II as the youngest pilot in the Navy. In every government job he held, his guiding question was, "What can we do to help the country?"

The prime example of a man who could have been a spectacular leader if he had possessed a servant's heart was Douglas MacArthur. This man showed incredible bravery as an officer in the First World War, he led U.S. forces in the Pacific during World War II with his imaginative "leap-frogging" campaign, and he pulled off a miracle in the Korean War with his bold landing at Inchon. He was a skilled organizer and a man who could give crisp, clear orders. Even his biggest detractors had to admit he had great talent. However, he craved recognition; he wanted grandeur. He worked hard at creating and maintaining his iconic image, forever posing with his battered general's hat, pipe, and sunglasses. One of his top lieutenants once said he would rather put a rattlesnake in his pocket than have a newspaper article give him credit for something MacArthur did. When President Truman removed him from command in 1951 for disobeying orders, MacArthur came back and toured the country, hoping the people would rally to him and give him the presidency. Fortunately, the people grew weary of his show and saw through his self-aggrandizement and phony claim that he wanted to serve the people, and they dropped him cold.

At the time of this writing, there is another man gaining popularity who is running for president. This man, just like MacArthur, is seeking power for its own sake. He is getting a free ride at the moment and is riding high in the polls, as he constantly reminds everyone. Just like MacArthur, he will fall to Earth as increasing numbers of people realize he doesn't want to serve, he wants to wield power.

4. A good leader projects an image of self-assurance and bravery.

No one can lead very well if he or she appears to be timid, vacillating, or afraid. Teddy Roosevelt proved his courage at San Juan Hill in the Spanish-American War, and after that, everyone knew he had the chops to stand up to banker J.P. Morgan or any other big shot, foreign or domestic, who tried to push him or our country around. Most leaders don't get the chance to prove their courage by facing enemy bullets, so they sometimes have to fake it, but they better fake it well. Dwight D. Eisenhower, who was general of our armies in World War II, admitted later, in his memoirs, that he kept fearful thoughts for his pillow at night. He had many doubts about how things would go, but in front of his troops, he showed nothing but confidence. After the famous photograph was taken of Ike giving his pep talk to the paratroopers just before D-Day, he went back to his headquarters and spent a sleepless night smoking endless cigarettes. He never let the men know he feared for them. It was important as well that his soldiers knew he cared about them as people—he truly did—and I will say more about that later.

Probably the best example of how important it is to project confidence and courage in leadership comes from Franklin Roosevelt. He always conveyed an image of sunny optimism and self-assurance, with his ready smile and up-tilted cigarette holder, but one event sorely tested those qualities. On Sunday, December 7, 1941, when FDR got the news of the Japanese attack on Pearl Harbor, he was totally devastated. The fact that our forces had been caught so completely unaware, that so many men had died and so many ships had been destroyed, and that all of this was *his* responsibility, almost completely shattered him. Those close to him said he came close to suffering a mental breakdown, and, yet, the next morning, he appeared before a joint session of Congress and delivered a stirring speech that was broadcast all over the world. Who could have guessed that the president had been utterly shattered just a few hours earlier? "No matter how long it may take us," he proclaimed, "the United States will win through to ultimate victory, so help us God!"

Roosevelt's response to Pearl Harbor has always served as a great example of how a leader should pull himself together in the face of adversity, take charge, and lead the people.

5. A good leader is a people person.

It should go without saying that a person who does not really like people, all kinds of people, really has no business leading *anything*. Every morning, Abraham Lincoln used to throw open the doors of the White House and welcomed whoever wished to visit. He always said he was refreshed by his daily bath in public opinion. All of the truly great presidents loved to get out and meet the people.

No president or leader, of course, should simply follow public opinion at all times. If John Adams had done that in 1799, we would have gone to war with France, which would have been a bad idea. If Harry Truman had done that in 1951, he would have let General MacArthur bomb China, which also would have been a bad idea.

A leader needs to be aware of how the people are thinking and work very hard to acknowledge their point of view, sympathize with what they are thinking, and ease them toward his or her way of thinking. Lincoln was a master at this. Had he lived to complete his second term in 1865, he very likely would have been able to bring the Union back together and provide basic rights and economic stability for the freed slaves far better than the ham-fisted men who carried out reconstruction after Lincoln was gone.

One of the important strengths of our great presidents has been their ability to reach out to and work with leaders in Congress, even if they are members of the opposing political party. Ronald Reagan and other leaders like him were famously able to put aside the heated debates when socializing time arrived and form bonds of friendship with their worthy opponents. Presidents who failed were very often not able to do this. They saw their opponents as enemies and always impugned their motives. Richard Nixon is the classic example of a leader who suffered from this shortcoming.

There is paralysis in today's government because there is so much partisan warfare. Our current leaders should take a lesson from the great leaders of the past and develop the ability to debate, socialize, and compromise. If leaders can't do that, then government becomes ossified, nothing gets done, and the people suffer.

6. A good leader sets forth clear goals and inspires the people to share them.

Every great or near-great president has set forth clear goals at the start of his term, and there was never any doubt about what they hoped to achieve. Following are a few examples:

Washington: Establish the protocols and procedures of the new government; get the economy off on sound footing; establish the nation as a neutral in world affairs

Jackson: Make the country more democratic; destroy the power and privileges of the National Bank and the very wealthy; move the Native Americans to lands west of the Mississippi (a clear goal, not a good one!)

Polk: Annex Texas; acquire California; acquire Oregon

Lincoln: Destroy secession and restore the Union; build the infrastructure for a burgeoning industrial economy; contain (later abolish) slavery

T. Roosevelt: Protect the public from unfair business practices; give labor a square deal; protect our natural resources; build a canal across Panama; make the United States a respected and powerful nation

Wilson: Bring big business under control; maintain our neutrality, then win the war against Germany; secure a just and lasting peace; create a world peace organization

F. Roosevelt: Put people to work; reform the economy so depression does not happen again; defeat Germany and Japan; create a world peace organization

Truman: Contain communist expansion

Eisenhower: End the Korean War; contain communist aggression; balance the budget; create an interstate highway system

Johnson: Protect South Vietnam from communism; expand civil rights for all Americans; fight the war against poverty

Reagan: Reduce the size of the federal government and lower taxes; build a strong military to stand up to the Soviet Union

Barack Obama: End the wars in Iraq and Afghanistan; guarantee health insurance for all Americans

Besides having these goals, these presidents had to inspire the people into getting on board with them. They had to make the people believe that the goals were worthy. Some of these men were better at it than others. The truly great ones will be covered in the next chapter on the power of words. Those leaders not only *sold* the people their vision, they *convinced* the people to make enormous sacrifices to achieve their vision. Clearly, an important quality any good leader must have is the ability to deliver an effective speech. It is almost impossible to imagine a great leader who is not a dynamic and convincing speaker.

Some presidents take office and don't deliver inspiring or moving speeches; instead, their message seems to be, whatever comes up, I'll deal with it. This is not what most people want to hear from their leader.

7. A good leader chooses competent, honest people to work for him, gives them freedom to do their jobs, but guards against incompetence and corruption.

The presidents whose administrations are often denigrated as being the worst in American history are the ones who really fell down in this regard. Ulysses S. Grant and Warren G. Harding appointed their old friends to high government positions and then got blindsided by horrific scandals. In 1973, many people thought Richard Nixon was suffering the same fate—that his underlings had engaged in illegal wiretappings and obstruction of justice—only to find out that *he* was involved.

When a person is running for office, and even when he or she first takes office, it is a little difficult to tell if he or she is a good judge of character and will run a clean, honest, and efficient administration; however, this is one of the most important qualities a good leader should possess. We should try to assess this talent in leaders who are asking for our vote.

If we are fortunate enough to get a leadership role, the quality of the people we bring in to help us is critical. If you are relying on incompetent or dishonest people to get things done, then your leadership is almost certain to fail. There are presidents in American history who have proved that at the highest level.

8. A good leader always takes time to get it right.

Dwight D. Eisenhower lived mostly by this principle: Never make a mistake in a hurry. He always wanted his staff to present his options to him in clear, one-page summaries. He would weigh the costs and benefits of each choice, but would not make a final decision until the last possible moment, after he had all the facts. When he felt confident that he knew everything possible, he would make a firm decision and stick with it.

Two American presidents offered the best examples of this important principle.

When Lincoln took office on March 4, 1861, seven southern states had left the Union and formed the Confederate States of America. Eight other slave states were wavering, having not decided whether to secede or remain loyal. The Confederate states had seized all federal installations in their territories except Fort Sumter in Charleston, South Carolina, and Fort Pickens in Florida. Fort Sumter soon became the focus of everyone's attention. It was a symbol of Union power right in the harbor of the southern state that had been the first to secede after Lincoln's election. If there were to be a civil war, it would probably start there. Lincoln had to decide what to do because the fort would soon run out of food and have to surrender to the Confederates.

Even though many people around him, including members of his cabinet, were screaming for action, Lincoln remained calm and waited. He found out the exact date when the fort would run out of provisions and set that date, April 12, as the date when he would act. That was six weeks away, and he wanted to use every one of those days to let things evolve before deciding what he would do. As the days went by, Lincoln made it clear that he would maintain federal facilities, just as he had said he would in his inaugural address. If there were to be a war, the

South would start it. He also made it clear that if war came, it would be a war to end secession and restore the Union, not a war to end slavery. He was determined that it would be very clear, especially to the states that had not yet seceded, that he was a moderate president who was only doing his job of enforcing the laws.

Finally, as time ran out, Lincoln sent a supply ship to Sumter. He made it very clear the ship did not bring reinforcements or weapons; it only brought "food for hungry men." On the morning of April 12, the guns along the shore of Charleston harbor opened fire on Fort Sumter. After a two-day bombardment, the fort surrendered. In response, Lincoln issued a call for volunteers to put down the southern rebellion. Now the remaining slave states had to decide. Four of them, Virginia, Tennessee, North Carolina, and Arkansas, joined the Confederacy. The other four slave states (Delaware, Maryland, Kentucky, and Missouri) did *not* secede. They saw that the Confederacy fired the first shots—the Confederacy had started the war—and since Lincoln had so far shown himself to be a moderate, they decided to wait and see what he actually did about slavery.

By moving cautiously, keeping his options open, and assuring everyone he was not a hotheaded abolitionist, Lincoln kept those four crucial border states loyal to the Union. This is one of the major reasons the North won the Civil War

In the Cuban Missile Crisis of October 1962, John F. Kennedy also remained calm and did not rush to a hasty decision. When he discovered the Soviets were installing intermediate-range nuclear missiles in Cuba, Kennedy could have followed the advice of his generals and immediately launched air strikes against the missile sites and/or invaded Cuba. Instead, he asked the intelligence people how long he had until the missiles became operational, found out he had approximately two weeks, and decided to use that time to consider the options, allow the Russians time to think, and hopefully avoid a nuclear war.

Kennedy brought his top military and intelligence people together to form an executive committee (EXCOMM), with his brother Bobby Kennedy, the attorney general, in charge. He told them to evaluate the options. When I read the minutes of these meetings, I was amazed at how little the committee panicked as they rationally discussed the possible outcome of each course of action. The president ultimately decided on a blockade of Cuba. This would be a first step. It would prevent further missiles from reaching Cuba, and it would throw down the gauntlet to the Soviets without going to war, at least not right away. It would give the Russians time to reconsider what they were doing. The result, as I described in Chapter IV, was a peaceful resolution to the Cuban Missile crisis.

Eisenhower's maxim and these two examples have served me well as guides for what to do when I'm in a leadership role and a crisis occurs. The paradigm is this: determine the point at which you will have to decide what to do; evaluate your options carefully using all the time available; and at the last moment, commit to a decision and then stick with it unless some new development occurs.

9. A good leader always asks, "What next?"

The 1975 World Series was memorable, and every older Red Sox fan knows that Carlton Fisk hit a dramatic home run in the twelfth inning to win the game. What is usually forgotten is the home run Bernie Carbo hit in the eighth inning that *tied* the game and made Fisk's heroics an hour later possible. Carbo launched one into the centerfield bleachers after almost striking out, and the crowd went wild. As the camera focused on the Red Sox dugout, we saw the fans delirious with joy and the players swamping Carbo and clapping him on the back. I noticed, though, that over on the right side of the screen, Daryl Johnson, the Sox manager, was standing there pensively, not showing any emotion whatsoever. At first I thought, "What's wrong with *him*? Why isn't he excited?" Then it occurred to me; the home run had only tied the game—we still had to win. Questions needed to be answered: Who would pitch the ninth inning? Who was available to pinch hit? Johnson didn't have the luxury of celebrating; he had to decide what to do next.

It was Eisenhower who again articulated this leadership principle. "What next?" was always his first question after someone suggested a course of action. When in 1954 his advisors suggested that we send troops to South Vietnam to support the government, he asked his usual question, but he didn't like the answer he got: no one knew what would happen next, so he decided to keep combat troops out of the jungles of Southeast Asia.

Lincoln, of course, provides an excellent example of this leadership principle. During the Civil War, the entire country was steeped in the momentous things that were happening: the Union being preserved and the slaves being freed. Lincoln, however, was also thinking ahead. What would happen after the war was won? How would the southern states be reunited with the Union? How would the leaders of the rebellion— Jefferson Davis, Robert E. Lee, and many others—be treated? Would they be tried for treason and executed? Most crucially, how would the former slaves, the freedmen, be aided in adjusting to their new situation? Lincoln was planning for these things long before Lee surrendered at Appomattox. The last great tragedy of the Civil War was that Booth's bullet prevented Lincoln from leading the all-important reconstruction effort.

The most tragic example of a president *failing* to ask the question "What next?" happened in 2003. In that year, George W. Bush decided to go to war to drive Saddam Hussein from power in Iraq. There were several reasons why Bush decided for war: Hussein might be concealing weapons of mass destruction that he might use himself or put into the hands of terrorists; Hussein was developing nuclear weapons with which he could annihilate Israel; and Hussein was a brutal dictator who should have been toppled in 1991. George W. Bush would finish the job his father had failed to do. I do think Bush truly believed Hussein had weapons of mass destruction, and, as he says in his book *Decision Points*, he was responsible for the safety of the nation and did not have the luxury of having it be of no consequence if he were right and did nothing. However, Bush did not get a complete picture from his advisors, both military and intelligence, of what would *follow* Hussein's removal from power. The nasty tyrant had run a secular government for decades and had kept the feuding Shia and Sunni factions of Islam under his militant thumb. What would happen once he was gone? Who would write a new constitution, and how would the sectarian and tribal feuds be mitigated?

The tragic result was we kicked a hornet's nest in Iraq and then we got stung many times. A new war began pitting the various factions against each other and against the occupying Americans. It dragged on for eight miserable years and is, in reality, still going on in the war against ISIS. George W. Bush, and all of us with him, learned the hard way what happens when a leader does not ask "What next?"

10. Once he makes a decision, a good leader carries it out with all the powers at his command.

George Washington set the tone for this important principle when he personally enforced the new excise tax on whiskey in 1794. Farmers in Western Pennsylvania rebelled against the tax, and Washington personally mounted his horse and led a force of thirteen thousand men to squelch the Whiskey Rebellion. The rebels gave up before he even got there.

In 1832, when South Carolina nullified the tariff, President Jackson determined that nullification could not be permitted. He believed the concept would make the Union "a rope of sand." He issued a proclamation to the people of South Carolina, telling them, and the people of the entire nation, that he would enforce the tariff and the South Carolinians would have to obey it. More to the point, he proceeded to put together an armed force, asserting that he would lead it into South Carolina and hang John C. Calhoun and every other nullifier on which he could get his hands. Given Jackson's militant reputation, Calhoun and the other South Carolinians believed he would make good on his threats, which made them a little more amenable to compromise.

In 1862, after Lincoln had determined the time had come to free the slaves, he acted under his powers as commander in chief and enforced a war measure in time of actual armed rebellion against the United States. He gave the South one hundred days to reconsider their secession and return to the Union before he acted. No one took him up on his offer and so, on New Year's Day, 1863, he issued his Emancipation Proclamation, freeing all the slaves in the Confederate States of America.

In 1940, when Franklin Roosevelt feared that England was about to be invaded and defeated by Hitler's Germany, he made a deal with Prime Minister Churchill to send Britain fifty destroyers in return for eight naval bases in the Atlantic. He presented the deal as a *fait accompli* to the Congress and to the American people, a clever "executive agreement" that would allow us to form a line of defense hundreds of miles out in the Atlantic while we gave up fifty old boats for which we had no use. The people and the Congress were in no mood to get involved in the war, but FDR took a bold step to save Britain, using his power to make executive agreements.

In 1981, President Reagan determined that the air traffic controllers (ATC) were breaking the law by going on strike. He ordered them to return back to work and declared he would fire all who did not. When his deadline came, he used his executive authority to fire every striking ATC in the country. This drastic action shocked the country, and the world. It served as notice that this president was a man who did not make idle threats. This reputation served Reagan well when he entered negotiations with foreign leaders in later years.

President Obama could have profited from Reagan's example when the situation in Syria began to spiral out of control. In 2013, Obama said he was drawing a "red line" in Syria, a line against the use of chemical weapons. If Syrian President Assad used chemical weapons, the United States would take military action against him. Not long after that, Assad *did* use chemical weapons against his own people; he called Obama's bluff. Obama did nothing. Consequently, the American word was devalued in the Middle East and Obama was less able to influence events in the region. My criticism is not that Obama failed to send troops into Syria after Assad used chemical weapons; that probably would have been a mistake that would have bogged us down in another fruitless war. His mistake was drawing a red line and making a threat *in the first place*. A leader should never proclaim he is going to do something unless he is totally sure he is going to follow through.

11. A leader should know when to stand tough and when to compromise.

In 1860, after Abraham Lincoln won the presidency and the southern slave states began to secede, Senator John J. Crittenden of Kentucky tried to step up with a compromise, just as his old mentor, the late Henry Clay, had so often done. Crittenden's proposal would have guaranteed the South the right to extend slavery to the Pacific Ocean, south of the 36°30' line. The southern states said they would accept his proposal if President-elect Lincoln would also accept it. From his home in Springfield, Illinois, where he was waiting to take office, Lincoln made it clear he would have no part in the compromise. As a Republican, he had been elected on a platform of non-extension of slavery, and he wasn't about to double-cross the people who voted for him before he even took office. "Stand firm (against the compromise) as like a chain of steel," he wrote to his friend Lyman Trumbull in the Senate. Lincoln was going to stand by his platform; besides, he was still convinced that the pro-Union people in the southern states would ultimately prevail. I wonder if Lincoln would have accepted the Crittenden deal if he had known that rejecting the compromise was going to result in a four-year-long war that would kill more than 600,000 people. Of course, he had no way of knowing, and I think he was totally right to reject compromise and stand by the platform on which he had just been elected.

A less understandable refusal to compromise came in 1919, after President Woodrow Wilson returned from Paris with the Treaty of Versailles. The treaty included his beloved League of Nations, and he was certain that this organization would be the key to avoiding future wars, especially if the United States were a part of it. "I am convinced," he said, "that in twenty years, there will be another world war unless the nations of the world adopt this means by which to prevent it." The problem was that the Republicans controlled the Senate and they were not ready to ratify Democrat Wilson's treaty without important input of their own. Senator Henry Cabot Lodge, chairman of the Foreign Relations Committee, had fourteen reservations, the most important of which was that the United States would not enter into any military actions by the League without the approval of Congress. Wilson refused to compromise, and he wouldn't allow such language into the treaty. Even when it became clear that the treaty would not pass the Senate without the Lodge amendments, he would not change his mind. The Senate defeated the Treaty of Versailles, the United States did not join the League of Nations, and just as Wilson had predicted, another world war began exactly twenty years later. Admittedly, it is hard to know when to stop fighting for what you want and agree to a compromise, but in this instance, it was very clear that without some backing down on his part, Wilson would get nothing. Perhaps it was the stroke he suffered that made him so stubborn, but, in my opinion, Wilson's refusal to compromise in 1919 knocks him from the ranks of the great presidents.

12. A good leader thinks creatively and is not stuck in old ways.

It is not always good for a leader to be hard, unbending, and tough. The people don't want a wishy-washy leader who cannot make up his mind, but they also don't deserve a leader who is hard and ossified to the point of being brittle. Sometimes a leader needs to be a little less like an oak tree that stands straight but blows over if its roots are rotten and more like a willow tree that is strong yet flexible in the wind.

Our best example for this comes in the year 1933. The country was deeply mired in the worst economic depression of all time, and President Hoover was unbending in his economic philosophy. In hard times, he believed the government must keep its budget balanced and that people need to take care of their own needs. He was willing to create the Reconstruction Finance Corporation to loan government money to private enterprises, but he could not create programs for direct federal relief to the unemployed people in the country. That sort of thing would create dependency in the people and unbalance the federal budget. By March of 1933, the economy of the nation was on the brink of complete collapse.

Franklin Roosevelt had a completely different approach. He was not a laissez-faire capitalist, but he was also not, as some people claimed, a socialist. The best word to describe him would be pragmatist. He would try anything, see if it worked, and if not, would scrap it and try something else. People who tried to put labels on him called him everything from a fascist to a communist, but they were all wrong. He was simply flexible enough to try anything, regardless of what it was called, and pray that it lifted the country out of the Depression. Some of his programs had never been tried before, at least on a national level, and they worked beautifully. My father-in-law was unemployed in Cleveland in 1933 when he went to work for FDR's Civilian Conservation Corps (CCC). He spent three great years planting trees and digging drainage ditches in Oregon. Afterward, he looked back on his CCC days as the best in his life. He was doing useful work, and he was sending money back to his family in Cleveland.

Critics of FDR will say that he never really ended the Depression with his New Deal, that he spent billions, and unemployment persisted. There is a modicum of truth to that, but the bigger story was that he did give millions of people jobs, and he gave everyone hope and the feeling that the government was working for them and that things would get better. One of the most important things a leader does is uplift the people, give them a sense of movement and purpose, and create a positive environment. An imaginative person who constantly tries new things will often inspire people, as FDR did in the 1930s.

In my analysis of leadership in American history, I have been rather impressed at the quality of the leaders we have had. Even the uninspired leaders have at least left the country no worse than they found it. Much of the credit for this should go to the Constitution and the checks and balances system that so beautifully keeps our leaders in line. We also should realize that our electoral process, while certainly not perfect, does put would-be presidents through quite a few rigorous tests, and the voters have been pretty intelligent about winnowing the field down to the ones who would do the best job.

It amazes me that the right people have been in power during the most severe crises in our country's history. Maybe it's a case of mediocre men rising to the occasion, but I think it has more to do with the American people knowing what they were doing when they cast their votes. As we move forward, we must pay close attention to our actions even more. We need to evaluate leadership in the light of history, as I have tried to do here, so that we can vote wisely. The choices we make in the future may be even more crucial than the ones we have made in the past.

CHAPTER IX

THE POWER OF WORDS

Mark Twain once wrote, "The difference between the right word and the almost right word is really a large matter; it's the difference between the lightning and the lightning bug." Many people who have made a difference in history seem to have known the truth of Twain's aphorism instinctively, and they worked hard at it because they knew it was important. I have been captivated by many memorable expressions or statements made in pithy ways. A history professor I had in college called such lines "historical nifties," because they were either so clever or so well said that they made it into the history books and are well known. Today, political analysts would call such words or phrases sound bites. Whatever you call them, I have marveled that some singular words or simple sentences were so memorable and stirring that they changed public opinion overnight.

I learned a long time ago that historical nifties did not happen by accident. They were the product of considerable thought and sometimes countless revisions. Franklin D. Roosevelt's speech the day after the Japanese attack on Pearl Harbor is an instructive example of the importance of just the right words. As FDR rode to Capitol Hill to deliver his war message to Congress, he looked over his speech and decided that the line "… a date which will live in history" lacked impact. After some thought, he drew a line through *history* and above it scribbled *infamy*. Within an hour, he was speaking to the joint session of Congress and the entire nation on radio: "Yesterday, December 7, 1941, a date which will live in infamy …" The date became embedded in everyone's memory as the "day of infamy." The entire country was aroused for the formidable war effort that lay ahead. Almost certainly the people would have been just as aroused if FDR had stuck with *history*, but *infamy* gave the speech a little more of a wallop and made it a lot more memorable. Throughout the war that followed, FDR always motivated the people with the idea that they were making history together. Branding December 7, 1941, a "date which will live in infamy" implanted it in memory and truly did make it "live in history."

Let's talk about some moments in American history when a single word or phrase had the power to reverse the direction of the historical winds.

GENERAL BRADLEY'S RHETORICAL DEVICE DEFLATED THE GREAT MACARTHUR.

One of the best examples of how a clever use of words changed the thinking of the nation was General Omar Bradley's testimony before Congress during the Korean War. With one sentence, he punctured General Douglas MacArthur's high-flying balloon and brought it down to Earth.

On April 11, 1951, President Truman relieved the very popular General Douglas MacArthur from his command in Korea for insubordination: failure to refrain from criticizing in public the administration's policy of keeping the Korean War limited to the Korean Peninsula. MacArthur began touring the country, receiving wild acclaim wherever he went. On April 19, 1951, he got off his own historical nifty when he spoke to a joint session of Congress. He told them there was "no substitute for victory" in Korea, and opined that a broader war in Asia, possibly involving China and the use of atomic bombs, was the best strategy for defeating world-wide communism. Then, in melodramatic tones, he closed with the memorable line from an old army ballad: "Old soldiers never die, they just fade away." Over sixty percent of the American people thought President Truman was wrong to fire the general and that MacArthur was a true American hero who would bring down communism in Asia if he were only given the chance. There was considerable talk of MacArthur running for president against Truman in 1952.

On May 15, Bradley, as chairman of the Joint Chiefs of Staff, gave the administration's rebuttal to MacArthur. Speaking in calm, measured tones, Bradley explained that widening the Korean War into a war with China, perhaps even on the Chinese mainland, as MacArthur was advocating, would be a huge mistake. It would bog us down in a fight against eight hundred million people in China, leaving the Soviet Union free to advance in Europe. It would be, Bradley asserted, "the wrong war, at the wrong place, at the wrong time, and with the wrong enemy." That sentence, so succinct, so easy to remember with its cadence and its repetition of the word "wrong," was quoted the next day in every newspaper and every television and radio account of Bradley's testimony. It made people think, do we really want to fight China now? Is a land war in Asia desirable? If we were battling China, would the Russians take advantage of our huge distraction?

In the summer that followed Bradley's address, General MacArthur's crowds grew increasingly smaller and less enthusiastic. At the Republican Convention the following year, MacArthur gave a speech that the delegates barely listened to, and the party went on to nominate Bradley's old friend Dwight D. Eisenhower for president. It is likely that the people would have tired of MacArthur even without Bradley's speech. MacArthur was so pompous and so sappy with his constant references to God, motherhood, and country, that the people were almost sure to grow weary of listening to him, but there is no doubt that Bradley's clever sentence hastened the great general's decline and helped eliminate any chance he had to become president.

Bradley's use of repetition and cadence was not the first, and certainly not the last, time this rhetorical devise moved the nation. Lincoln famously ended his speech at Gettysburg with "… that government of the people, by the people, and for the people shall not perish from the earth." Since I will take up the Gettysburg Address again in another context, I will not dwell on these words now except to say that they were probably the single most important reason the Gettysburg Address was remembered and quoted.

THE REVEREND MARTIN LUTHER KING, JR. INSPIRED THE NATION WITH HIS DREAM.

Certainly the most memorable use of repetition and cadence was Dr. Martin Luther King's "I Have a Dream" speech at the August 1963 March on Washington. "I have a dream," he said, "that one day this nation will rise up and live out the true meaning of its creed: 'We hold these truths to be self-evident, that all men are created equal.' I have a dream today." Even fifty years later, almost everyone knows that line because even when it was being delivered to the two hundred thousand people in front of the Lincoln Memorial and the millions who were watching on television, it was powerful and inspiring. It grew even more powerful as he went on to give several manifestations of his dream, such as, "I have a dream that my four little children will one day live in a nation where they will not be judged by the color of their skin but by the content of their character. I have a dream today."

At the time Dr. King delivered his speech, I was a nineteen-year-old college student living in a white, upper middle class suburb of Detroit. I had not had much connection with the efforts of African-Americans to achieve equality. My high school history classes had covered slavery in a superficial way, but as a sophomore at the University of Michigan, I was just then becoming aware of the awful brutality of American slavery and of the century of segregation, discrimination, and violence that followed emancipation. Dr. King's speech forced me to confront the horrific crimes the white race had committed against the black race in our country. It inspired me to hope that if we all woke up and worked together, King's dream of equality would become a reality.

My efforts at working to end racial discrimination were sincere, but as I review them now, they were quite inadequate. At Southfield High

School, where I taught in 1966, I led a club called the Community Relations Seminar. Southfield High School was all white (fifty percent Jewish), so if we were going to have an impact in the black community, we thought we were going to have to travel to inner city Detroit, five miles away. Every Saturday morning, we drove downtown to an all-black elementary school. Several of our members tutored first and second graders in reading and math, and a group of twenty others painted the walls of every classroom in the building. We formed friendships with many of the young children, as well as the school principal, and we really felt like we were making a smidgen of progress toward improving race relations in our own little corner of the world.

One day, however, the principal pulled me up short when he said, "It's great that you folks come down here on Saturdays and do the work you are doing, but if you really want to make a difference, stay in Southfield and work on changing attitudes there." He gave me a pile of bumper stickers, white ones with black letters that said "I Have a Dream!" I was at once stung and inspired. We all put the stickers on our cars. We continued our tutoring program for the rest of the year and finished painting the classrooms, but our new focus was on bringing the message to Southfield. We put on a black history exhibit at the school and invited Frank Ditto, a black activist in Detroit, to come speak to the Southfield students.

Ditto's visit was an eye opener. He was a militant man in combat boots and a black beret, but he gave the class of thirty white students a sly grin and said, "Look at you all. You're looking like you're afraid of me. I'm the only black man within five miles of here and YOU'RE afraid of ME? Do you think I'm going to attack you? I know you think black people are stupid, but we're not THAT stupid! I'm outnumbered five thousand to one as I stand here. And let's get this straight; who's been violent toward whom in this country? It's the white man who has been beatin' on the black man since slave times. I'M the one who should be afraid … and I AM!" Mr. Ditto made quite an impression on all of us that day.

Whenever I visited my parents and parked my car in front of their house, they had a fit. My father asked me to remove the sticker from the rear bumper. "What will the neighbors think?" I said I hoped they *would* think, and I refused to remove it. Every time I drove into their neighborhood, I felt like I was making a statement. Of course, no one probably even noticed what I had on my car.

As I've said, though, this was all pretty insignificant. Dr. King's speech, as well as the marches, protests, and the like, inspired *others* to do a lot more than I did. In the spring of 1964, signs posted on the University of Michigan campus called for students to join a crusade called "Freedom Summer." Thousands of college students from around the country would travel to Mississippi and spend the summer registering black people to vote. Dozens of students from Michigan inspired by the *dream* heeded the call and set out for steamy Mississippi. I, however, was not going to give up my summer of being the athletic director at a YMCA camp on Lake Ontario, so I did not go to Mississippi. In that fateful summer, the Ku Klux Klan murdered three of the volunteers. They gave their lives for the dream, and all the others risked a similar fate as they went door-to-door down dusty back-country roads and tried to convince the great-grandchildren of slaves to sign up to vote. Meanwhile, white people sneered at the "nigger loving Yankees" and threatened to kill them. I have always felt a little guilty that I was playing baseball with the campers by the lake while many of my peers were down South on the front lines fighting for the dream.

Of course, as I've said before, in all these examples of the powerful effect of words, events might have followed the same or a similar course even if the speakers had used other less effective words; however, I truly believe that a powerful word or expression that plants an idea simultaneously in millions of minds does produce a sea change that moves events in a new direction. The "I Have a Dream" speech moved me and it moved an entire generation.

More recently, the statement "black lives matter" became a motivating force after numerous incidents of police officers shooting young black men. It doesn't have the hopeful promise of "I have a dream," but it is succinct, it gets to the core of the problem, and it is already making an impact. I expect this will be the slogan of a new civil rights movement to fight for equal justice under the law. There is a danger, however, that some of the more extreme practitioners of Black Lives Matter will turn their anger toward hatred of police officers. Those who are walking the streets and shouting, "What do we want?" "Dead cops!" "When do we want it?" "Now!" are jeopardizing the movement to make people aware of the way police sometimes single out black citizens for special persecution. Dr. King's peaceful and effective approach that produced the Civil Rights Act of 1964 and the Voting Rights Act of 1965 was jeopardized by more radical elements, and now, fifty years later, we may be seeing the same dynamic happening again.

BOTH SIDES REFRAMED THE DEBATE TO THEIR ADVANTAGE.

In recent history, the choice of words made a crucial difference during the abortion debates that heated up after the Supreme Court's *Roe v. Wade* ruling in 1973. The Americans who supported the Court's ruling that no state could prohibit a woman from having an abortion during the first six months of her pregnancy, called themselves pro-abortion; the people who opposed the Court's ruling called themselves anti-abortion. During the 1980s, the pro-abortion advocates began to realize that their opponents were vilifying them as baby killers and that their name seemed to imply that they thought abortions were a good thing, so, they decided to turn the focus onto the woman and her right to decide whether to have a baby. They began to call themselves pro-choice, and that made a big difference in how they were perceived by the public.

Not to be outdone, the anti-abortion advocates decided to emphasize their view that a human life was being destroyed in an abortion, so they began to call themselves pro-life. Each side had adopted the most positive name possible, and the debate was on. I am convinced that if the supporters of a woman's right to choose had continued to call themselves pro-abortion, they would have lost even more ground than they did when ultrasound made possible the images of the human features in a three month old fetus. The pro-life side, meanwhile, was in a position to benefit from the new technology because they had taken the focus away from anti-abortion and put it on the life of the unborn baby.

In a similar way, the two sides in the debate over gay marriage have used different names to further their causes. Instead of calling themselves anti-gay marriage, the opponents of gay marriage tried to put themselves in a positive light by saying they supported traditional marriage. This was effective until it was trumped by the people who favored the rights of gay people to marry. They no longer said they supported gay marriage; instead, they said they were for marriage equality. This put them squarely on the side of the Fourteenth Amendment to the U.S. Constitution that guarantees "equal protection of the law" in every state. I am convinced that it was this change in terminology that propelled gay marriage to the victories it has achieved in the states and in the U.S. Supreme Court.

American history is full of many other slightly less weighty examples of how a clever word or phrase has an impact. Besides proving Mark Twain's maxim and providing me with some amusement, these clever words have proved to be very useful when I have been able to use them in conversation or as examples of something I am trying to say.

Following are a few of the choice *nifties* that have intrigued me and that I have sometimes used:

HARRY TRUMAN'S "GIVE 'EM HELL."

In his bid for reelection in 1948, President Harry Truman trailed his Republican opponent, Governor Thomas Dewey of New York, by as many as sixteen points in the polls. Always a fighter, Truman went on a cross-country whistle-stop campaign in which he spoke from the rear of his special train to crowds in towns and villages all across the country. At each stop, he lambasted all Republicans back to, but not including, Abraham Lincoln, and referred to the Republican-controlled Congress as the "do-nothing" congress, because it would not pass any of his bills for social reform. The reporters nicknamed him Give 'em Hell Harry because of his aggressive style. They all still thought he was going to lose by a big margin and were shocked beyond belief when Harry pulled out a solid victory in November. Years later, Truman was asked about his *give 'em hell* reputation and he replied, "I didn't give them hell. I just told the truth and they *thought* it was hell."

I've always thought Truman's response to that question was pretty clever, and I have used it myself. Recently, a parent of one of my students accused me of being sarcastic to her daughter. I replied that I wasn't sarcastic, I had only told the truth and she *thought* it was sarcastic. That quickly ended the conversation, and I never told her that I had summoned Harry Truman to help me out.

THEODORE ROOSEVELT CALLED THE PRESIDENT SOFT.

Probably the funniest personal attack in American history was a jab Theodore Roosevelt made against President McKinley in 1898. Roosevelt was assistant secretary of the Navy, and he was exasperated that McKinley was not moving toward war with Spain, even though the Spanish had brutalized the Cuban people for decades and had, it was assumed, blown up the battleship USS Maine in Havana Harbor. "The president has no more backbone than a chocolate éclair!" Roosevelt exclaimed to a friend. The image of the president as a squishy éclair was certainly vivid, and TR, as usual, had made his point in a very colorful way. In reality, it was wise for McKinley to proceed cautiously because it was not known for sure if it was the Spanish who attacked the Maine, and he had fought in the Civil War, had seen the bodies piled up, and was not eager to see that again. Two months later, McKinley gave in to public pressure and asked Congress for war. It could be argued that it was then that he showed his backbone *was* an éclair!

Regardless of its fairness, the chocolate éclair metaphor has always amused me and I have used it several times. Once, at a teachers' union meeting in a school where I was teaching, I commented that we couldn't rely on a certain administrator to support us because he "has no more backbone than a chocolate éclair." Everyone laughed because the description fit the person perfectly, and no one knew I was quoting Theodore Roosevelt. (I can't remember if I told them; I don't think I did.)

IKE COINED A PHRASE ON MY BIRTHDAY.

I celebrated my seventeenth birthday on January 17, 1961. During cake and ice cream, we all sat down in front of the TV because the president was going to speak to the nation. Dwight D. Eisenhower was about to leave office and he was delivering his farewell to the American people. He said one thing that night that made a big impression on all of us and it has become part of the American political lexicon. This five-star general and commander-in-chief of the armed forces warned us that there was a symbiotic relationship between the large manufacturers—steel, automobiles, airplanes, etc.—and the U.S. military that purchased materials from them. There might be times, Ike warned, when their interests in profit and increased power might not be in the best interests of the American people as a whole. In a way, he was echoing the warnings of the people in the 1930s who asserted that the United States went to war in World War I because the munitions makers (the merchants of death) stood to make big profits in a war. Ike called this relationship between the major industries and the military the "military-industrial complex."

Almost immediately after Ike's warning, the concept of the military-industrial complex was used to explain and disparage U.S. involvement in Vietnam. The fact that the term was invented by a man who was a military man and the most pro-business president in decades was soon forgotten. I never forgot who said it because I heard it while eating birthday cake. The fact that Ike said it gave it more credibility for me, and it contributed to my growing opposition to the war in Vietnam. Ever since the sixties, I have been alert to the possibility that our leaders may want to get involved in wars mostly because their friends in big business might profit. It was partly for that reason that I opposed the U.S. invasion of Iraq in 2003. If more people around the country had been aware of Ike's warning, they could have pressured Congress in

2003 to vote down the war, and the whole history of the last two decades might be different.

JFK CALLED ME TO SERVE.

Just three days after he warned the country about the military-industrial complex, Dwight D. Eisenhower, the oldest man up to that time who had ever occupied the White House, turned over the presidency to John F. Kennedy, the youngest man ever elected president. As Ike sat nearby and watched, Kennedy delivered a great inaugural address. His voice rang out through the crisp January air as he said, "Ask not what your country can do for you; ask what you can do for your country." As a teenager in high school, I found his command thrilling. Booker T. Washington had inspired me to become a teacher, and now JFK was making me feel that by teaching, I would be serving my country.

It was a devastating blow to me three years later when the inspiring President Kennedy was shot dead in Dallas. Many years have passed and JFK's reputation for me has diminished, as I've learned that some of the rumors about his mafia connections and infidelity to his wife were true, but I am still inspired by his words from that cold January morning in 1961. I have been much happier being a server than I would have been doing any other job.

SPEECHES, DOCUMENTS, AND BOOKS THAT CHANGED THE COUNTRY

Beyond catchy words and clever phrases, several writings and speeches have had a profound impact on public opinion and have changed the course of world events. The old adage "the pen is mightier than the sword" has been borne out many times in American history. The writings and speeches of Thomas Paine, Thomas Jefferson, the authors of the United States Constitution and its amendments, Harriet Beecher Stowe, Abraham Lincoln, William Jennings Bryan, and Franklin Roosevelt have all had a profound effect on our lives. Learning and teaching about these people has given me a profound appreciation for the power of words.

THOMAS PAINE RADICALIZED THE PEOPLE OF AMERICA.

By early 1776, the English subjects of the King of England who inhabited the North American colonies were in turmoil over the brutality of British rule. The injustice of taxation without representation, the occupation of Boston by British troops, and the battles at Lexington, Concord, and Bunker Hill had all outraged Americans. They were ready to go to any lengths to protect their rights as Englishmen, but they were not ready to declare their *independence* from the British crown. Even in early 1776, that still seemed too radical to contemplate.

In January, Thomas Paine, an unemployed corset maker who had just arrived in America from Britain, changed that reluctance within a few months. Paine published a small pamphlet called *Common Sense*. In plain and simple language, he explained the logical reasons why the English colonies in North America should declare their independence from the British crown.

He argued that it was absurd that a small island (Great Britain) should be ruling a gigantic continent three thousand miles away. The laws of physics tell us that a large sphere always dominates a smaller one; it is always the smaller one that rotates around the larger one, as the earth does around the sun or the moon does around the earth. British rule of the vast North American continent violates the laws of nature. Furthermore, the very distance of North America from Great Britain militates against any effective and sympathetic rule. Issues that arise in the colonies will not be heard of in Britain for several months, and action to deal with those issues will take more months to be realized in the colonies. Rule by Great Britain, just in practical terms, does not make any sense.

"We must always remember," Paine told his readers, "that Britain rules her colonies for her own benefit, even if it is at the expense of the American colonies. We should not deceive ourselves into thinking she has our interests at heart. We speak of her as our mother country, but what mother would ever treat her children as cruelly as she has treated us? And as for the trade benefits we derive from being connected to Britain, we would have flourished as much, and probably much more, if we had never had any connection with her." He went on to say, "The commerce by which she has enriched herself are the necessities of life, and will always have a market while eating is the custom of Europe." In other words, America can sell its corn and wheat to Europe without Britain's help.

The Puritans who founded one of the first settlements in America came here to find religious freedom away from rule by the Church of England. By remaining politically connected to the British crown, Paine declared, "We find that kind of freedom increasingly difficult to maintain. Furthermore, whenever Britain becomes involved in wars with European powers on the continent, we shall be obliged to participate in those conflicts as long as we are connected to Great Britain." (The origins of America's long-held policy of neutrality can be found in the pages of *Common Sense*.)

It is said that as Englishmen, we owe allegiance to the British crown, Paine said, but, in fact, we are not all Englishmen, not by a long shot! The North American colonies are populated by people from all over Europe: France, the Germanic states, Holland, Sweden, and many others. We are becoming a polyglot people who hail from many different places of origin, and we should think of ourselves as Americans, not Englishmen.

Paine next ventured where few before him had dared to go. He blamed not the parliament but the king himself for the tyranny under which the colonists were suffering. American colonists had been thinking that the source of their problems was parliament, with its unfair legislation: the Stamp Act, the Townshend Duties, The Tea Act, the Intolerable Acts, and many more outrages that had trampled on their rights as Englishmen. Paine argued, though, that the real tyrant was the king himself. Forget turning to him for a redress of our grievances, Paine seemed to be saying. He is the source of all the trouble. It is he who sent the troops to enforce parliament's laws; it is *he* who has hired Hessian soldiers to brutalize our people.

Finally, Paine's most revolutionary point, the point that caused many Americans to pause and say, "Yes, I never thought of it that way," was his assertion that the whole concept of a king, an absolute monarch with powers he inherited from his ancestors, was outdated and absurd. Why should an educated people who were accustomed to making their own laws, in their own legislative assemblies, have to obey the dictates of a pampered monarch in London who had never even been to North America?

Paine's ideas, expressed so clearly, spread like wildfire around the thirteen colonies. Within a few weeks, thousands of copies of the forty-eight-page pamphlet were sold. By the spring of 1776, virtually every American had read *Common Sense* or had heard the points Paine had made. (The total sales of Paine's book, based on the size of the population available to buy it, make it the top bestseller of all time, except for the Bible.)

By June of 1776, the delegates to the Continental Congress in Philadelphia had read *Common Sense* and had detected a sea change in public opinion back home. They were ready to vote for complete independence from the British crown. A few stalwart moderates, such as John Dickinson of Pennsylvania, held out for more attempts at reconciliation with King George III, but the tide had turned against them. On July 2, 1776, Congress voted for independence from Great Britain, and on July 4, they adopted the Declaration of Independence.

Whenever I think that what I say or write to someone won't make any difference, I think of the profound effect Thomas Paine had on the entire North American continent with his simple pamphlet. Paine also reminds me how important it is to write in clear and simple language and make your points as compellingly logical as possible.

THOMAS JEFFERSON EXPLAINED THE THEORY OF DEMOCRACY.

I have to hold my nose a little bit when I expound on the beauty of Thomas Jefferson's masterpiece, The Declaration of Independence, because the hypocrisy of a man who owned slaves writing "all men are created equal" is a little hard to take. I wonder if he had his slave fanning him to lessen his suffering in the stifling Philadelphia heat as he wrote those words. Is it possible he *didn't* sense the irony of the moment?

When I was at the University of Michigan in the early 1960s, Professor Bradford Perkins, whose American History course I enjoyed very much, always gave his lecture on Thomas Jefferson to a packed lecture hall. Dozens of people who were not even taking the class would show up that day to hear Perkins shred the reputation of the founding father who stands memorialized in stone next to the Potomac River, surrounded by his words carved in marble. Besides repeating the usual charges of Jefferson's sexual immorality with the slave girl, Sally Hemmings, Perkins accused Jefferson of being a mere tinkerer, a man who took the ideas of others and merely tinkered with them enough to call them his own. Perkins almost went so far as to call Jefferson a plagiarist. The point was that Jefferson's masterpiece was, in many ways, simply a restatement of the theory of government put forth by the English philosopher John Locke, almost one hundred years earlier.

Perkins' criticism is valid up to a point. It is true that Jefferson was indeed simply restating the political theory that many Americans, who knew very well that it came from Locke, had already accepted. The significance of what he did was that he expressed Locke's theory in language that was superior to what Locke had used and thereby made it a guiding light for the American people as they slogged through the difficult years of the American Revolution.

The second paragraph of the Declaration of Independence is one of the most beautiful pieces of writing in American political literature and it should be required reading in every high school history class. In fact, and I may be old-fashioned in saying this, I think it is a document that every American ought to memorize, because it is the bedrock of our nation's culture. At the very least, Americans should know the basic argument Jefferson makes in that paragraph:

1. All men (all human beings) are created equal and God gives them certain unalienable rights, including the rights to life, liberty, and the pursuit of happiness.

2. The *people* create governments to *protect* their rights. (This is a loaded statement. The people, not God, give governments their powers, and governments are there to protect the people's rights.)

3. When a government *fails* to protect their rights, the people have the *right*, indeed the obligation, to change it or to abolish it and replace it with a new government that *will* protect their rights.

4. Surveys have been done in which Americans have been given a copy of the second paragraph of the Declaration of Independence, without being told what it is, and have been asked what they think of it. Most of them do not recognize it and many of them think it is far too radical. It must be the work of some communists or degenerate hippies!

5. How sad. People should know what is in their country's founding document, and they should understand its meaning! Americans in 1776 knew every word of it, and those words inspired them to keep fighting for their freedom through the Revolution's darkest days.

THE U.S. CONSTITUTION USES PRECISE LANGUAGE TO SAY HOW THINGS WILL BE DONE.

The United States Constitution would never be called great literature, but as a legal document, precise in its language, it has no equal. The true beauty of the Constitution is that it creates a republican form of government that is flexible enough to adapt to the enormous growth of the nation for which it was written. When James Madison and the other founders wrote the Constitution, the United States was a struggling string of thirteen states hugging the Eastern Seaboard. Within the next century, the nation expanded across the entire continent, and by the twenty-first century contained fifty states and well over three hundred million people, yet the same instrument of government they wrote is still in effect.

The Constitution very logically divides the powers of government between the national (federal) government and the states. The national government has the power to declare war, raise an army, make treaties and alliances, coin money, regulate trade between the states and with other nations, and, very significantly, promote the general welfare of the people. That last power has opened the door for the federal government to do all sorts of things, such as create a social security system and a Medicare program. It was on that power that the Supreme Court declared the Affordable Care Act constitutional.

The states, meanwhile, are left with the authority to do anything not specifically delegated to the national government or denied to the states. The states regulate marriage and divorce and all matters of probate, they establish and operate public schools, and perform a myriad of other functions, many of which have the most impact on our everyday lives, such as traffic laws and water supply.

The authors of the Constitution were very realistic about human nature; they believed, as Abigail Adams once wrote to her husband John, that "all men would be tyrants if they could." So they built into the Constitution a system of checks and balances that effectively prevents one person or group of people from gaining too much power. The president is the commander-in-chief of the armed forces, but Congress has the power to declare war and also controls military appropriations. The president may propose legislation, but Congress must pass his proposals through both the House of Representatives and the Senate. The president may veto a law passed by Congress, but Congress can override his veto with a two-thirds vote in both houses. The federal courts interpret the laws—decide their meaning in individual cases—and the Supreme Court has expanded this power to include the ability to declare laws unconstitutional. Congress has the impeachment process at its disposal to remove federal officials or judges for unlawful behavior. This perfectly balanced system has kept the country going without a dictator taking power for over two and a quarter centuries.

Equally remarkable have been the amendments. The first ten, added almost immediately after the Constitution was adopted, protect the rights of the American people from the possibility that their government might try to abuse them. A careful reading of the Bill of Rights shows that they cover almost every contingency, but there were some questions involving interpretation. In the 1960s, the Supreme Court ruled that the right to have counsel for your defense meant that the states have to provide an attorney for people who are too poor to hire a lawyer. The court also ruled that a defendant, because he or she is protected from self-incrimination by the Fifth Amendment, must be informed that he or she has the right to remain silent and does not have to answer questions without the presence of an attorney.

After the Civil War, Congress proposed, and the states ratified, three more amendments that, in effect, expanded the Bill of Rights. The Thirteenth Amendment declared that slavery would no longer exist in the United States. The Fourteenth Amendment gave the newly freed African-Americans their basic rights as citizens, and it has become the most important part of the Constitution that exists. In all my years of teaching, I have made a huge point of the power of this amendment. I have been so adamant about this that one group of students actually presented me with a framed copy of the Fourteenth Amendment to hang on my classroom wall.

The amendment begins by defining citizenship: "All persons born or naturalized in the United States and subject to the jurisdiction thereof are citizens of the United States and of the state wherein they reside." This bestowed citizenship on all the freed slaves, even in the states that were not inclined to give it to them. In recent years, it has been attacked by foes of immigration who claim that people come into the United States just to have their children born on American soil, thus enabling them to claim American citizenship for the new child.

The amendment goes on to prohibit actions by the states that would deprive citizens of their privileges and immunities and their right to due process of law. The amendment then attempts to change the entire fabric of American society when it says, "(No state shall) deny to any person within its jurisdiction the equal protection of the laws." This is the first time the word "equal" appears anywhere in the Constitution, and its presence has been the cause of explosive arguments right up to the present day. For one hundred years, the southern states declared that their black populations were treated equally even though they were required by law to be segregated. Black facilities were separate, the argument went, but they were equal. In 1896, the Supreme Court gave sanction to this ruse and it continued until the Civil Rights Act of 1964 finally ended segregation.

Equally as significant, the "equal protection" clause has been used by women to advocate for their equality in inheritance, in the workplace, and in the military. On another front, in 2015, the Supreme Court ruled that states could no longer deny marriage licenses to gay couples because it would deprive them of *their* equal protection of the laws.

There is so very much in the United States Constitution that affects our everyday lives. Most people have very little idea what is in the document—and what is not in it. They would have a better understanding of what is going on around them today if they did. I am no constitutional scholar, but I have always been happy to know the basics of how the government works and how our constitutional rights have been interpreted. Stories I see in the news make much more sense to me because I know the Constitution. I also marvel at the way the framers of the Constitution were able to express complex procedures and concepts with such efficiency and clarity. The language may be too lawyerly for some people, but I admire its precision and I find it comes in handy occasionally when I try to explain something in a short and efficient yet complete way.

HARRIET BEECHER STOWE WROTE A STORY THAT HELPED START A WAR.

By the 1850s, William Lloyd Garrison, Theodore Weld, and other abolitionists had been telling the public about the miseries of the slave population in the South for over twenty years. Frederick Douglass published his memoir detailing the travails of his own life as a slave, but none of these efforts had anywhere near the impact that a story about a fictitious slave named Uncle Tom had after 1852. Tom was the creation of Harriet Beecher Stowe, a Northerner whose only firsthand view of slavery was the few runaways she saw when she lived in Cincinnati, just across the Ohio River from Kentucky. Beecher told Tom's story in her novel *Uncle Tom's Cabin*. Her book sold over three hundred thousand copies in its first year of publication and became the biggest selling book in the nineteenth century, except for the Bible, of course.

It is easy to understand why Tom had such an impact on readers in the 1850s. He is a Christian man who exudes kindness, compassion, and generosity. His fate, however, is not his own, as he is sold from one owner to another, and he is powerless. At the moment when his owner is about to set him free, the owner dies and Tom is sold again. Clearly, as a slave, he has no control over his life. His final master is a hideously cruel man named Simon Legree. Stowe makes Legree a transplanted Northerner to show that the slave system debases all people who become part of it; cruel behavior is a product of *slavery*, not a southern characteristic. In the climactic scene of the book, Legree orders his overseers to whip Tom to death. Even as he is dying, in a final act of Christian love and forgiveness, Tom forgives the overseers and Legree.

Readers of Stowe's novel always finish the book dissolved in tears and filled with hatred for Simon Legree and the slave system that produced a man like him. Even though Tom and Legree were characters in a novel, Northerners began to think of all slaves as Uncle Tom and all slave owners as Simon Legree. When the southern states began seceding from the Union in 1860, Northerners were much more united against slavery than they would have been in 1850, before Ms. Stowe's book.

The story is often told that Lincoln met Harriet Beecher Stowe in the White House during the Civil War and said to her, "So, you're the little lady who wrote the book that started this big war." It is very likely that story was fabricated, but it does make the point that *Uncle Tom's Cabin* united the North against slavery like nothing before had ever done. Anti-slavery unity made Southerners paranoid about the intentions of the North when Lincoln was elected and, thus, probably contributed to their decision to secede. Northerners' sympathy for the slaves made them willing to fight rather than see the South leave the Union and form a slave republic. So, whether Lincoln said those words or not, Harriet Beecher Stowe did a great deal to create the conditions that led to a civil war between the slave-owning and non-slave-owning sections of the United States.

ABE LINCOLN INSPIRED THE NATION AT GETTYSBURG.

We can see now that the Battle of Gettysburg was the high watermark of the Confederacy. The southern armies were never again going to be able to mount a serious offensive against the forces of the Union. At the time, however, it seemed as though this was just another in a series of horrible, gory battles that would go on forever. Lee's army had slipped out of Pennsylvania after the battle and was back in Virginia preparing to fight on. General Meade of the Union Army had failed to follow up on his victory and deliver a knockout blow. Meanwhile, in New York City, riots were breaking out against the military draft, and some of the soldiers who fought at Gettysburg were being dispatched to the city to quell the disturbances.

In Gettysburg, the dismal task of collecting and naming all of the dead went on for weeks after the armies had retreated. At first, the corpses were tagged and placed in shallow graves to cut down on the stench of rotting flesh that permeated the area. Later, permanent coffins were constructed and the bodies were moved to their final resting places. By the fall, the Gettysburg Soldiers' National Cemetery was nearing completion and a dedication ceremony was scheduled for November 19, 1863. The program for the event included an opening prayer, music by the Marine band, and a major two-hour oration by the greatest speaker of the day, Edward Everett. The president of the United States would also make a few dedicatory remarks.

On the eighteenth, Lincoln took the train up from Washington and took lodging in the home of a local resident. He had rewritten his speech several times and spent some time that night at a small table revising it still further. The story that he hastily scribbled it out on the back of an envelope on the way to Gettysburg was a complete myth. Lincoln always took great care in his choice of words and in his phrasing, and he certainly did in this speech. Great writing took time. One of my favorite Lincoln stories is the one in which he writes a letter to a friend, saying, "Please excuse the length of this letter. I didn't have time to write a short one." In other words, I rambled because I didn't take the time to figure out a concise way to express my thoughts.

The next day, under a leaden November sky, Lincoln sat on the platform with his tall hat removed and listened to the prayers, the hymns, and the band; then, for two hours, he listened as Edward Everett regaled the crowd with his Gettysburg Address. The speech was very good and was well received by the large crowd standing before the platform. He concluded with what he hoped would be a memorable line: "… wherever throughout the civilized world the accounts of this great warfare are read, and down to the latest period of recorded time, in the glorious annals of our common country, there will be no brighter page than that which relates the Battles of Gettysburg." I find this awkward and cluttered, with too many words, and I don't find it memorable at all.

When Lincoln finally rose to speak, the crowd had been on its feet for almost three hours, but people in those days were used to long speeches; in fact, they craved them. When Lincoln spoke for only two minutes, some in the crowd were disappointed. Only a few people appreciated the beauty and eloquence of his short address, and as he resumed his seat, Lincoln judged that his effort had been a failure. It was only in the days afterward, as people read the speech in their newspapers, that they discovered its impact. Edward Everett realized immediately that

Lincoln had captured the essence of the moment and had delivered a speech that would inspire the nation. He wrote Lincoln a letter in which he commended the president on the "eloquent simplicity and appropriateness of your remarks." He went on to extend a very generous compliment: "I should be glad if I could flatter myself that I came as near to the central idea of the occasion, in two hours, as you did in two minutes." (Everett's letter, by the way, is another useful lesson I have learned from American history. I always try to be as gracious toward someone who has outdone me as he was!)

Lincoln's remarks are another part of American lore that students would do well to memorize. There was a time when high school students in many towns were required to recite the Gettysburg Address as part of their graduation requirement. I never asked students to memorize it, but we always read it and analyzed it in class, with the goal of understanding why those two hundred forty-two words have such an honored place in American history and what Lincoln's beautiful address might teach us about how to write and speak.

In a sense, Lincoln began poorly with "Four score and seven years ago" when he could have simply said, "eighty-seven years ago." I suppose the words he used might have attracted attention because of their uniqueness, but the phrase is in conflict with his usual attempt to be as direct, simple, and clearly understood as possible. Lincoln's opening words sound a bit pompous today.

After establishing the time reference, Lincoln reminded his audience that the founders established a "new nation, conceived in liberty, and dedicated to the proposition that all men are created equal." Lincoln's Emancipation Proclamation a year earlier had made it clear that the war was being fought not just to preserve the Union, but also to achieve true equality for *all* people. What a noble and inspiring goal this was! (He might have added that this was beyond what the author of the Declaration of Independence had in mind.)

"Now we are engaged in a great civil war," he went on, "testing whether that nation, or any nation, so conceived and so dedicated, can long endure. We are here to dedicate a cemetery as a final resting place for those who fought here to preserve that nation. It is altogether fitting and proper that we should do this. But in a larger sense, *we* cannot dedicate, *we* cannot consecrate, *we* cannot hallow this ground. The brave men living and dead who struggled here have consecrated it far above our poor power to add or detract." Here, Lincoln chose his words perfectly: *hallowed, consecrated, add or detract.* They are so concise and express exactly the right concepts.

Having established the cause for which men died and the valor the gathering was commemorating, Lincoln concluded with a view to the future: "... from these honored dead we take increased devotion to that cause for which they gave the last full measure of devotion—that we here highly resolve that these dead shall not have died in vain— that this nation under God shall have a new birth of freedom, and that government of the people, by the people, and for the people, shall not perish from the earth." The *new birth of freedom* was the emancipation of the slaves. In this last, beautifully crafted sentence, Lincoln exhorted his countrymen to continue fighting for the preservation of our glorious democracy and for freedom for all people.

During the weeks following the Gettysburg dedication, people all over the North read Lincoln's address. Because every word in the speech was potent, almost everyone was inspired by it. Steven Spielberg's *Lincoln* begins with a couple of Union soldiers standing in front of Lincoln near a battlefield and reciting back to him his Gettysburg Address. I think the scene is a bit contrived, almost hokey, but it does make the point that Lincoln's speech motivated the people of the North, soldiers and civilians alike, to keep on struggling. And they *needed* motivation because the casualty lists were long. More soldiers died in the battles after Gettysburg than died in the Korean and Vietnam wars combined, and Gettysburg was fought at a time when the whole population was only twenty percent what it was in the 1950s and 1960s. There was no chance to speak to the nation on television during the Civil War. The mothers who lost sons, the wives who lost husbands, and the soldiers themselves had *only* Lincoln's words to keep them going. The Gettysburg Address is the best example there is of the power of words.

WILLIAM JENNINGS BRYAN SKEWERED THE ONE PERCENT.

We hear a lot these days about the one percent, those very rich people at the top of society who seem to have everything and to have gotten much of it by getting special favors from the government and by ripping off the middle and lower classes. In 2016, Vermont's Bernie Sanders is basing his run for president on the idea that he will take on the rich and powerful by taxing some of their fortunes and using the money to benefit the poor people and the nation as a whole.

People who know American history are aware that the Sanders' candidacy and the concept of the one percent are not really new. The concept traces its origins all the way back to rebellions against the wealthy Eastern Seaboard landowners in colonial times by ferocious frontiersmen, such as Nathanial Bacon. After that, there were Thomas Jefferson and the even more Democratic Andrew Jackson, who both despised banks and bankers. But the true apostle of the crusade against the one percent would have to be William Jennings Bryan, who stirred the passions of the entire country with an explosive speech in 1896.

By the summer of that year, the farmers (who still made up fifty percent of the population) and the factory workers were in an uproar over the struggles they were having against the big business plutocrats. Every time the workers tried to achieve better conditions through unionizing and strikes, the employers beat them down. The farmers consistently felt they were being screwed by the railroads and banks. Worst of all, it was clear that the government, state or federal, Republican controlled or Democrat controlled, always supported the wealthy. On several occasions, presidents or governors of states had sent in troops to bust up strikes and arrest the organizers. The Supreme Court had stymied the farmers' attempts to regulate the railroads through state legislation. Mary Lease, a farm organizer from Kansas, shouted that we had a government not "of the people, for the people, and by the people" but, rather, "of Wall Street, by Wall Street, and for Wall Street." That was a historical nifty, and she got off another one when she opined that farmers should "raise less corn and more hell!"

In 1892, the discontented farmers in the Midwest organized a new political party to advocate for their interests. Called the People's Party, or Populist Party, the platform called for government ownership of the railroads, an eight-hour workday, a graduated income tax, and the coinage of silver. Adding silver to gold in the nation's currency system, the Populists argued, would inflate the currency and thus drive up farm prices and make debts easier to pay off. In 1892, James Weaver, the Populist candidate for president, won five states. The fiery organizers of the party looked to 1896 as the year when they would really make their mark and carry their message of "free and unlimited coinage of silver" to greater heights. But when that year arrived, someone stole their thunder.

At the Democratic Convention in 1896, William Jennings Bryan, a relatively little known congressman from Nebraska, gave a speech that none of those who heard it would ever forget. Bryan was a young man, only thirty-six years old, but he had a powerful presence, and he had developed a dynamic speaking style that any politician, or actor, would envy. His message focused on the plight of the poor farmers and workers in the country and the solution the Democratic Party should adopt: the free and unlimited coinage of silver.

Using strong words and vivid metaphors, Bryan brought the delegates to their feet again and again to applaud and cheer. A complete reading of the speech lets you really appreciate the dynamics of it. In my classes, I always have a volunteer student, preferably a good actor, assume the role of Bryan and regale the class. Following are a few of Bryan's best lines:

"(When you say our proposal for silver will disturb the business interests of the country), we say to you that you have made the definition of a businessman too limited in its application. The man who is employed for wages is as much a businessman as his employer; the attorney in a country town is as much a businessman as the corporation counsel in a great metropolis; the merchant at the crossroads store is as much a businessman as the merchant of New York; the farmer who goes forth in the morning and toils all day, who begins in the spring and toils all summer, and who by the application of brain and muscle to the natural resources of the country creates wealth, is as much a businessman as the man who goes upon the Board of Trade and bets upon the price of grain …"

The crowd went wild at this elegant explanation of how the lower classes create wealth, as well as at its accompanying skewering of the pretensions of the upper classes that sniff that *they* are the only ones who create wealth.

Later in the speech, Bryan put forth the basic difference between Republicans and Democrats with a clarity most of the delegates had never before heard: "There are two ideas of government. There are those who believe that if you will only legislate to make the well-to-do prosperous, their prosperity will leak through on those below. The Democratic idea, however, has been that if you legislate to make the masses prosperous, their prosperity will find its way up through every class which rests upon them." Today, the idea of this last sentence would serve Democrats well in attacking the Republicans' "trickle down" theory of economics. It was novel in 1896 and brought big applause.

Bryan then responded to those who claimed that "free silver" only benefitted the farmers: "You come to us and tell us that the great cities are in favor of the gold standard; we reply that the great cities rest upon our broad and fertile prairies. Burn down our cities and leave our farms, and your cities will spring up again as if by magic; but destroy our farms and the grass will grow in the streets of every city in the country." After a moment's reflection, we can easily see the truth of what Bryan was saying, and the delegates were once again on their feet cheering loudly.

As he neared the end of his speech, Bryan already had the delegates at a fever pitch, but his closing brought the delegates to such a level of excitement that they rushed the platform and carried Bryan around the hall on their shoulders. "If they dare to come out in the open field and defend the gold standard as a good thing, we will fight them to the uttermost," Bryan shouted. "Having behind us the producing masses of this nation and the world, supported by the commercial interests, the laboring interests and the toilers everywhere, we will answer their demand for a gold standard by saying to them, 'You shall not press down upon the brow of labor this crown of thorns, you shall not crucify mankind upon a cross of gold!'"

The last line became so famous that the speech is always referred to as the "Cross of Gold Speech," and it is always ranked as one of the ten greatest speeches of all time. The delegates were so enthralled that they gave up any loyalties they had to other party leaders in the nomination for president and, instead, nominated Bryan for president on the first ballot. Because of his speech, William Jennings Bryan became the youngest man ever to be nominated by a major party for president. He was only one year older than the constitutional requirement for the office, and he was seven years younger than John F. Kennedy would be when he became the youngest elected president in 1960.

You might well be asking, If Bryan's speech was so great, why did he lose the general election to the Republican candidate, William McKinley? Bryan did win the rural states across the South, the Midwest, and the far West, but McKinley won the states in the industrial, heavily populated Northeast, where many of the electoral votes were. The Republican forces had a big advantage in that election in that they had much more money than the Democrats, and they were able to get their message out to the factory workers and even some farmers in states such as Ohio and Illinois. Their message was that abandoning the gold standard would inflate the currency and make the price of everything go up. This would stifle business and harm everyone. Bryan and the Democrats (and the Populists who also nominated Bryan) were just too radical, the Republicans proclaimed; they wanted to go too far. "Do you really want the value of the dollars in your pay envelopes to go down?" Republicans asked. Enough workers did not, and Bryan went down in defeat.

Bryan's speech has never been forgotten, however, and the concepts he set forth live on today. Congress members such as Elizabeth Warren or Bernie Sanders could dust off the "cross of gold speech" and almost use it word for word in their campaigns. The Populist party died off in the early 1900s, but the concept that the rich have more than they deserve and that the banks and Wall Street financiers are getting all the breaks lives on and is often referred to as "populism." The colorful populists of the 1890s ("raise less corn and more hell") and William Jennings Bryan (mankind is "crucified upon a cross of gold") got the movement off to a strong start over a hundred years ago, and the movement could someday win a major election if its proponents are as articulate and use words as effectively as did William Jennings Bryan.

FDR BANISHED FEAR.

The winter of 1933 has to have been the dreariest period in American history. The economic depression that had started in 1929 was getting worse by the day. Twenty-five percent of the people were unemployed, and thousands of people were homeless and living in shacks made out of scrap lumber or discarded boxes. On the farms, crop prices were so low that many farmers couldn't make their mortgage payments and were losing their land to their creditors. Most frightening of all, banks by the thousands were failing, closing their doors and leaving all their depositors without the money they thought they had. By March 4, when newly elected President Franklin Delano Roosevelt was scheduled to take office, the entire financial system of the country was tottering and appeared to be on the brink of total collapse. The American people were desperate. They had great expectations for the new president to take charge.

Twelve years earlier, Franklin Delano Roosevelt was one of the rising stars in the Democratic Party firmament when he ran for vice president in 1920. Even though the ticket of Cox and Roosevelt lost that year, everyone thought the young, charismatic Roosevelt had the personal charm—not to mention the name—that would take him far. He had his sights on the presidency, but then, suddenly, in the summer of 1921, FDR fell ill with infantile paralysis (polio) and was left paralyzed from the waist down. In those years, way before the Americans with Disabilities Act and laws requiring handicapped access to buildings, a man could hardly think of running for town council, let alone president, without the ability to walk. Most people concluded he was through at this point.

One of the greatest stories in American political history is FDR's return to politics after paralysis struck. Much like his distant cousin Theodore Roosevelt had built up his body as a weak and sickly child, FDR spent five years in the mid-1920s building up his leg muscles and developing powerful shoulders and arms that could hold up his body on crutches and braces. He also perfected techniques for creating the illusion that he was walking. By 1928, he was able to walk to a podium by leaning on the arm of his son, James, and swinging his heavily braced legs forward from the hips. He would grasp the speaker's rostrum and, with his shriveled legs hidden from view, project the image of a powerful man delivering a rousing speech. In 1928 he was elected governor of New York; in 1930 he was reelected governor; and in 1932 he won the presidency by promising the American people a *new deal.*

On a cloudy, raw March 4, the crowd at the Capitol Building watched as their new president approached the podium where he would take the oath of office. The cluster of dignitaries walking toward the podium in front of FDR was moving slowly, so no one in the crowd could see that he was clinging to his son's arm and inching his legs forward. When their new president stood and swore the oath of office, he looked dignified, straight, and strong. The people stood silent, eager to hear what he would say. Across the nation millions of people sat by their radio sets to listen to the man on whom they were placing so much hope.

I can only imagine how energized and tense FDR must have felt at that moment. Any time you are about to speak in public it is a nerve-wracking experience; your stomach turns over and your mouth gets dry, at least that's what happens to me, but everyone experiences anxiety in a different way. Imagine how *you* would feel if you were about to speak in front of thousands of people, with a hundred million more listening at home, in their cars, and in their offices, all of them expecting you to lift them out of the worst disaster they and their country had ever faced! Add to that the anxiety FDR must have felt about his physical limitations.

Almost as soon as FDR began to speak, the fog that was enveloping the country began to lift. His voice was clear and his tone was confident and strong. The country was in such bad shape that no one had any idea what to do, but this man seemed to have things under control. He recited the oath of office from memory in a calm and confident voice, and then he turned toward the microphone to address the nation.

I have listened to recordings of FDR's speech that day several times, and it is clear to me that the people responded as much to the manner of his delivery as they responded to his words. An interesting exercise is to read aloud a speech such as FDR's first inaugural. Speak rapidly and with no inflection in your voice. The whole thing loses its impact. But FDR spoke distinctly, his voice ringing clearly out over the crowd and rising and falling according to the meaning of his words. The American people were mesmerized. They were afraid, but here was a leader who was *not* afraid; they were confused, but here was a leader who *knew* what to do.

People often misquote the most memorable line FDR spoke that day. He is often quoted as saying, "We have nothing to fear but fear itself." That line expresses the basic idea, but it carries nowhere near the punch of the sentence the way he *did* say it: "So, first of all, let me assert my firm belief that the only thing we have to fear is fear itself: nameless, unreasoning, unjustified terror, which paralyzes needed efforts to convert retreat into advance." Those words, and the way they were delivered, electrified the nation.

No one would ever claim that FDR ended the depression with his inaugural address. Seven long years of economic hard times still lay ahead. With this speech, though, Roosevelt gave the people hope and the positive feeling that something was being done and that the government did care about them.

Nine years after his first inaugural address, FDR rallied the nation again with the Pearl Harbor address that I referred to at the beginning of this chapter. Roosevelt's speaking style and interesting choice of words and images rallied the people and kept a majority of them with him as he led the nation for twelve years.

I have always thought that a person who aspires to be a great public speaker would be well advised to listen to as many FDR speeches as possible. His style really connected with his audiences and is well worth emulating. I always have a little FDR image in my brain when I speak in public. It helps me to speak distinctly and with great attention to cadence and phrasing. Of course, you can make a fool of yourself by obviously trying to imitate another person, so I try not to do that! If you take a little dose of FDR and mix it with the techniques of some other famous speakers in American history, you will become a better speaker and you will be able to be a discerning listener when orators are trying to impress you with their words.

OTHER WORDS THAT HAD IMPACT

Like a senator filibustering, I could go on at great length with many other examples of the books, speeches, and other forms of communication that have had a major impact on me; however, in the interest of brevity, I will leave it at the ones I have just described, except to draw your attention to several others that might also interest you and to suggest that there are many more that you might discover on your own if you study American history with an eye toward gaining worthwhile knowledge. The point is that words can be impactful; by listening to some of the great speakers or reading the writings of some of the historical greats, you can become a great communicator too. What follows are a few of the other gems that have benefited me.

ANDREW JACKSON THREATENED JOHN C. CALHOUN AND THE OTHER NULLIFIERS.

I have said negative things about Andrew Jackson in previous chapters because he was basically a racist and a hothead; however, his handling of the attempt by South Carolina to nullify the tariff provides us with a great example of how powerful words can have an impact. Jackson's reply to the South Carolina Ordinance of Nullification is a long and masterful document (probably written by someone else in his administration), but his offhand remark about his vice president, John C. Calhoun, who had resigned his office to return to South Carolina and lead the nullification fight, was a gem. If the nullification ordinance were not repealed, Jackson said he would personally lead an army into the state and hang Calhoun and every nullifier he could get his hands on from the nearest tree he could find! Eventually, a compromise tariff was agreed upon and the nullification crisis ended, but Jackson had set an example for clarity in dealing with South Carolina that Lincoln, in more dignified and nuanced ways, would follow twenty-nine years later.

WILLIAM LLOYD GARRISON PROCLAIMED HE WOULD BE HEARD.

I have already said a lot about my admiration for Garrison and his willingness to take an unpopular stand, but he deserves to be mentioned again because I believe his forthright and hard-hitting writing in every speech and every edition of *The Liberator* was masterful, especially when we consider that he had very little formal schooling when he was young. (It amazes me, by the way, how many great writers and speakers in the eighteenth and nineteenth centuries came from such primitive educational backgrounds, Garrison and Lincoln foremost among them. How did they do it? I believe most learned to read at home and that the only book available to many of them was the Bible. They devoured it because it was the only "entertainment" they had. The Bible is written in beautiful language and has wonderful stories that teach great lessons. They were nurtured by it, and it most likely helped them become great speakers and writers. I defy anyone to produce any other possible explanation.

Every speech and edition of *The Liberator* contained memorable quotes, but the greatest is the statement Garrison made in the very first edition, on New Year's Day, 1831. It is worth repeating, and I urge you to take note of his clarity and his obvious dedication to the cause of abolishing slavery:

"I am aware that many object to the severity of my language; but is there not cause for severity? I will be as harsh as truth and as uncompromising as justice. On this subject I do not wish to think, or speak, or write, with moderation. No! No! Tell a man whose house is on fire to give a moderate alarm; tell him to moderately rescue his wife from the hands of the ravisher; tell the mother to gradually extricate her babe from the fire into which it has fallen, but urge me not to use moderation in a cause like the present. I am in earnest ... I will not equivocate ... I will not excuse ... I will not retreat a single inch ... AND I WILL BE HEARD!"

Many historians claim that Garrison had very little influence because his views were so extreme. I beg to differ. It was the extremity of his views that caused southern slave owners to react violently, first against Garrison personally and later in response to anyone, including the very moderate Abraham Lincoln, who seemed to be the least bit in Garrison's camp. As Garrison predicted early in his career, his words shook the nation with their mighty power.

JOHN BROWN WARNED THE NATION ABOUT ITS FATE.

In 1859, John Brown led twenty men in a raid on the federal arsenal in the town of Harper's Ferry, Virginia. Their intention was a bit vague, but apparently they hoped to procure guns from the arsenal, distribute them among the slaves in the area, and ignite a slave rebellion. Their plan, which never really had a chance, failed when a U.S. Army contingent under Colonel Robert E. Lee surrounded Brown and his men in the arsenal, killed most of them, and took Brown himself prisoner.

At his trial, Brown asserted that he was only trying to bring slaves, in a peaceful way, out of the South and off into Canada, where they would be free. He had not intended, he claimed, to incite a slave rebellion. Nevertheless, he was found guilty of treason and sentenced to hang.

On the day of his execution, Brown handed a note to a guard just before the rope was placed around his neck. The message he left to the American people was prophetic: "I, John Brown, am now quite certain that the crimes of this guilty land can never be purged away but with blood."

When news of Brown's execution reached northern cities and towns, church bells rang to honor the martyr to freedom. Less than two years later, thousands of northern soldiers were marching off to war against the Southern Confederacy singing "John Brown's body lies a moldering in the grave, but his soul goes marching on." John Brown's willingness to die for the freedom of the slaves and his prophetic words inspired countless young men to emulate him and march off to war against slavery.

ABRAHAM LINCOLN ENVISIONED REUNION.

In March of 1865, as the seemingly endless Civil War was finally drawing to a close, Abraham Lincoln took the oath of office for the second time. His second inaugural address focused on why the war had come and why it had dragged on for so long with so much bloodshed. His explanation for the cause of the war was, as one would expect from Lincoln, concise and clear:

"Both parties (the Union and the Confederacy) deprecated war, but one of them would make war rather than let the nation survive; and the other would accept war rather than let it perish. And the war came."

As for why the war had been so lengthy and bloody, Lincoln turned to the Bible for explanation, as he often did:

"Fondly do we hope—fervently do we pray—that this mighty scourge of war may speedily pass away. Yet, if God wills that it continue until all the wealth piled by the bond-man's two hundred and fifty years of unrequited toil shall be sunk, and until every drop of blood drawn with the lash shall be paid by another drawn with the sword, as was said three thousand years ago, so still it must be said, 'The judgments of the Lord are true and righteous altogether.'"

In other words, the nation committed the great sin of slavery and God is using the war to punish the nation for its sin and will not stop until the debt has been paid.

Finally, and this, for Lincoln, was the most important part of his address, he looked ahead to peace and the reuniting of the nation once the war was over. Here Lincoln was at his most eloquent and profound, and here Lincoln revealed his almost Christ-like compassion:

"With malice toward none; with charity for all; with firmness in the right as God gives us to see the right, let us strive to finish the work we are in; to bind up the nation's wounds; to care for him who shall have borne the battle, and for his widow and for his orphan, to do all which may achieve and cherish a just and a lasting peace, among ourselves and with all nations."

The wording of this beautiful paragraph is not from the Bible, but the sentiment is pure Christianity. Jesus, in the same situation, would have said the same thing. Six weeks later, when Lincoln was murdered on Good Friday, the irony was complete, but, of course, unlike Jesus, Lincoln could not return. His message of unity, peace, and forgiveness, which he had espoused so beautifully, was left to much lesser men to carry out. They failed.

UPTON SINCLAIR TURNED THE COUNTRY'S (AND THE PRESIDENT'S) STOMACH.

In 1906, a socialist writer named Upton Sinclair was disgusted with the conditions in the meat packing factories in Chicago. To alert the public to the atrocities of the slaughterhouses and canneries, he published a novel called *The Jungle*. His book tells the story of a Lithuanian immigrant named Jurgis Rudkis, who takes a job at Durham and Company, meat processors, and finds himself working in conditions that are positively obscene. One paragraph from the book gives you the flavor, so to speak:

"Worst of any (of the workers), however, were the fertilizer men, and those who worked in the cooking rooms. These people could not be shown to the visitor, for the odor of a fertilizer man would scare any visitor at a hundred yards, and as for the other men, who worked in tank rooms full of steam, and in some of which there were open vats at the level of the floor, their peculiar trouble was that they fell into the vats; and when they were fished out, there was never enough left of them to be worth exhibiting; sometimes they would be overlooked for days, till all but the bones of them had gone out to the world as Durham's Pure Leaf Lard!"

Sinclair's solution to these appalling conditions was socialism, a people's revolt to throw over the rich, selfish capitalist owners, have the *people* take over the factories, and make them public enterprises that would care about workers' benefits more than profits. At the end of *The Jungle*, Jurgis Rudkis joins the socialists and marches in the streets for revolution.

Millions of people read *The Jungle*, and it had a profound impact on them, but not the kind of impact Sinclair wanted. Sinclair thought people would feel bad for the workers who fell into the fat vats, but, instead, people felt revulsion over the food they were eating. President Theodore Roosevelt read the book and moved to get Congress to pass two important regulatory pieces of legislation: the Meat Inspection Act and the Pure Food and Drug Act. These laws put the food industries under federal government regulation, so now we can be reasonably sure our food is sanitary; however, I still hesitate to eat sausage, and I won't touch lard! Sinclair was only minimally satisfied with these changes, important though they may have been. His hope for a full throttle socialist revolution did not materialize.

THE "MUCKRAKERS" DUG UP DIRT.

Sinclair was one of several writers in the early years of the twentieth century who focused the public's attention on what was wrong in the country and, in some cases, got action to correct the problems. Theodore Roosevelt grew a little tired of their constant focus on the evils of society and called them "muckrakers," characters in John Bunyan's book *Pilgrim's Progress* who constantly rake the muck and never look up to the sky to see the celestial crown being offered to them. Teddy thought these writers should at least give a nod to some of the improvements that were being made.

The most famous of the muckrakers was Ida Tarbell, who wrote a series of magazine articles about the oil tycoon John D. Rockefeller. Her "History of Standard Oil," which appeared serialized in McClure's magazine and was later published as a book, charged Rockefeller with using unfair business practices and driving rival operators out of business in order to eliminate competition and achieve an oil monopoly. Rockefeller responded with silence and then indignation, asserting it was only his better business practices and efficiency that had won him his success. Still, Tarbell's articles had an effect on the public's perception of Rockefeller and his Standard Oil Company. In 1911, the U.S. Supreme Court broke up Standard Oil, stating it was a "conspiracy in restraint of trade" and thus in violation of the Sherman Anti-Trust Act.

Ida Tarbell's friend and colleague Lincoln Steffens also wrote articles for McClure, but his focus was the political corruption in the cities of America. Starting with an article called "Tweed Days in St. Louis," Steffens went on to investigate the political corruption in several major cities, including Minneapolis, Chicago, Pittsburgh, and Philadelphia. His focus was not so much on the corruption itself, because the fact that it existed was well known; instead, his articles drew attention to the business people and private citizens who allowed the corruption to continue because of their lack of interest in politics. The result was that reform movements grew up in cities across the country, dedicated to cleaning up the corruption.

A new type of political leader emerged in many of the states. Calling themselves *progressives*, their goal was to make progress toward clean, honest government, and in many states they succeeded. National leaders such as Theodore Roosevelt, William Howard Taft, and Woodrow Wilson caught the progressive spirit of regeneration as well. Those three presidents initiated many reforms at the federal level, including the Pure Food and Drug Act, the Clayton Anti-Trust Act, and the practice of "trust busting." Thus, it is largely the muckrakers, with their powerful pens, who started the Progressive Era we hear so much about. An entire era of reform (1901-1920) was begun with the power of words.

RACHEL CARSON WARNED THAT THE BIRDS WOULD STOP SINGING.

In the early 1960s, most of us were pretty oblivious to the effect our automobiles, garbage, pesticides and, indeed, everything else we used was having on our environment. Many of us would have been hard pressed to explain what it meant to say *our environment*. In 1962, Rachel Carson, a marine biologist, published a book called *Silent Spring*. It opened many of our eyes to what we were doing to the planet. Focusing on the indiscriminate use of pesticides, particularly the chemical DDT, Carson concluded that the balance of nature would be severely disrupted if this continued. Many of the pesticides were carcinogenic; their continued use in large quantities would kill more than just insects. Birds would die—hence, we would have *silent springs*—and so would other animals, even humans. Moreover, thoughtless use of pesticides would result in insects that would be resistant to the chemicals. "… the insect enemy," she wrote, "has been made actually stronger by our efforts."

Because of Ms. Carson's work, the United States and many other countries around the world banned the use of DDT and began to look closer at the actual effects of all chemicals used in the environment. Environmental awareness became much more popular, and in 1970, the first Earth Day was observed. Two years later, Congress established the Environmental Protection Agency to conduct research on threats to the environment and, most importantly, to enforce environmental legislation. Although Ms. Carson has her critics, especially the chemical industry, no one disputes the fact that she raised the public's awareness as to how everything we do affects the natural world around us.

BETTY FRIEDAN TOLD WOMEN THEY WERE RIGHT TO FEEL BORED AND DISRESPECTED.

In the 1950s, Betty Friedan was a typical American housewife doing *housewifey* things: cooking the meals, doing the laundry, vacuuming the floors, and deferring to her husband on almost everything. She was profoundly unhappy. In 1957, as she prepared to attend her fifteenth college reunion, she conducted a survey and found that many of the women in her class were as unhappy as she was. The endless tedium of grocery shopping and housework, the mind-numbing loneliness, and the lack of self-respect were all common complaints. Most of the women who answered the survey were relieved to find that they were not the only ones who were experiencing this dissatisfaction.

Six years later, Betty Friedan published *The Feminine Mystique*. The book described the panic women experienced as they sat in their houses, waiting for their husbands to come home from work, and thinking, "Is this all there is to my life?" Friedan argued that women were fully as capable as men of performing any kind of work, of earning a paycheck outside the home. The book spoke for women all over the country and quickly became a bestseller. In 1966, Friedan cofounded The National Organization for Women (NOW), an organization dedicated to fighting for legal equality for women. Friedan became NOW's first president, and the message she spoke around the country and on television was that women needed to break away from the roles assigned to them by men.

By 1970, the women's liberation movement was under way. Even women as traditional as my mother were affected by it. She would proclaim, "I'm no women's libber," because she didn't like the radical talk and the marches women were staging to draw attention to the cause. She hated the bra burning demonstrations—"Men don't wear bras, so why should we?"—and she despised the glib chant "A women needs a man like a fish needs a bicycle." But one Sunday night, as ten people sat around Mom's dinner table, she noted, "Every one of you will be expected at work somewhere tomorrow, but *I* won't be. No one will give a damn about me because I don't have a job." Women's lib was making her think in ways she never had before.

One of the saddest aspects of my mother's life was that after she got married in 1940, she was never able to make use of her skills in a way that was truly satisfying. She was a great typist, able to type seventy words a minute on a manual typewriter without a mistake, and she was the world's greatest organizer—she would have made a superb office manager—but she could never break out of the role my father prescribed for her. She was precisely the kind of woman Betty Friedan wanted to liberate, but, for her, liberation never came.

For most women after 1970, liberation *did* come. By the turn of the century, half of the workforce was women. Soon after that, the majority of people in the United States with college degrees were women. By 2015 there were three women on the U.S. Supreme Court, and there were even female generals in the Army. As I write this (December 2015), it is very possible that the next president will be a woman. Betty Friedan's book played an important part in launching a movement that was destined to change the face of the nation.

MALCOLM X TOLD AFRICAN-AMERICANS TO BE PROUD OF THEIR RACE.

It was noted earlier that Dr. Martin Luther King, Jr. had a profound influence on the country. His speeches and marches led directly to the passage of the major legislation that brought the African-American people out of the shadows of segregation. Malcolm Little played an equally important role because he changed the way black people thought about themselves; in fact, it is because of him that I just used the word *black*.

In the 1950s, Malcolm Little seemed to be yet another "Negro" man, spending most of his time on the streets, getting into drugs and petty crime. He was arrested and sent to prison. In prison, however, he converted to Islam, the faith he believed was the true religion of the African race. He emerged from prison as Malcolm X, substituting X for Little, which was his slave name, the name given to his ancestors by their white owners. He did not know what his real name was; therefore, he was X.

From the time he became a Black Muslim to his assassination in 1965, Malcolm X preached Islam. He was disgusted with the way black people accepted the religion the white man had forced upon them. The "white devils" of slave days wanted their slaves to accept Christianity, because it promised them a great afterlife in heaven. With that thought planted in their minds, the slaves would accept all the crap the white man was dishing out to them!

Malcolm X also hated the way black people tried to imitate the whites in the forlorn and ridiculous hope that they would be accepted as equals. He particularly hated the way blacks tried to straighten their hair with harsh chemicals, and even bleached their skin in an effort to look white.

In 1965, Malcolm published *The Autobiography of Malcolm X*, a bestseller that told his story from childhood to his conversion to Islam. Some of his stories were shocking, including the lengths to which he and his friends would go to straighten their hair. The conk was a hairstyle popular among African-American men from the 1920s to the 1960s. Achieving it involved applying lye and other harsh chemicals to the scalp, which burned it almost beyond endurance, wearing a bandana on the head all day until the conk took, and then applying huge quantities of grease and brushing it through repeatedly. "We looked ridiculous," he said, and he urged black people to forget the conk and to wear their hair in its natural state. By the end of the 1960s, almost every African-American wore his or her hair natural, in an "Afro."

Malcolm X also hated the words "colored" and "Negro." These were words the white people used, supposedly in an effort to be *nice*, pretending to cover up the fact that black people were, um, black. "We should be proud of our skin color," Malcolm said repeatedly in his speeches. In one of his addresses that he gave when he was in a mellow mood, he told his black audience, "You need to stop thinking you are inferior to the white people. You are *better* than the white people. Do you know they lie in the sun all day just trying to get to look like you?"

By the end of the 1960s, the expression "Black is Beautiful" was part of black culture. There was also the Black Power movement, which demanded that black people take control of their own destinies, that they elect their own leaders, and that they stand up for their rights, even using violence if necessary. Militant groups such as the Black Panthers emerged ready to engage in "armed defense of the ghetto" against the police who, they believed, targeted black people for brutal treatment.

By the late 1960s, a new paradigm in race relations had emerged because of Malcolm X. Black people were no longer asking for equality, they were demanding it. Blacks who acted the least bit subservient to whites were denigrated as Uncle Toms. At the end of *Uncle Tom's Cabin*, you may recall that Tom took his whipping, and he even forgave Simon Legree. Now, no black man would take a whipping and forgive. I recall a cartoon showing a young black man with a huge Afro admonishing a wide-eyed young black child. The older man says, "Look, I don't care if my name is Tom and I'm your uncle, DO NOT CALL ME 'UNCLE TOM'!"

In the early 1970s, one of the cultural shifts we saw was the emergence of white people perming their hair to mimic the Afro—white people trying to look black! If only Malcolm X had lived to see what his words had accomplished.

I hope this chapter is proof that words—beautiful words, carefully chosen words—can have a huge impact and that they often propel people, and the country, in new directions. I hope the stories about these famous speakers and writers have sparked your interest. Perhaps these individuals can even serve as role models for how to be a great *wordsmith*. If you aspire to any kind of success in life, even in a field as number oriented as engineering or finance, you have to be able to communicate effectively, and words play an important role in doing so. Why not learn from the great men and women whose words accomplished much in American history?

CHAPTER X
THE POWER OF IMAGES

Not everyone is a personal witness to a particular event, so we depend on accurate descriptions and images to tell the story. Early on, artists—and later, photographers—performed an invaluable service to the public by showing what was happening in visual form. But there was, and is, a down side to this. Before 1835, an artist could dramatically affect people's opinions about an event by portraying it in a way that suited his own prejudices. In the age of photography and video, we like to think "the camera never lies," but there are numerous examples of how the camera *does* lie, or at least shades the truth.

In this chapter you will learn about the power some images have had on public perception and how, in a few instances, images have changed the course of history. People may never have been aware of what was happening if they hadn't seen "those damn pictures," as Boss Tweed derisively called them. Photographers' images often raised public awareness about what was happening at the time, and that was a good thing, but they occasionally focused on just one aspect of a particular event, or one moment in time, when in fact many things happened before and after the picture was taken, and in some cases, the result was a warped impression of reality.

Understanding the power some images have had in American history helps me to better evaluate the impact some photos have today. Some of these images will be the only experience of the event that people will have, but this also makes me a little bit skeptical of the veracity of these images, often displayed in the pages of a magazine. I am aware that some photos may not be telling the whole story.

PAUL REVERE MADE AN INCIDENT A MASSACRE.

In March of 1770, when British soldiers fought off an angry mob by firing their muskets into the crowd and killing five men, most Americans had not seen the event and had no clear image in their minds of what happened. Within a few weeks, the silversmith, Paul Revere, who himself had not seen the shootings, put out a drawing of what had occurred, at least according to his friend Sam Adams, who also was not present. In Revere's rendering, the British soldiers are standing in a disciplined line, firing their muskets in unison at the command of their commanding officer, who is standing next to their line with his sword held high in command posture. The wounded Americans are sprawled on the street, with blood pouring from them in rivers of red, the very same color as the uniforms of the scowling British soldiers.

Revere's picture was published all over the thirteen colonies. Soon, the incident was called the Boston Massacre, and Americans were convinced that the British had shot like a firing squad into the gathering of innocent Americans. Hardly anyone outside of Boston learned later that John Adams, cousin of Sam, had defended the soldiers in court and that the court had ruled that the soldiers were duly provoked by the actions of the unruly, brick-throwing mob.

In the years that followed, the American colonists often referred to the Boston Massacre as one of the primary examples of British tyranny. Paul Revere is most remembered for his midnight ride before the

Battles of Lexington and Concord in 1775, but it might be that his biggest contribution to the American struggle for independence was his rendering of what happened in front of the Old State House on March 5, 1770.

JACOB RIIS SHOWED AMERICANS THE FACES OF POVERTY.

In the late nineteenth century, a Danish immigrant named Jacob Riis, a New York reporter who worked for *The Sun*, took advantage of the new developments in photography, such as flash equipment, to take pictures of the poor people he encountered as he traveled around the city. The photographs he took were startling and depressing. Following are a few descriptions:

1. A group of young boys spending the night in a city stairwell, sleeping on the cold concrete, huddled together for warmth;

2. A back alley named Bandit's Roost, inhabited by several young thugs, several of whom glare menacingly at the camera;

3. Families cramped into tenement rooms, often eight or nine to a room, working on sewing garments or assembling cigars. The people are so dirty you can almost smell them in the photograph;

4. Men in a flophouse, crowded two or three to a mattress.

In 1890, Riis wrote a book titled *How the Other Half Lives*. In it, Riis vividly described the poverty and squalor that was widespread in New York and illustrated his text with his photographs. The effect was dramatic. No one who read his book was able to put it down without being profoundly affected by it.

Theodore Roosevelt, who became police commissioner of New York in 1895, read Riis' book. It was Riis who accompanied TR when he made his midnight rambles around the city to check on the work his police officers were doing, or not doing. When Roosevelt became president, he regarded Riis as his favorite "muckraker," a man who called the public and the government on its duty to improve things, but who did not wallow in despair or see only evil. Roosevelt wrote a glowing tribute to Riis that said, in part, "The countless evils which lurk in the dark corners of our civic institutions, which stalk abroad in the slums, and have their permanent abode in the crowded tenement houses, have met in Mr. Riis the most formidable opponent ever encountered by them in New York City."

In the years following the publication of Riis' photographs, reformers in many fields—those who worked to clean up the slums, those who advocated public works to clean up the water supply, those who worked for better care for the homeless, particularly homeless children, and those who demanded less corruption in government—all saw *How the Other Half Lives* as the definitive view of poverty in large American cities. Prior to Riis, people would hear about poverty, and a few had ventured into the Lower East Side and other known slums to see it for themselves, but now *everyone* could see very vividly just how heart-rending true poverty was.

DOROTHEA LANGE MADE THE GREAT DEPRESSION REAL.

When the Great Depression struck in the early 1930s, millions of people lost their jobs and many also lost their homes. In the farm regions of the Midwest, particularly Oklahoma, Texas, and Kansas, drought added to the people's miseries. Parched earth and dust storms drove people from their farms and onto the roads to California, where they hoped to find work. The countless stories of despair, fatigue, anxiety, and starvation were enough to make even the most callous person weep.

Yet there were millions of people in the country who were doing very well, thank you very much, during the Depression. They had very little awareness of the suffering that was going on hundreds of miles away on the farms, or down the road in the nearest city. Not everyone was unemployed. For many, the Depression meant lower prices at the stores and life going on pretty much as it always had.

Two such insulated people were my parents. My mother's father worked for Otis Elevator Company, and he had a very good job installing and then maintaining the elevators in the brand new Empire State Building in New York City. He also owned a few apartments that he rented. There was no suffering in the Elliott household. In fact, my grandmother got a new fur coat in 1933, when the Depression was at its worst. My father's father owned a grocery store in Quincy (MacDougall's Market). To be sure, he had many customers who could not pay their bills, and he was very generous about extending them credit, but he was always able to pay his own bills, and he, too, owned a few apartments to rent. There is a picture of my parents taken when they were juniors in high school (1933), showing each of them in snappy outfits and looking very satisfied with life. What was happening in the "dust bowl" concerned them not in the least.

Three years later, a photograph finally snapped my parents, and many others, out of their complacency. A photographer named Dorothea Lange, who worked for the Resettlement Administration, gave a picture to a newspaper editor in San Francisco that she had taken at a migrant camp where "pea pickers" had assembled to set up lean-tos and tents and look for work. In the photo, a mother, looking sad and care worn, holds her hand to her face while two of her children nestle their heads on her shoulder. The family is clearly struggling to survive.

First published in San Francisco, the photo made its way to the Resettlement Administration, which responded by sending thousands of pounds of food to the camp in California where Lange took the picture. Ultimately, the photo made its way into magazine articles, newspaper stories, and textbooks about the Depression. Even people as isolated and insulated as my parents saw it and became aware of the deprivation and torment other people were suffering.

The picture is often referred to as the iconic photo of the Great Depression: the "dust bowl" and the dispossessed who migrated to California looking for work. No other picture captured the despair and hopelessness quite as dramatically as this one did. Forty years after

Lange took the photograph, the identity of the migrant mother finally became known. She was Florence Owens Thompson, only thirty-two years old at the time; she looked to be in her forties. She died at the age of eighty, in 1983. Her life was unremarkable—she worked hard following the crops, picking vegetables, and raising a family of seven children—but she made the Depression real to many people, like my parents, who had no idea what it was like to be homeless and destitute.

FDR AND MACARTHUR USED SMOKING AS A PROP.

I hate cigarettes with a passion, and have hated them ever since the days when I was a kid. I remember my brother and me feeling trapped in the backseat of the car on a rainy day, with the windows closed and our parents up front, puffing away and filling the car with noxious fumes. During my first decade of teaching, the faculty room was always filled with smoke, and I could barely stand to be in there. It is one of the true miracles of the twentieth century that, by its end, smokers were relegated to the outdoors and the inside rooms were all declared, by law, to be smoke free.

Still, even I have to admit that cigarettes, cigars, and pipes, when used correctly, can be excellent props. Probably the two greatest practitioners of using the smoking habit to enhance their image were Franklin Roosevelt and Douglas MacArthur. One succeeded, the other failed.

Franklin Roosevelt was a chain smoker (which explains why he aged so quickly and died suddenly at age sixty-three), and he preferred to use a cigarette holder to keep the foul nicotine stains off his fingers. Of the thousands of photos taken of FDR, the one showing him sitting at the wheel of an automobile with his cigarette holder pointing straight up out of his smiling mouth is by far the most famous. In fact, the silhouette of that image even appears on the sign that welcomes people to Hyde Park, New York, the site of FDR's ancestral home. The impression it gives is one of a happy, self-assured man who has a positive approach to everything. The cigarette points straight up, as if to designate the direction the economy will go. The thirties and forties were a time when very few people had negative attitudes about smoking—more than half of all adults were smokers—so FDR's cigarette was an unsullied symbol of confidence and hope for the future. Most Americans loved the image they had of their president, with his jaunty, up-tilted cigarette.

General Douglas MacArthur's favorite purveyor of tobacco smoke was a corn cob pipe. He claimed that drawing smoke from the contraption increased his powers of concentration, and he liked to be seen as a general who was a thoughtful strategist. A battered officer's hat that he had worn through many campaigns and a pair of sunglasses completed the ensemble. MacArthur was very self-aggrandizing and he sought publicity at every opportunity. If he could be photographed with his pipe, sunglasses, and cap, all in place and looking bold, everything was great; he was pleased. He could envision himself as the brilliant military leader, heralded when he returned from the wars as the conquering hero, and crowned president by a grateful republic. The writer William Manchester, in his biography of the man, captured the essence of MacArthur's egocentric character. That is why he titled his book *American Caesar* and chose for the cover the famous picture of the general with all his props.

Unlike FDR, however, MacArthur was never quite able to get the public to buy into his image of himself. It is true that, after President Truman fired him, stores sold MacArthur kits, each of which contained a pipe, a cap, and sunglasses, so children could imitate the hero; however, the fad, as I've described earlier, quickly wore off, and most of those kits are no doubt in a landfill somewhere. The fact was that many of those who served in his army, as my father did, thought of MacArthur as a pompous ass.

The lesson I take from these two men is that the only way to present yourself in an admirable and iconic way is to do so naturally. If you try to *create* your image, most people will see right through you, and you could come off looking like a jerk.

THE 1960S WAS A DECADE
OF ICONIC IMAGES.

By the 1960s, photojournalism had reached full stride. Left far behind were the clumsy cameras Jacob Riis lugged into the slums. Now, high-speed and telephoto lenses made it possible to take action photos and shots from far away of people who did not even know they were being photographed. Beyond that, television cameras were now mobile, filming action as it occurred and transmitting the images instantly into almost every home in America. Nearly every day, new images were being created that would give lasting witness to the events taking place at the time.

The decade began with a photo of a vigorous looking John F. Kennedy, young, tan, his hair tousled by the wind, looking forward to his run for the presidency. The decade ended with a grainy shot of an astronaut, Neil Armstrong, taking one small step for man and one giant step for mankind onto the moon. In between, there were thousands of still photos and miles of film that captivated the nation and defined the events they depicted.

Several images stand out in my memory of the sixties. Three involved the Civil Rights Movement. The first was a photo of the Birmingham, Alabama police manhandling and searching Dr. Martin Luther King, Jr., whom they were arresting for holding a civil rights demonstration; the second was a photo of the Birmingham Fire Department using the powerful spray from the fire hoses to knock the black civil rights demonstrators off their feet and roll them across the pavement into telephone poles and buildings; and the third was the photo of Bull Connor's police dogs attacking black demonstrators on the streets of Birmingham, Alabama.

Birmingham was the epicenter of the Civil Rights Movement in 1963. I lived in Birmingham, Michigan, that year, which was a very different place. Or was it? Our town was lily white and rich. The only black people who ever appeared were the "colored" maids who took the buses out from Inner City Detroit in the mornings and who very quickly got themselves onto those same buses in the afternoon to go "back where they belonged." Our family didn't have a maid. My mother wanted to at least do *that* job, but my father always said that the maids who were hired by Birminghamites were lucky to have the rich white people around who could afford to give them jobs. I cringed when he said those words, even then. When I walked home from high school every afternoon, I passed the maids waiting at the bus stop and felt embarrassed. When I saw the demonstrators being hosed on the evening news, I felt sick. Those images affected me a great deal, but as I related earlier, I didn't do much to affect change, other than put an "I have a Dream" bumper sticker on my car. I'm sure that "impressed" the maids waiting at the bus stop when I drove by.

Other images that defined the decade for me were those that captured the Kennedy assassination. The photo of the president and his wife, she in a pretty pink suit (that was later to be soaked with blood), he looking tanned and cheerful, riding in the black presidential limousine and oblivious to what was about to happen to them, made all of us sad beyond words when it appeared the following week in *LIFE* magazine. Almost too painful to watch was the color film taken by amateur photographer Neil Zapruder, which captured the very moment when the bullets struck the president. It shows the reflexive movements of Kennedy's hands, the pitiful attempt by Jackie Kennedy to retrieve a piece of her husband's skull from the rear trunk lid, and the people in the background ducking for cover. Watching Jack Ruby gun down accused assassin Lee Harvey Oswald rattled the nation even more than we already were. Finally, watching President Kennedy's funeral on television brought the tragedy to its sad end. None of us who are old enough will ever forget the images: Jackie Kennedy, in black dress and veil; the two children, Caroline and John; three-year-old John saluting his father's coffin as it went by; the drums—none of us will ever forget those drums—beating a steady cadence as the caisson bearing the casket rolled along Pennsylvania Avenue and finally crossed the river to Arlington Cemetery.

The sixties took a terrible turn that week. A decade that seemed to hold so much promise was suddenly looking dark and foreboding. Sadly, the feeling we had was prophetic.

The following year, 1964, was the year of the Freedom Summer, described earlier. I shared with you the guilt I felt after the three civil rights workers were killed in Mississippi, and to that end, the image that really sticks in my mind, and in the minds of many others, I'm sure, is the photo that appeared in *LIFE* magazine of Sheriff Lawrence Rainey and Deputy Cecil Price awaiting court action for their part in the killings. Both men are smiling, and Rainey is reaching into a pouch of Red Man chewing tobacco. To them, the charges against them are a big joke. The photograph made me sick. When I found out they were never charged by Mississippi state authorities and were only brought up on charges of civil rights violations in federal court, I was really upset. Price only served four and a half years for delivering the three young men to the Ku Klux Klan to be murdered.

Nineteen sixty-four was also a presidential election year. A TV commercial that aired in the fall made a big impression not only on me, but on the entire country as well. The ad was for Democratic candidate Lyndon Johnson, who had succeeded John F. Kennedy after the terrible assassination and was now running for his own term as president. The ad was so controversial that it only aired once.

To understand the commercial and its impact, you have to know the situation in which the country found itself during the fall of 1964. A major issue in the presidential campaign was the war in Vietnam that Johnson inherited from Kennedy. During the summer, Johnson had responded to the attacks on two U.S. Navy vessels in the Gulf of Tonkin (off the coast of North Vietnam) by getting Congress to authorize the use of military force in Vietnam. As the fall election campaign heated up, Johnson's Republican opponent, Senator Barry Goldwater of Arizona, charged that Johnson was not doing enough to win the war in Vietnam. He asserted that if he were president, he would conduct the fight against the communists with more vigor. He even said he would use tactical nuclear weapons if that would win the war. Until Goldwater said that, I never knew there were such things as tactical nuclear weapons, and they sounded pretty scary. They would produce Hiroshima-type explosions, only not as powerful.

On the night of September 7, during the NBC Monday Night Movie, the Johnson campaign aired the ad we have since come to call "Daisy." The ad begins with a cute little two-year-old girl picking daisies in a field of flowers. As she holds a flower and counts the petals, a scary male voice can be heard when she reaches nine, and he begins counting down: nine … eight … seven … six … The little girl appears to see something in the sky and looks up. As the viewers look into her innocent eyes, the countdown reaches zero, a flash of light fills the screen, an explosion and a mushroom cloud appear, and the voice of President Johnson says, "These are the stakes: to make a world in which all of God's children can live, or to go into the dark. We must either love each other, or we must die." Another voice then says, "Vote for President Johnson on November 3. The stakes are too high for you to stay home."

The effect on those who saw the ad was dramatic. It was so powerful that even though the Johnson campaign pulled it, news programs for the next week continued to air it. I saw it replayed on the news; I did not see it on the Monday Night Movie. The effect was to make people believe that a vote for Johnson was a vote for reasonableness and peace; a vote for Goldwater was a vote for nuclear war and annihilation. During the next six weeks leading up to the election, Goldwater was never able to shed the image of a mad warmonger who would have his finger on the nuclear button if he were president. With that view in mind, which I thought was confirmed by some of Goldwater's militaristic comments and the fact that he had been a major general in the Air Force, I voted for Johnson. Johnson won the election with sixty percent of the vote. The image of the sweet little girl in the daisy field getting incinerated by a nuclear explosion had done its work!

Many of us who voted for Johnson felt betrayed the following year when he escalated our troop commitment to Southeast Asia and authorized

Operation Rolling Thunder, the bombing of North Vietnam. A vote for Johnson had not turned out to be a vote for loving each other.

The Vietnam War, which began escalating in 1965, produced hundreds of images in the sixties that shocked us all. In its own way, each photograph had a tremendous impact on the outcome of the struggle. One photograph in particular was the most appalling for me, and it turned me permanently against the war, but that was partly because, for many years, I didn't know the full story behind it.

In January 1968, just when we all thought the war might be winding down because the North Vietnamese and Vietcong hadn't conducted an offensive in six weeks, the Viet Cong launched surprise guerrilla attacks all over South Vietnam. They even sent a contingent into the American Embassy in Saigon. Although the Cong who breached the walls were all eventually killed, those of us back home were shocked that they had the ability to make such an attack. Photos of American soldiers battling the guerrilla invaders and crouching behind the shrubbery and well-manicured gardens in the embassy grounds were very unnerving, but the worst was yet to come.

On February 1, an NBC news photographer was on hand when South Vietnamese General Nguyen Ngoc Loan (pronounced Lo-ahn) calmly walked up to a handcuffed Vietcong prisoner in a plaid shirt, drew his .38 caliber revolver from its holster, and quickly shot the man in the head, killing him instantly. The photographer, Eddie Adams, caught the event on film, and the still photo of Loan pointing his gun, and the Vietcong man wincing as he anticipates what is about to happen to him, was shocking. Film footage of the execution showed the man in the plaid shirt crumble to the ground as blood from his head rolled out onto the street. General Loan re-holstered his pistol and walked away slowly. I remember thinking, "The general who is so cruelly shooting the poor man in handcuffs is the guy on *our* side. We're sacrificing our lives for *that* kind of person? This war is too ugly for me to support any longer; how can we be supporting such brutality?" The picture had the same effect on millions of other people across the country and around the world. I really believe the war was lost the day that photo appeared.

What I didn't know at the time was the back story of the photo. The guy in the plaid shirt was Nguyen Van Lem, a Viet Cong leader of a death squad who, earlier that day, had executed in cold blood a South Vietnamese colonel, Nguyen Tuan, and his entire family: his wife, his children, and his grandmother. The guy in the plaid shirt was not an innocent civilian; he was a killer who was fighting South Vietnamese and United States soldiers in civilian clothing. Since there was ongoing street fighting in Saigon at the time, General Loan's action, while brutal, was probably within the limits of the rules of war, and he was never prosecuted.

Eddie Adams always regretted the effect his picture had not so much on public perception of the war, but on the reputation of General Loan. Loan became infamous around the world. When the war ended, he was one of the ones who escaped from Vietnam and came to the United States. He opened a pizza restaurant in Virginia, but he had to close when people in the area became aware of who he was. He died in 1998, still vilified as the brutal executioner in the photo.

THE SEVENTIES WERE AN INCREDIBLE SHOW.

I usually think of the Vietnam War as a 1960s event, but it certainly extended into the seventies. My friend from elementary school, Tony Miller, died in Vietnam in 1971. All of the images of that war are depressing, unnerving, and gross, but there are two from the seventies that stand out: the Kent State shootings and the last day of the war, when defeat finally came. These last two photos completed the picture of the war, which was, for most of us who lived through it, the most ghastly experience in American history since the Civil War. (Of course, more Americans died in the two World Wars, but they at least died in successful causes.)

As the 1970s began, it seemed to many of us that the Vietnam War might at last be drawing to a close. President Nixon's Vietnamization policy of gradual withdrawal of U.S. troops was starting to produce fewer American casualties, and many of us were beginning to look forward to the day when we would be out of Vietnam entirely. But on April 30, 1970, Nixon went on television to announce that American forces would be going into Cambodia, the country just to the west of South Vietnam, in an effort to eliminate Vietcong supply bases. Despite Nixon's efforts to show that the Cambodian incursion would only last three months and would have limited objectives, many people across the country believed this was just another widening of the war and reacted with outrage. The negative reaction was particularly strong on college campuses.

At Kent State University in Ohio, students began demonstrating against the Cambodian invasion on Friday, May 1, and throughout the weekend, the demonstrations grew larger and more violent. On Saturday, the ROTC building was set on fire and student anti-war protesters cut the fire hoses in an attempt to keep the firefighters from extinguishing the blaze. On Saturday evening, Governor Rhodes called in the National Guard to keep order.

On Monday, May 4, a rally took place in the center of campus attended by almost two thousand students. The guardsmen ordered the students to disperse, and when they refused, a group of seventy-seven troops with fixed bayonets began advancing on the crowd. Confusion ensued, with some students retreating and others slowly advancing toward the guardsmen. Suddenly, several of the guardsmen knelt to the ground and opened fire on the crowd. Of the seventy-seven troops, twenty-nine fired their weapons. The results were devastating. Four students were shot dead, and nine were seriously injured, including one who was hit in the back and permanently paralyzed from the chest down. Not all of the students who were hit were part of the demonstration; some were simply watching or were on their way to class.

News photographers, of course, were all around that day, and several got photos of the guardsmen shooting. One of them, John Filo, saw a girl rush over to one of the students who had been shot and was lying motionless on the ground. (It was Jeffrey Miller, who had been shot in the mouth and died instantly.) The girl, a young runaway who was not even a student at Kent State, kneeled next to Miller, realized he was dead, spread her arms, and screamed in horror. Just as she did that, Filo took the picture. Within days, the image of Miller lying dead on the pavement and the girl, Mary Ann Vecchio, formed the story of what happened at Kent State in everyone's minds.

The immediate response, of course, was horror, and then came anger. Across the country, student protests erupted on thousands of college campuses. Many schools had to close their doors or cancel graduation plans. On May 9, one hundred thousand people demonstrated against the war in Washington, D.C. It appeared to some of us that the country was disintegrating into a civil war.

In the years that followed, for most people who were old enough to be aware of what was happening in May of 1970, the photo of Ms. Vecchio anguishing over the body of Jeffrey Miller is all we think of when we recall Kent State. What we fail to recall is that eight of the guardsmen were indicted for manslaughter by a grand jury, but the charges were dropped when a judge ruled the evidence was insufficient. The result of all the legal proceedings, including lawsuits filed against the guardsmen by families of students who were killed and wounded, was the payment of a total of six hundred seventy-five thousand dollars to the families and a statement of regret for what happened. Public opinion polls generally showed a slight majority of the American people sympathetic to the guardsmen. I thought the guardsmen truly overreacted and should have, at least, fired warning shots into the air before they did anything deadly.

In the passage of time, the Kent State shootings take their place in history alongside the Boston Massacre as examples of what happens when cruel authority figures possess lethal power and use it against innocent citizens. I have kept this in mind when incidents occur such as the police shooting in Ferguson, Missouri, in 2014. Officer Darren Wilson, a white man, was accused of wantonly shooting a robbery suspect, Michael Brown, a black man, who, it was said, had his hands up and was surrendering. Pictures were drawn and paintings were produced of Brown with his hands in the air and pleading, "Don't shoot!" The immediate reaction from many people was outrage against Wilson and police officers in general. Many people assumed that Wilson, acting on racist impulses, shot Brown with no cause. Aware of what transpired legally after the Boston Massacre and the Kent State shootings, I deferred judgment. In the weeks after the incident, state and federal grand juries exonerated Officer Wilson and dismissed the charges. Personally, after reading all of the eye witness accounts, I think Wilson could have handled the situation better, but I also think Brown was not totally innocent and was not standing motionless with his hands in the air. Being aware of the way photos sometimes skew a story kept me from condemning officer Wilson in my classes and among my friends and family.

The ugly, disgusting, and traumatic Vietnam War finally ended in April 1975. President Nixon's Secretary of State, Henry Kissinger, had negotiated a peace accord with the North Vietnamese in January 1973. It stipulated a cease fire, return of American prisoners of war, and North Vietnamese troops to remain in place in South Vietnam. The last stipulation set up a ticking time bomb; the fragile cease fire held until early 1975, when the North Vietnamese Army and the Vietcong renewed their offensive against the South. On April 29, 1975, as the communists advanced into the outskirts of the city, American helicopters evacuated as many South Vietnamese people who had supported the government as possible. There was little doubt that these people would be treated severely by the communists once Saigon fell. Many photos were taken that day, but one in particular captured the moment of defeat for posterity. The photo depicts a chopper on the roof of a building near the American Embassy, awaiting dozens of people, eager to board it. They are lined up on a ladder and crowded onto the rooftop, and they are all desperate to get on board. They do not want to be left behind, but, clearly, there will not be enough room for all of them. Some will be stranded, left to whatever their fate may be when the communists arrive.

When I stared at the picture on the day it appeared in *Newsweek* magazine, I was deeply saddened. We had spent twenty years in Vietnam and lost more than fifty-eight thousand lives, only to have it come to this, an ignominious flight from a doomed city. It was heartening to know that several thousand South Vietnamese bravely took to small boats to escape, and quite a few made it to Thailand and other safe havens. These "boat people" came to the United States in large numbers, and they all had sad tales of family members who drowned or had to be left behind. The man who runs the nail salon where my wife goes was one of the boat people. He told her of his harrowing escape, and he feels bitter that the American Army did not destroy the Vietcong.

DID WE SEE THE START OF WORLD WAR III?

I could describe dozens of images of the last forty years that have played a large part in establishing history as we know it; however, there is one image that I believe will go down as the start of the third world war, and it may also be the image that sets the course of history for the entire twenty-first century. That image, of course, is the one burned in the minds of everyone on September 11, 2001, of the jets crashing into the World Trade Center towers. That ghastly attack touched off a war between radical Islam and the West. That war has seen many permutations in the last fifteen years, but in broad outline, it is radical Islamic terrorists attacking their perceived enemies across the world: in the Middle East, in Europe, in Africa, and in the United States. No one is calling this World War III, as far as I know, but it will not surprise me at all, should I live that long, if the history books of the future show a picture of the assassination of Archduke Franz Ferdinand as the event that began World War I, grainy photos of the Japanese attack on the U.S. Navy base at Pearl Harbor as the event that brought the U.S. into World War II, and clear color photos of the World Trade Center buildings silhouetted against a clear blue sky with a jetliner crashing into one of them as the event that started World War III.

There are so many images that have defined events and determined the course of history; an entire book could be devoted to them. I hope that I have clearly demonstrated that images, whether drawings, paintings, photographs, or motion pictures, have tremendous power. They frequently determine reality for many, and they are sometimes the only evidence people have that an event occurred. More importantly, they sometimes represent a "reality" that is not quite, or not at all, what it seems to be. The more we know about the images in history, the better we are able to evaluate the images of our own time.

On a final note, what is truly troubling today is that we may never know if a photo or video footage of a particular event represents any reality at all. At least in 1968, the photo of General Loan shooting the Vietcong in the head was a real photo and the issue we had to deal with was why did he do it? Today, with the sophisticated technologies, we would have to first be skeptical about whether the event even occurred. The old adage "Don't believe everything you read" doesn't go far enough. We should add to it "Don't believe everything you see."

CHAPTER XI
TO DIE FOR

Dialogue on the TV show Frasier:

Niles Crane: *"Dad, the food at that restaurant is to die for."*

Marty Crane: *"Son, your family or your country are to die for; food is to eat."*

1960s anti-war poster: *What if they held a war and nobody came?*

In the two hundred forty years of our country's existence, Americans have been called upon to give their lives in twelve major wars and dozens of other smaller military enterprises. On each of those occasions, the people had to decide if the objectives of the conflict were worthy of their support. After all, they or their loved ones might end up dead because our leaders decided our country needed to fight. A thorough study of our country's motives for using military force has helped me get a better grip on the question "under what circumstances would I be willing to give my own life or see my family and friends risk theirs?"

In this chapter I will give a brief history of the wars our country has fought and analyze how I would have responded, had I lived in those times. In preparing this, it has surprised me a little bit to realize what wars I would have willingly fought, which wars I would have tried to avoid, and which wars I would absolutely have opposed. Along the way, I will take up the one war in our history during which I actually was called upon to serve in the Armed Forces. It was then that all my knowledge of the history of our country's past military engagements helped inform my decision about what I would do.

THE REVOLUTIONARY WAR, 1775-1783: WOULD I BE A REBEL OR A LOYALIST?

In the 1760s and 1770s, the American colonists were becoming increasingly roiled about the way their rights as Englishmen were being abused by the British government in London. Beginning with the Stamp Act in 1765, Parliament repeatedly attempted to raise revenue in the colonies. The colonists, in response, were angry that they would have to pay taxes passed by a legislative body in London in which they had no voice. The feud began to come to a head when young men in Boston threw tea owned by the British East India Tea Company into the harbor and the British government responded by imposing military rule on the city. Soldiers would run the city until the tea was paid for. At that point, the Americans began to meet in a Continental Congress in Philadelphia to decide on united action.

The situation in and around Boston grew increasingly tense until, in April of 1775, a detachment of British soldiers marched out of the city to seize the weapons they believed the rebels were storing in Concord and to capture the major rebel leaders. On the green in Lexington, the British regulars fired into a gathering of Minutemen, killing eight of them. Later, at a small bridge in Concord, Americans drew British blood for the first time when they shot and killed two British soldiers in a brief skirmish. After that, the embattled farmers killed many more soldiers as the pitiable Redcoats made the long march back to Boston. The time was clearly coming when all Americans were going to have to choose sides.

Two months after the battles of Lexington and Concord, the British Army marched up Breed's Hill to dislodge the Americans who were entrenched there. The ensuing Battle of Bunker Hill was very bloody, and it was now becoming clear that the issues that set the colonists against their mother country would be decided by "blows," to use King George III's word.

Still, it was over a year before the American colonists actually declared their independence from Britain. At that point, July 1776, it became very difficult to remain uncommitted. You would have to decide if you supported the revolution and if you would enlist in one of the armies in the field. General Washington, General Gates, and others were always looking for volunteers.

If I had been a young man living in Boston in the 1760s and 1770s, I probably would have sympathized, to a degree, with the radicals, the Sons of Liberty, as they called themselves, but I would not have been part of the mob harassing the British soldiers, and I certainly would not have thrown tea into the harbor. I know this because when I was in my twenties and thirties, I agreed with some of what the counter culture stood for, especially opposition to the Vietnam War, but I was never a *hippie*, and I certainly did not set fire to ROTC buildings!

When the move for independence started taking hold, I probably would *not* have joined. Thomas Paine's *Common Sense* might have convinced me to join, because his arguments were very persuasive, but I would have seen many advantages to staying with Britain, especially the security the British Army offered against other hostile countries. Furthermore, living in Boston, I probably would have had to make my decision before I was able to read Paine's pamphlet. Most likely, when the British Army evacuated Boston in March of 1776 and a thousand *loyalists* went with them to Nova Scotia, I would have been among them. If I were older than forty at the time, I *know* I would have gone to Canada. It would not have seemed worth it to me to fight a war—to kill or be killed—to make our lives marginally better or, quite possibly, lose and be executed.

It is interesting to note that some of my MacDougall ancestors immigrated to the United States from Canada in the early 1900s. It would not surprise me to learn that they were descendants of loyalists who had fled to Nova Scotia in 1776. If that's the case, then my feeling that I would not have been a revolutionary in 1776 is inherited. It seems my innate attitude is why shed blood if the situation isn't all that bad and can be resolved peacefully?

WAR OF 1812:
WOULD I FIGHT IN MR. MADISON'S WAR?

In June of 1812, President Madison asked Congress to declare war on Britain because the British Navy was stopping American ships on the high seas, taking cargo they deemed to be contraband (articles of war), and impressing American sailors into their navy. He was responding to the War Hawks in Congress who were mostly from the West and who were angry about the maritime incidents, but even more furious about the British support for Indian raids on American settlements along the frontier. The War Hawks also proclaimed that Canada was ripe for picking and a victory over England would enable us to add that vast region to our domain.

The War of 1812 is often called America's second war for independence because even though the fighting was inconclusive, we held our own against our former mother country, we won some significant battles, and we had a galaxy of heroes to adore: Andrew Jackson, William Henry Harrison, Oliver Hazard Perry, and the great warship the USS Constitution (Old Ironsides). Never mind that our attempts to invade Canada were utter disasters and that the British-occupied Washington drove the president and Congress out of the capital city and burned the executive mansion. The people had a new love for their country, a new love for the flag, and a poem to go with those loves: the "Star-Spangled Banner."

If I had lived in New England then, as I have for most of my life, I would have opposed the war against Britain, and I certainly would not have volunteered to fight in it. I would have found plenty of support for my view among my neighbors, who would have felt our trade was still prosperous in spite of British interference. A war would only shut trade down completely and create an economic depression, which it did. Britain's war with Napoleon would end, and when it did, English interference with our trade and impressment of our sailors would end also. Besides, if we fought and lost, which was very possible since Britain was one of the most powerful nations on Earth, we might very well lose some of the hard-won gains we had made in the Revolutionary War. Furthermore, if we fought Great Britain, we would actually be allying ourselves with Napoleon! Did we really want to do that?

I would not, however, have joined the Federalists in New England, who opposed the war so much that they actually talked about withdrawing the New England states from the Union. This idea of secession would have bothered me. Hardly anything was provocative enough to break up our country.

In studying our country's first two wars, it pains me to realize the anguish so many people suffered, not to mention all the lives that were lost, since discussion and compromise may have gone far to resolve the issues at hand. I'm not a "peace at any price" person. I understand that principles must be upheld and that sometimes fighting for a cause in the present helps to avoid a greater fight in the future, but I don't think the Revolutionary War or the War of 1812 involved either of those two situations. Surely the rights of the Americans could have somehow been resolved peacefully. To support my claim, I offer the example of Canada, which did not fight a war with Britain, and in 1867, it very peacefully became a dominion with self-rule. Couldn't we have done the same?

I am also quite a bit of an Anglophile (a person who loves Great Britain). The British had a long-standing tradition of upholding liberty and the rights of man. Recall in the chapter on the power of words that Jefferson got all of his ideas for the Declaration of Independence from the Englishman John Locke. Imagine how things might have been different if we and Canada had *both* remained in the British Empire! The history of the nineteenth and twentieth centuries would certainly have been very different. Hitler might never have come into power in Germany; if he had, we, the great Transatlantic British Empire, would have crushed him like a bug! Just sayin'.

THE MEXICAN WAR, 1846-1848:
WOULD I FIGHT IN MR. POLK'S WAR?

James K. Polk came into the White House in 1845 with territorial expansion occupying most of his brain. Expansion occupied his thinking twenty-four seven, and he wouldn't rest until he had acquired Texas, Oregon, and California for the United States. Any Mexicans, Englishmen, and, of course, Indians, who happened to object had just better get out of the way!

Texas came into the Union even before Polk took power. Congress voted to annex it on March 1, 1845, and Polk took the oath of office on the fourth. The Mexican government was furious because it had never recognized the independence of its northeastern province when Texas proclaimed its independence in 1836.

Now, Polk immediately began taking the steps to acquire California from Mexico. He sent a representative, John Slidell, to Mexico City with an offer to buy all of the territory between Texas and the Pacific Ocean. The Mexican government refused to even talk to Slidell and reasserted its continued possession of Texas. Polk was enraged. He was about to ask Congress for a declaration of war against Mexico on the basis of Mexican intransigence, but then a better cause for war presented itself.

General Zachary Taylor, commanding U.S. troops in Texas, moved his force from the Nueces River, which Mexico said was the southern boundary of Texas, down to the Rio Grande River (one hundred fifty miles south), which the Texans claimed was their southern boundary. On April 25, 1846, a Mexican cavalry detachment of two thousand men attacked an American patrol of approximately seventy men, killing sixteen. When word of this incident reached Polk he immediately sent a war message to Congress: "American blood (has been) shed on

American soil." Congress agreed, voting to declare war against Mexico on May 13, 1846.

The Mexican War was a lopsided victory for the United States. In a year and a half, the Mexican Army was defeated and American troops were occupying Mexico City. The Treaty of Guadalupe-Hidalgo that ended the war gave the United States immense territory: the Rio Grande as the southern boundary of Texas, California, and the lands between California and Texas (the present-day states of Nevada, Arizona, Utah, and New Mexico).

This is one war I am sure I would not have supported in any way. I'm sure I would have been a disciple of William Lloyd Garrison and the other abolitionists who saw the war for what it was: a flat out war of aggression fueled mostly by the greed of the slave interests who wanted to acquire additional territory for slavery and slave states. Polk was a slaveholder, and most of the soldiers who volunteered for the Army were Southerners. The officers were mostly from the South, and their names constitute a roster of the major Confederate leaders in the Civil War that came thirteen years later, including Robert E. Lee and Jefferson Davis.

When Abraham Lincoln became a congressman in 1847, he opposed the war and demanded to know how Polk could claim the United States had been attacked. "Where was the spot on American soil where American blood was shed?" he asked, noting that the lands between the Rio Grande and the Nueces Rivers were disputed. Lincoln did not approve of a war of aggression, especially one that had the extension of slavery as its goal. The issue of slavery's extension had already caused enough quarrels over the Louisiana territories; we certainly did not need new lands for the sections to quibble over.

If I had lived in Concord, Massachusetts, I might have joined Henry David Thoreau in refusing to pay taxes that would support this immoral war. Perhaps I would have spent the night in jail with Thoreau discussing civil disobedience and the prospects for the abolitionist cause. Most people in New England opposed the Mexican War for the reasons I think I would have opposed it. For them, it was Mr. Polk's war, a war he provoked for the selfish interests of slave owners. My opposition to the Mexican War makes it clear to me that I would oppose any war that was fueled by lust for conquest or simple greed.

THE AMERICAN CIVIL WAR, 1861-1865:
WOULD I FIGHT TO SAVE THE UNION? WOULD I FIGHT TO FREE THE SLAVES?

When the Confederate States of America attacked Fort Sumter in Charleston Harbor on April 12, 1861, President Lincoln issued a call for volunteers to "put down the southern rebellion." My immediate response would probably have been to wait before I signed up, because Lincoln was making it clear that the slave system would remain intact if the rebellion could be put down. It was simply going to be a war to save the Union. William Lloyd Garrison believed slavery would be doomed if the South did not have the Union to protect its interests, and so he had been advocating *northern* secession for years. In the first weeks after Fort Sumter, I would have advocated letting the seven seceding states go in peace. They would not last long as an independent slave republic. They would come back into the Union when they saw the other slave states, who did *not* leave, doing reasonably well under President Lincoln.

Garrison soon became a supporter of Lincoln's war effort, however, because he could see that the president would eventually have to develop an emancipation policy if the South were not defeated quickly. By 1862, after the war had been grinding on for more than a year, it became obvious to Lincoln that he needed to adopt a more drastic approach to weaken the South, and he began taking steps towards emancipation. Finally, in September 1862, he announced a Preliminary Emancipation Proclamation, stating that as of January 1, 1863, all slaves living in areas that were then in rebellion against the Union would be "thenceforth and forever free." Legalistic and cautious as always, Lincoln was giving the seceded states one hundred days to reconsider their rash acts and come back into the Union without losing their slaves. None of the Confederate states took him up on his offer, and on January 1, 1863, the war officially became a war against slavery as well as a war to restore the Union.

At this point, I would have been willing, if not eager, to join the Union ranks. Now the war had a moral element to it that I could get behind. Saving the Union with slavery still intact did not do it for me. Saving the Union with freedom for all of the four million slaves was a cause worth fighting, and, yes, dying for. The brutal way the war was fought in the final two years made it very likely I *would* have perished on behalf of the slaves.

As I write these words, I find myself wondering if I am being contradictory in *not* being willing to fight for the Declaration of Independence—freedom for the Americans from British rule—and being *willing* to fight for freedom for the slaves? My answer to that is that I don't think freedom was an issue for the American colonists. Democracy was part of the English heritage; certainly, better protections of our *rights as Englishmen* could have been worked out without a war. The slaves, on the other hand, were in the iron grip of their owners and the Confederate States of America. Without a military defeat of the Confederacy, it was likely that slavery would continue for many years to come. It is worth noting here that the British government had freed the slaves in the British Empire in 1833. If we had remained in the British Empire, slavery might well have ended thirty years before it did— another reason we should not have fought a war for independence in 1776.

THE SPANISH-AMERICAN WAR, 1898:
WOULD I JOIN THE "SPLENDID LITTLE WAR"?

In the 1890s, Americans were aroused to a fever pitch over what was happening in Cuba. Stories were emanating from that sorry island of Cubans rebelling against Spanish rule and Spanish military authorities herding the people into concentration camps and beating and starving them. American newspapers such as Hearst's New York *Journal* and Pulitzer's New York *World* were vying with each other to put out the most lurid stories possible, even if they weren't true. "You supply the pictures," Hearst supposedly told a reporter, "I'll supply the war."

In February 1898, the USS Maine, which President McKinley had sent to Havana Harbor to protect American interests in Cuba, suddenly exploded, and two hundred sixty-two American seamen lost their lives. The newspapers and many politicians blamed the Spanish for the incident—it was found in the 1970s to have been a boiler explosion—and demanded a declaration of war against Spain. Finally, in April, McKinley gave in and the people had their war. No one was happier about this than Assistant Secretary of the Navy Theodore Roosevelt, who immediately resigned his post, enlisted, and began organizing a volunteer cavalry regiment that eventually became dubbed The Rough Riders.

The war lasted only four months. Roosevelt got his chance to prove himself in battle; the Spanish military was completely humiliated; and the United States took possession of Cuba (temporarily), Puerto Rico, Guam, and the Philippines. With great strategic acquisitions, coming from a war with so few casualties and coming so quickly, what was not to like? No wonder Secretary of State Hay called it a "splendid little war."

This is one war for which I might actually have enlisted. I wouldn't have believed all the atrocious stories in the newspapers, but even if they were only half true, the Cuban people were suffering grievously at the hands of their Spanish rulers. Theodore Roosevelt was the kind of leader who would have captured my imagination. The thought of following such a man to liberate an oppressed people would have stirred my blood.

If the United States Army had sent me to the Philippines after the war in Cuba ended to help put down the Filipino rebellion against American rule, I would have had a very different reaction. Emilio Aguinaldo and his fellow Filipinos thought we were fighting Spain to set them free, as we had the Cubans. When he was told otherwise, he launched a rebellion against U.S. forces that lasted almost three years. It took one hundred thousand American soldiers to put down the Filipino revolt, and it was one of the most brutal wars in American history. Aguinaldo's insurgents fought guerrilla style, melting into the jungle after each encounter with American troops and blending in with the local populations. Desperate for information about guerrilla plans, American soldiers used torture, such as the infamous water torture, to extract details from prisoners. Attempting to enforce our will against an alien culture in Southeast Asia among people who deeply resented our presence should have taught us a lesson about our limitations. Sadly, it didn't, and we went into another part of Southeast Asia fifty years later, as if the Filipino War had never happened.

I would not have wanted to be part of this war, but I would have stuck it out. Desertion gets you shot. Also, I would have told myself that if we didn't take over the Philippines, some other power, certainly nastier than us, such as Germany, would. Furthermore, the ultimate American plan was probably going to benefit the Filipinos in the long run. We would build better roads, bridges, railroads, harbors, and schools. All of this did come about, and we set the Philippines free in 1946.

I looked back to our country's experience in the Filipino War years later when deciding how I felt about U.S. involvement in Vietnam.

WORLD WAR I, 1917-1918:
WOULD I FIGHT TO MAKE THE WORLD SAFE FOR DEMOCRACY?

The First World War raged on for two and a half years before the United States got into it. During that time, the armies of the Central Powers (Germany and Austria-Hungary) and the Allied Powers (Britain, France, and Russia) suffered terrible casualties. The armies on the Western Front (northern France) were dug in with trenches running from the English Channel to the Swiss border. Most Americans were not fully aware of the horrors of the Western Front, but we knew for sure that we did not want to be part of it. In 1915, less than a year after the shooting started, we almost got into it when a German submarine sank the Lusitania, a British passenger liner, with Americans on board—one hundred twenty-eight perished—but President Wilson got the Germans to apologize and promise not to do such a thing again, and the crisis passed. The following year, Wilson was reelected on the slogan "He kept us out of war."

I would have been very glad we were neutral. Even though I might not have known all the details, just the broad outlines of what was happening—the machine guns, the poison gas, the barbed wire—would have made me quite glad to care very little about which side won, as long as we didn't have to get involved.

Our happy isolation came to an end in 1917, however, when the German government, in an effort to starve England into submission, decided to begin sinking American merchant ships headed for Britain. If this brought the United States into the war, their generals reasoned, they were sure they would have England on its knees before any American troops arrived in France. To make matters worse, the British intercepted a telegram sent by the German foreign office to their ambassador in Mexico, instructing him to offer an alliance with Mexico if war began between the United States and Germany. Should the alliance prove successful in the war, Mexico would receive the lost territories of Texas and California as prizes. Naturally, this arrogance outraged all Americans.

In February and March of 1917, German subs sank several unarmed American ships, and Wilson reached the end of his patience. On April 2, he went up to Capitol Hill and delivered a speech to Congress, asking it to declare war on the Central Powers. He cited the submarine attacks on our ships, but he also gave our involvement in the war an idealistic motive. We would defeat the German and Austro-Hungarian empires and "make the world safe for democracy." Congress cheered and four days later passed a declaration of war.

There is a story in my family regarding the start of U.S. involvement in World War I. My mother was born nine days after the declaration of war. Soon after that my grandfather volunteered for the U.S. Army and left to go to basic training. My grandmother stood in the doorway with her new baby in her arms, cursing my grandfather as he strode off in his khaki uniform. I doubt there was much idealism in his action. He was only eighteen years old and was probably looking for adventure and a chance to duck the responsibilities of being a father to a new baby.

If I had been a young man at the time, I certainly would have supported the war effort, but I probably would have waited to get drafted. I want to help a worthy cause, but I'll admit that I would have been pretty afraid of those machine guns, to say the least. When my draft notice came, I would have willingly, if fearfully, answered the call, because I would have been convinced that a German victory would be bad for the civilized world. The Kaiser was easy to hate; the villainous mustache and pointy helmet made him an icon of evil. More rationally, it really did seem to be a war of the democracies against the tyrants: Britain, France, and the United States were all democracies, as was Russia, now that the Czar had been overthrown. We didn't know yet that Russia would be a communist country soon. Unlike my grandfather, I would have had real idealism in my soldiering.

When the war ended, I would have been sorely disappointed in the peace that was made. The Treaty of Versailles was not really based on Wilson's fourteen-point plan for a generous peace, and it was sure to create a desire for revenge in Germany, and then, because Wilson refused to compromise with the Senate on the League of Nations, the United States did not join the League and we left the world to solve its problems without us. I think I would have gone back to civilian life totally disgusted that we had suffered so much and had achieved so little.

As a student of history, I see a real lesson to be learned from the First World War: It is very possible to win the war but lose the peace. When we get into a war, we need to go all out to win, of course, and then we need to stay engaged in the issues so that we can make the peace a lasting one. We did go all out to win World War I, but the politicians in Washington blew it when it was over. The Republicans did not want to support Wilson's League of Nations unless Wilson compromised with them, and Wilson was too stubborn to do so. The result, as Wilson himself predicted, was another world war that my father had to fight just twenty-four years after my grandfather had marched off.

WORLD WAR II, 1941-1945:
WOULD I FIGHT THE *GOOD* WAR?

In the 1930s, Hitler came to power in Germany and began a military buildup and the annexation of Germany's immediate neighbors, Austria and Czechoslovakia. Meanwhile, in Asia, Japan invaded and annexed Manchuria and then began a major invasion of China. People in the United States wanted nothing to do with any of this. When Roosevelt proclaimed in a 1937 speech that the peace loving nations of the world should "quarantine" the aggressors, a huge uproar ensued, as people screamed he was leading us to war. Roosevelt backed off and said no more for two years. Congress had passed neutrality legislation designed to prevent any of the problems that dragged us into the First World War from dragging us into another war. The Neutrality Acts said, in sum, no Americans on ships of nations at war (no Lusitania this time!), no loans or credits to nations at war, and no sales of weapons to nations at war. This time, if a storm broke out in Europe or Asia, the United States would be like a turtle: We would withdraw into our shell and wait for the storm to blow over.

When war came in 1939, Americans were shocked at the ferocity of it. Hitler conquered Poland in less than a month. The following spring, he subdued most of Western Europe, including France, and began aerial bombardments of Britain in preparation for an invasion of the only country that still stood against him. By the fall of 1940, German planes were bombing London every night, and Britain appeared to be going down to defeat.

As we watched all of this from our "safe" perch three thousand miles away, most Americans were willing to offer some help to Britain—the British could buy arms from us on a "cash and carry" basis—but we still wanted to remain aloof from any fighting. There were even some Americans, such as Charles Lindbergh and Joseph Kennedy, the U.S. Ambassador to Britain and John Kennedy's father, who foresaw a German victory in the near future, and they were okay with that!

The Americans I admire the most in the World War II story are the young men who went over to England in the days of the German bombings of London (the blitz) and volunteered to serve in the Royal Air Force and fight the Germans. They were the ones who saw very early on the evil the world was up against and were willing to give their lives, as some of them did, to fight it. The German air forces (Luftwaffe) never did gain control of the skies over the English Channel, and without that control, Hitler never attempted to invade Great Britain. When Churchill said, "Never have so many owed so much to so few," he was referring to the Royal Air Force, but that included a few stalwart Americans.

As 1941 wore on, the Axis powers were winning on every front. Japan was penetrating deep into China, and England was on the brink of starvation because German U-boats were active in the Atlantic, cutting off trade. By now, the United States had a military draft in place and men were being called into the armed services. No one in my family, including my father, was called at this point, and they were hoping the war would end before they were called. I'm not sure how they thought that would happen, at least not without a victory by Germany. Had I been in their shoes, I probably would have waited as well. We have to realize today that in 1941, no one quite knew the horrors of the Nazi and Japanese systems. The existence of concentration camps was thought to be an exaggerated rumor, and most Americans were unaware of the Japanese atrocities in China. Had I known how brutal the Nazis and the Japanese were, I might have enlisted and not waited to be drafted. If ever there were nations that needed to be defeated, it was the Axis Powers.

Finally, The Japanese woke us up with their attack on our naval base at Pearl Harbor. This was a clarion call to arms that I'm sure I would have heeded. I would have enlisted even before I was drafted. No one who served in World War II was happy that the war came, but almost every veteran I ever talked to after the war was over was glad that he had been part of it and had helped defeat the most evil forces that ever existed. When I was a kid in the fifties, I heard stories from the men in our neighborhood who had been all over the world: Italy, France, North Africa, Guadalcanal, and the Philippines. They fought evil on a thousand different fronts, and they saved their old uniforms, combat badges, and service knives as mementos. One man, who lived down the street in Melrose, Massachusetts, had a giant Nazi flag that he had torn off a building in Belgium. I certainly would have been willing to die to help win that huge struggle against evil.

Along with the men, the women had stories to tell as well. Not only did they battle extreme loneliness when their husbands or boyfriends were off in the service, they also had to carry much of the burden of keeping the home front going, serving in the medical corps all over the world, and manufacturing the equipment and supplies the armed forces would need. Rosie the Riveter was a fictional character, but she actually existed in factories all across the country. Children, too, were enlisted to scour the neighborhoods for scrap metal and to buy war stamps at school to support the war effort. Many people who lived through World War II actually remember the period with some nostalgia, because everyone was pulling together for a very worthy cause.

When it became evident in the final stages of the war what the concentration camps in Europe were like and how the Japanese treated their prisoners in their disgusting camps, the sacrifices that were made to defeat these demons became even more acceptable. This truly was a war that had to be fought, and those who fought it, against odds that seemed almost impossible when it began, truly were the Greatest Generation.

World War II ended with the signing of surrender documents and huge celebrations in America's cities. General MacArthur, ever the master at staging ceremonies to mark significant military events, put it best as he spoke to the world from the Battleship Missouri in Tokyo Harbor, where the Japanese emissaries were about to sign the surrender documents. "The issues involving divergent ideals and ideologies have been determined on the battlefields of the world and, hence, are not for our discussion or debate," he said. "It is my earnest hope, and indeed the hope of all mankind, that from this solemn occasion, a better world shall emerge out of the blood and carnage of the past...." Americans were very hopeful at that moment that this war had finally done it, that peace would be permanent!

Almost five hundred thousand Americans died in World War II. There are impressive cemeteries all across the world where American soldiers and sailors are buried, their graves marked by seemingly endless rows of crosses and Stars of David. I have visited several of these cemeteries, and as I walk through, reading the names and the memorials inscribed nearby, I always think, this is a sad place, but it's also a place of pride and hope, because these soldiers died for a worthy cause. There was and is no question about it; World War II was a war worth fighting.

KOREA, 1950-1953:
WOULD I FIGHT FOR CONTAINMENT?

After the joyous conclusion of World War II, the American people got to savor only five years of peace before war came again. On June 25, 1950, communist North Korea crossed the thirty-eighth parallel and attacked South Korea. Committed to a policy of containing communism, President Truman sent General Douglas MacArthur to Korea to assess the situation; MacArthur determined the South Koreans could not hold on without our help. Within days, American forces that had been stationed in Japan since the war were on their way to Korea. The UN Security Council voted to authorize collective military action against North Korea, and by the end of the summer, more than one hundred thousand UN troops, mostly Americans, were in Korea fighting the communists along a one hundred fifty mile front near the southern port city of Pusan.

For a while, it looked like the South Koreans and their UN allies might be driven into the sea and that the communists would take control of the entire peninsula, but MacArthur, in one of the most brilliant maneuvers of his career, landed a force of U.S. marines at Inchon, just north of Seoul, and far behind enemy lines. The UN forces down at Pusan, meanwhile, launched a counterattack and, suddenly, the North Koreans found themselves retreating into a giant vise: MacArthur's force in the North and the UN force in the South closing in on them. Within a week, the North Koreans were back on their own side of the thirty-eighth parallel.

At this point, having held the line against aggression—having contained communist North Korea—the UN and the United States could have declared victory and ended the war; instead, the UN and President Truman authorized MacArthur to pursue the North Koreans into North Korea to destroy their capacity to fight. MacArthur pursued the North Koreans all the way to the Yalu River, the boundary between North Korea and communist China. At this point, the Chinese "jumped in with both feet" (as MacArthur put it) and attacked across the Yalu with two hundred fifty thousand men. American and UN forces were driven in headlong retreat back across the thirty-eighth parallel.

Not accustomed to retreating, MacArthur wanted to strike back against the Chinese by bombing their bases north of the Yalu River and authorizing Chiang Kai-shek on Formosa to attack the Chinese mainland. Truman did not want to risk a third world war with China, and probably the Soviet Union, which would come into the war on the side of its communist friends. He ordered his general to fight a limited war in Korea and not to publicly air their disagreement. MacArthur disobeyed Truman's order and, in fact, wrote a letter to the speaker of the House of Representatives, complaining that he was fighting with his hands tied and proclaiming that "there is no substitute for victory."

Truman, furious that the general had disobeyed orders from his commander-in-chief, fired the general; more accurately, he removed him from command in Korea. The fighting continued on under General Matthew Ridgway and finally came to an end in 1953, when an armistice (ceasefire) was signed. A demilitarized zone was established along the thirty-eighth parallel (approximately), and prisoners of war were exchanged. The situation in Korea has remained like this ever since. The communist regime of North Korea is a pariah among nations; its leader, Kim Jung Un, is a mad man; and it is one of the few nations of the world that possesses nuclear bombs.

People who adore MacArthur as a hero argue that none of the difficulties we face in Korea, or, for that matter, in China, would exist if Truman had listened to MacArthur. We were the only power in Asia that had an atomic bomb in 1951, so MacArthur's supporters argue we could have used it, or threatened to use it, and driven the Chinese out of North Korea and perhaps even driven Mao Zedong out of Beijing. Such a view ignores the Soviet Union and the fact that China was a nation of almost a billion people. Most people think Truman was right, even though the end result was an unsatisfactory stalemate. The MacArthur people, without having to prove it, stand firm in claiming he would have solved all our problems.

The Korean War was the first world event I was aware of outside of my own little life. I was only six on the day it started, and I remember my mother worrying that my father would be drafted again. He was thirty-three, so it certainly was possible. The great baseball player Ted Williams, who had missed three years of his career serving in World War II, was called back to serve another two years in Korea. Dad was never drafted for this fight. If I had been fifteen years older, I would have answered the call if drafted, but I doubt if I would have volunteered. I have always thought *containment* was the best policy to follow against communism. It was better than appeasement, which had been such a disaster in the 1930s, and it was better than total war, which would possibly destroy the world with nuclear explosions. Korea was about as clear an example of containment as there would ever be. The policy was to hold the line against communist expansion, and in Korea, there was a clear and definable line: the thirty-eighth parallel. If we didn't hold that line, then the policy was a lot of sound and fury, signifying nothing.

I believe the Korean War was a victory for containment. That war made the policy seem simple enough. If a communist country (Soviet Union, China, North Korea) attacks a non-communist country, we employ force to stop it. If we keep doing that whenever communist countries try to advance, communism will eventually collapse of its own illogical contradictions. That's what George Kennan, the originator of containment, told us, and he eventually proved to be right. The problem was that a situation where containment applied might not always be totally clear. What should we do, for example, if the people within a country wanted to adopt communism? What if, in a democratic vote, the people wanted to choose communism? Should the United States move in to thwart the will of the people because we didn't like the choice they were making? In the late 1950s, just as I was reaching military age, we were about to find out.

VIETNAM, 1964-1975:
WOULD I FIGHT FOR THE FIRST DOMINO?

When I registered for the draft in 1962, there was no war going on and there seemed to be no prospects for one. There was the Cold War with the Soviet Union, of course, but we all figured if war came with Russia, it would be nuclear, and we would all be killed before anyone got drafted. The Cuban Missile Crisis in the fall of that year seemed to confirm that "all or nothing" viewpoint.

It was with a mixture of surprise and concern that I watched a television news special in 1963 describing U.S. support for the government of Ngo Dinh Diem in South Vietnam, who was fighting against the communist National Liberation Front (also referred to as the Vietnam communists or Viet Cong). The voiceover said we already had thousands of advisors there, as I watched a film of a South Vietnamese Army unit heading into the jungle, accompanied by a few American soldiers.

Over the next three years, I completed college and was looking forward to starting a teaching career; however, by then, President Johnson had escalated our troop commitment to well over one hundred thousand combat troops, and we were fully engaged in a war to defend the government of South Vietnam against the communists from the North and the local Viet Cong. By 1966, the military draft was in full swing, and able-bodied twenty-two year-olds like me who had just finished college and were no longer covered by a student deferment were prime targets. In the summer of that year, I started a job as athletic director at a camp; I was in denial, I guess, totally oblivious to the fact that I was about to be tapped for military service.

My view on the Vietnam War at that time was based on a rather superficial knowledge of American wars in the past. If I had known my history better (I know; I was about to begin a job teaching it, so what was wrong with me?), I would have had some doubts about whether I would answer the draft call. It seemed to me that Vietnam was clearly part of the containment policy. It was just like Korea: the communists from the North were trying to take over the "good guys" in the South, and we had to stop those evil reds! If we didn't, we would be making the same mistake the democracies made in the 1930s, when they appeased Hitler. President Eisenhower had likened Southeast Asia to a row of dominoes standing on edge. If the first domino (Vietnam) fell to communism, the rest would cascade. We couldn't allow the first to fall. Naturally, I assumed that our military efforts would be "all out," just like they had been in all our previous wars, and that we would win.

My draft notice arrived in August, and it ordered me to report to Fort Wayne in Detroit for a physical. August 28 was the hottest day of the summer, and there we were, four hundred sweaty guys in just our underpants, shuffling along from one examination station to another. At one point, we all had to pull down our shorts and bend over while the examining officer came along behind and checked for hemorrhoids. At another station, we all had to sit in student desks, still wearing just our underpants, and take an intelligence test. In those circumstances, it was difficult to feel very intelligent.

The whole day was stinky, sweaty, and degrading. The guy in front of me had a big pimple in the middle of his back, and since we were required to stay in line the entire day, I got to stare at it for seven hours.

At the end of it all, a sergeant handed me my papers and informed me that I had a hernia, which would make me 1-Y, meaning temporarily physically unfit for service, and that I should get the hernia taken care of and then get back to them. Did he give me a wink and a slight smile when he said that? I couldn't say for sure, but I chose to think he did. What was clear was that I would be able to at least start my teaching job the next week and that I would have some time to get my mind around what I wanted to do. I'd had the hernia for years and wasn't bothered by it, but I could use it, at least for a while, as my pass out of 'Nam.

As the school year 1966-1967 moved along, I became increasingly aware that the Vietnam War was not really like Korea. Yes, we were trying to contain communism, but the situation was much more complicated than it was in Korea. The North had not just suddenly, without provocation, invaded the South. Elections to unite Vietnam under one government had been scheduled for 1956, and the United States had advised South Vietnam not to participate, mostly because we feared the popular communist leader of North Vietnam, Ho Chi Minh, would win. In the ten years since then, many people in South Vietnam had joined the communist movement in an attempt to overthrow the South Vietnamese government and bring Ho Chi Minh to power. As a result of this very fluid situation, there was no clear battle line in Vietnam. The enemy was everywhere, and he was invisible, posing as a peasant farmer by day and waging war as a Vietcong by night.

By 1967, I was becoming sympathetic to the growing anti-war movement. We seemed to be repeating in Vietnam the mistakes we had made in the Philippines at the turn of the century. We were an alien people trying to impose our views on a people that we did not really understand. Moreover, we seemed to be trying to do it "on the cheap." There was no total commitment to the war; President Johnson did not ask Congress to declare war, and he did not seem to make the commitment to the war that might be necessary to win. It was horrible to think that it might not be possible to win without totally annihilating the country. That thought was borne out in early 1968, during the Tet Offensive, when a U.S. commander said that we had to destroy the city of Hue in order to save it from the communists. That comment, coupled with the picture I described in the last chapter of General Loan shooting the Vietcong prisoner in the head, was the final straw. I became fully opposed to the war and decided to ride my hernia exemption to the end, if possible.

I never received another draft notice. The local draft board never asked me if I had my hernia fixed. At the time, I didn't really understand why they never asked, but I'm sure I know why now. The jurisdiction of my draft board included Pontiac, Michigan, which was a predominantly black town. It seems evident that the board was able to meet its monthly quota of recruits with black men from Pontiac without having to go after the white teacher from Birmingham. Cynics have said about every war that it was a "rich man's war and a poor man's fight." That was certainly true about Vietnam, and I am one of its best examples.

The Vietnam War was one of the greatest tragedies in American History. Fifty-eight thousand young Americans lost their lives and many thousands more were physically and/or psychologically maimed in a cause that was a fool's errand from the start. It was essentially a civil war, and the containment policy should not have even been applied to it. George Kennan, the originator of the containment concept, said so himself. Our leaders and the hawks that supported them did not know their history well enough. They should have seen the difference between Vietnam and Korea, as I've said, and they should have realized what we were in for from the Philippine experience of 1900-1902. Finally, they might have taken a lesson from the American Revolution. The British Army tried to fight the American colonists using conventional tactics, while the colonists fought in civilian clothes, used hit-and-run tactics, and blended into the local population. Sound familiar? The British Army did not lose many battles, but the government grew weary of the long, protracted war and finally decided to let the colonists go. In

Vietnam, *we* were the British; we could have completed the analogy by wearing red uniforms.

In the forty years since the Vietnam War ended, it's been difficult using that particular war as a guide for which wars are worth fighting. President George H.W. Bush often talked about the Vietnam Syndrome: the idea that we certainly did not want to make the same mistakes we made in Vietnam ever again. The problem is that not every infusion of American troops into a hostile situation is necessarily going to lead to more troops and a quagmire. It might be necessary to use American force to defend our interests or the interests of one of our friends, and we cannot let the Vietnam experience completely paralyze us. Compounding this problem is the fact that the world, in the last few decades, has become a much more confusing place. Hostile forces of varying colorations have cropped up everywhere, and they defy easy comparisons to enemies we have had to fight in the past. Nevertheless, a few truisms have emerged from the stories of our past wars that can still be applied:

1. The United States should never commit its military forces into a situation unless it has a firm resolve to win. Dwight D. Eisenhower, as general and as president, always believed in using *overwhelming* force in a situation once we decided to use force, and I think that is always good advice. As president, Eisenhower sent the One Hundred First Airborne—one thousand heavily armed paratroopers—to Little Rock, Arkansas, to escort nine black students into the high school. The mob on the school lawn stepped way back.

2. The United States should never try to insert itself into any conflict without a clear concept of what victory will look like. We should always have very clearly defined goals.

3. The United States should never send its military into a foreign culture that we cannot possibly understand. The Vietnam experience should have shown us that we cannot make people do what we want them to do if we continually offend them and they hate us.

4. The president should never send American troops into a conflict without fully informing the American people about the situation and the goals we will try to achieve. Furthermore, he or she should have the full support of the people as expressed in a vote of the Congress. Without public support, no war can succeed. (We should remember that Congress *did* vote to authorize the president's use of military force in Vietnam in the Gulf of Tonkin Resolution. The vote was almost unanimous. That means the people and their congressmen need to be fully informed and not react hysterically to provocative incidents.)

THE GULF WAR, 1991:
WOULD I FIGHT TO LIBERATE KUWAIT?

George H.W. Bush (Bush '41) was the president most qualified to handle foreign affairs since John Quincy Adams. Bush had been a member of Congress, ambassador to the United Nations, ambassador to China, head of the CIA, and vice president for eight years under Ronald Reagan. When Saddam Hussein invaded Kuwait in the summer of 1990, he was messing with the wrong president.

Bush had no intention of allowing Hussein to remain in Kuwait. Hussein would not only commandeer their oil fields, he would also threaten other Arab states in the region, such as Saudi Arabia, which was just across the Persian Gulf from Kuwait. The president stated his policy very succinctly: "This will not stand." Even as he said this, he was putting together a coalition of over twenty-five nations, including Arab countries, that would stand together to throw Iraqi forces out of Kuwait. Because of his many years of foreign policy experience, Bush personally knew many of the leaders and was able to convince them, even the Russians, to take a stand against aggression. If the peace of the world were going to rest on any kind of a firm foundation, Saddam Hussein could not be appeased.

By Christmas, the United States and its allies had a force of over half a million troops stationed in Saudi Arabia. Called Operation Desert

Shield, this force was there to protect Saudi Arabia and also to set up a base for launching an attack against Iraqi forces in Kuwait that would drive them out. Bush took the issue to the United Nations, and the UN gave Hussein an ultimatum: either leave Kuwait or the coalition would attack on January 16, 1991. In early 1991, Bush sent a personal letter to Saddam, urging him to comply with the UN ultimatum and withdraw his forces from Kuwait. Saddam did not respond.

Even though Bush could have proceeded with the action against Iraq without Congressional authorization by using his powers as Commander in Chief, he decided to seek the support of Congress anyway. Amazingly, the vote was close: fifty-two to forty-seven in favor of war in the Senate and two hundred fifty to one hundred eighty-three in the House. Nevertheless, Congress was now on record in favor of military action against Iraq.

On the night of January 16, 1991, Operation Desert Storm began. It was a massive aerial bombardment of Iraqi military installations in Kuwait, and it was very effective. As we watched the coverage on TV it looked like one of the new video games just out. Still, Hussein would not withdraw his forces, so on February 23, Bush ordered ground troops into Kuwait. Equipped with the most sophisticated equipment available, the coalition troops were able to subdue the Iraqi Army in less than five days. By the end of February, it was all over. Thousands of Saddam's soldiers had surrendered, had been killed, or had fled back across the border into Iraq.

In President Bush's address to the nation, he said, "We declared that the aggression against Kuwait would not stand, and tonight, America and the world have kept their word." There were some military advisors and some people in the country who wanted Bush to send coalition forces after Hussein's troops, pursue them all the way to Baghdad, and topple that rotten dictator from power. The temptation to do so must have been great, but Bush knew that the coalition, which included several Middle Eastern countries, would not support that extension of the mission. He also knew that Iraq was a conglomerate of many tribal groups made up of Shiite and Sunni Muslims, who are mortal enemies. Replacing Hussein with a stable, democratic government in that kind of environment would be a very difficult, if not impossible, job. Driving Saddam out of Kuwait completed the mission; it was best to leave it at that.

In many respects, the Gulf War of 1991 was even more a "splendid little war" (if there can be such a thing) than the Spanish-American War had been. It was over in two months; the casualties were light: one hundred forty-eight American lives. It was tragic for the soldiers who lost their lives and their families, but it was a small number as wars go. Most of all, it had stopped a nasty dictator in his tracks. And we did this for mostly altruistic reasons. The United States coveted no territory and took none. There were, of course, cynics who said Bush went into Kuwait to protect our oil supplies, but I would argue that our primary motive was to stop aggression. Besides, is it such a bad thing to protect the supply of a commodity vital to our national interest?

I totally supported the Gulf War. The United States does not want to be the world's policeman, but sometimes we have to be. Who else is going to do the job? And it is a job that *has* to be done.

People used two historical models when we first started to challenge Saddam Hussein in 1990 in order to judge whether they supported Bush's decision to fight. These models led to totally different conclusions, so the one you picked made all the difference. Your understanding of history was critical in 1991. The first model was the World War II model, which advised to never allow a dictator to take territory, because he would only try to take more. Fight now and avoid a bigger war later. Allowing Hitler to take over Austria and Czechoslovakia was a big mistake, and we should never make that kind of concession again. The second model was the Vietnam model, which advised that we must be very reluctant to insert our forces into regions we don't understand, as we will get bogged down in an endless war that leaves us with heavy casualties and no positive result. Before the actual fighting started in Kuwait, many people used this model, and that is why the vote in Congress to authorize the attack was so close.

The correct model, of course, was the World War II model. The Gulf War involved one rogue nation attacking its neighbor. We had to put him back into his box. We had allies—twenty-eight nations—fighting with us. The battle lines were clearly drawn; there were no Kuwaitis battling us guerrilla style. Kuwaitis welcomed us as liberators, just as the French, the Belgians, and the whole of Europe did in World War II. There are times when it is crystal clear that the United States needs to take a tough stand and fight. The Gulf War of 1991 was one of those times.

In his book about his father, George W. Bush says with pardonable pride that because of what his dad did, "The Vietnam syndrome was vanquished." After the Gulf War, American presidents would no longer be quite so fearful of quagmires or quite so timid about asserting American power around the globe, but his dad had also taught another important lesson in the Gulf War, and George W. Bush would have been well advised to pay a little more attention to it. American power has its limits, and they need to be recognized and observed.

THE WAR IN AFGHANISTAN: WOULD I FIGHT TO AVENGE 9/11 AND BRING DEMOCRACY TO AFGHANISTAN?

In the weeks that followed the attack on the World Trade Center, we all knew that President George W. Bush was going to launch an attack against the country that had given sanctuary to the man who was responsible for the attack, Osama Bin Laden. The disgusting Taliban government of Afghanistan had given Bin Laden and his Al Qaeda organization a home; that made the Taliban complicit in Bin Laden's horrific crime. In his speech to Congress a few days after the attack, Bush had said that the perpetrators of the attack, and "those who harbor them," would be brought to justice.

Once again there was almost unanimous support for the war—as unanimous as it is possible to get for *any* military action. For various reasons, there are usually twenty to thirty percent of the American people who *never* want to fight. There was even one dissenting vote on the declaration of war against Japan the day after the Pearl Harbor attack.

At first, the Afghan War went almost as swimmingly as the Gulf War had ten years earlier. Our better-equipped forces were able to drive the Taliban out of Kabul and into the southern provinces of Afghanistan very quickly, and we had Osama Bin Laden on the run. Unfortunately, he eluded our grasp and escaped into the mountains of Tora Bora and eventually into Pakistan. By the end of 2002, our mission in Afghanistan was no longer to capture Osama Bin Laden; it was to establish a democratic regime in the country that was friendly to the United States and to keep the Taliban from regrouping and returning to power. This job was going to occupy us for the next fourteen years and beyond.

We established a government there that was ostensibly democratic, but also exceedingly corrupt. On the plus side, we brought about some very important political and social changes, not the least of which was securing several important rights for women that they had never had: the right to go to school, the right to vote, and the right to testify in court, even against men. The news reports of Afghan girls joyfully attending school was heartwarming and, in my view, that result alone made the entire war effort worthwhile.

Unfortunately, not only was Osama Bin Laden still at large (he was not killed in Pakistan until 2011), but the Taliban was not dead. Like the villain in a horror movie, they were springing back to life and, within a few years, were once again a force to be reckoned with in Afghanistan. By 2015, their attacks were so successful in some areas that President Obama felt obliged to give up his plan to remove all U.S. troops and to leave five thousand in the country to advise the Afghan police and military and hopefully secure the country.

Despite all the setbacks, I think the invasion of Afghanistan was the right thing to do and I supported it from the start. By now, my children are of military age. The draft still exists, but it's currently not active. If it were, I can't say that I would be happy to see my son sent off to serve in Afghanistan or my daughter volunteer to enlist, but if it came to be, I would at least know they were laying their lives on the line for a good cause, even though it wrenches my gut to think about the possibility. But that's just a mental virtual reality for me. Millions of parents had to face that situation for real during World War II, and even though there was never a more important or more justified war than that one, it must have been very hard. So, when I say I would be okay with members of my family serving in Afghanistan, I don't say it lightly.

THE WAR IN IRAQ:
WOULD I FIGHT TO REMOVE SADDAM HUSSEIN FROM POWER?

This is not hindsight or Monday morning quarterbacking. At the time President Bush ordered the invasion of Iraq in March 2003, I thought it was a bad decision, for several reasons:

1. We had enough to do in Afghanistan.

2. We should focus on capturing, or killing, Osama Bin Laden by sending our special forces after the sumbitch and his lieutenants, wherever they were.

3. There were Sunnis and Shias in Iraq who hated each other. Invading Iraq would be like kicking a hornets' nest; what happened after we toppled Hussein would be really ugly. President Bush should have asked Ike's all-important question: "What next?" Apparently, he didn't.

Those who argue that ISIS, the scourge of our time, was spawned by the turmoil in Iraq and the hatred for the United States that our presence engendered are probably correct. The reasons Bush Sr. had for not invading Iraq in 1991 were still valid, and I wish—I wished even in

2003—he had taken his son out behind the woodshed and given him a lickin' for even thinking about doing it.

I am not a Bush hater who blames everything, including yesterday's weather, on him. He had his reasons for going into Iraq in spite of what I just said. In his book *Decision Points*, he reminds us that his job as president was to protect the country, and he had intelligence that showed that Hussein had weapons of mass destruction. He says, quite rightly, that those people who doubt the veracity of the intelligence have the luxury of hindsight and of not being responsible for the consequences of being wrong. Furthermore, I don't think the war has been a complete waste, as long as we stay in there long enough to keep the gains from coming undone. There is a democratic constitution in the country, and just as in Afghanistan, women are enjoying new rights they never had before.

Still, my three reasons for opposing the war remain, highlighted by the third. The Sunni-Shia conflict is the one thing that threatens the whole project in Iraq. Getting the two groups to cooperate in a stable government is like putting a mongoose and a snake in a box and expecting them to become pals.

What strikes me about our two most recent wars is how well our armed forces have been able to do in spite of the horrendously complicated situation they were thrown into. We broke some of the major rules of engagement that I listed earlier, especially the one about going into a culture we don't understand, and yet with incredible bravery and fighting savvy, they were able to stabilize, at least for a while, very volatile and dangerous situations.

I think many people, especially young people, believe their opinion about a war doesn't matter and that if they are called to fight in a war, they really have no choice. First of all, our opinion does matter. We have won major wars because the American people enthusiastically supported the war effort, but several wars have been lost or ended early with less than perfect results because the American people did *not* support them. The Vietnam War is a prime example. We might still have a military presence in Vietnam propping up an unpopular government if the people had not rallied so strongly against our involvement. The people supported the Korean War, and we have had thirty thousand troops in South Korea for the six decades since the ceasefire in 1953.

When it comes to our own personal involvement in fighting, we actually do have a choice: we can either support the war by volunteering for combat or we can wait to be drafted. At election time, we can campaign and vote for candidates who support the war. We can make our opinion known in social media, in editorials, and at rallies.

If we oppose a war, we can make our opinion known on that side as well. Even if we are drafted, we also *really do* have a choice. James Fallows wrote an article in 1975 that I often refer to in my classes when discussing the draft during the Vietnam War. In his article titled "What Did You Do in the Class War, Daddy?" Fallows described how he was called to the Boston Navy Yard during the Vietnam War for a draft physical and showed up with a folder of doctor's notes declaring him unfit for service. What struck him, as he waited in the long line, was how the poor kids from Chelsea, a working class town, just went along, obviously believing they had no choice. They were like sheep being led to the slaughter, with no thought whatsoever that they could do anything about it. Fallows and his college friends were thinking of all the angles and all the ways they could avoid the draft: physical disability, wealthy father pulling strings with the draft board for a deferment, etc. Most of the college kids went back to campus as free men, relieved of all military responsibility. The poor guys from Chelsea, meanwhile, were off to 'Nam.

For those who absolutely opposed the war or were too cowardly to fight, they had the option of "bugging out" to Canada until it was over—and there were thousands who did just that!

So, what we decide regarding U.S. involvement in a war is important. We have a role to play in the way public opinion is heard. More importantly, we can actually decide—in fact, we *have* to decide—whether we or our loved ones and friends will take part in the fighting. And what does history have to do with this? Everything! How can we make a rational choice about a war unless we have some idea about how wars have gone in the past? What happened when our country got involved in similar circumstances? If we have no knowledge of past wars, we will be making our decisions in a vacuum! I would hate having to make a decision about life or death based on nothing but my own emotions. If I did that, I would be opposed to every war, and I don't think that would be right.

THE BACK STORY

If you are generally aware of what is going on in the world around you, knowledge of American history will certainly help you understand events better. If you are still with me at this point, I have to assume you care about your world and would like to know more about it. To make my case, I have culled out several major news stories that have occupied the headlines during the last month, as of this writing. In the next few pages, I will summarize those stories and show how knowledge of American history helps you understand them and develop an informed opinion about them.

The *Boston Globe,* November 24, 2015:

　U.S. details an expansive security checklist

The Week, December 4, 2015:

　Trump's escalating anti-Muslim rhetoric

These stories describe both the efforts being made by the United States government to make sure that the ten thousand immigrants who might enter the United States from Syria as they flee the civil war are not terrorists and the fear mongering that Donald Trump (and other candidates) are using for political gain. For several weeks, this has been a major issue for the United States Government and the American people, but it has gotten really heated up since November 13, 2015, when Islamic terrorists attacked several sites and murdered over one hundred thirty people in Paris.

Knowledge of American history helps me understand these stories in several ways. I understand why Islamic terrorists exist and why they might want to target people in the West, particularly Americans. I also understand the impulse many Americans feel to keep those out of the country who might be a threat, although I don't approve of this tactic.

The hostility between some Muslims and the United States can, in a way, be traced back to Jefferson's fight against the Barbary pirates of Tripoli, from 1801 to 1805. Jefferson refused to pay the bribes the pirates were demanding for safe passage through the Mediterranean Sea, and instead fought a war ("to the shores of Tripoli," as the Marine hymn says) that was mostly successful. There was a Muslim versus infidel element to that war because the pirates were Muslims, but the war was mostly about national pride and shipping rights.

The real conflict between Muslims and the United States arose in 1948, when the United States was the first country in the world to recognize the state of Israel. Since that year, our policy has been to support Israel at all costs and to assist in her defense with large amounts of military aid. All of the Arab countries, and the Palestinian Arabs who lived in the land that became Israel, are predominantly Muslim, so, of course, it's a short leap from hating the United States for its support of Israel to hating the predominant religion of the United States, Christianity.

There is much more driving the extremists, though. In fact, our support for Israel itself might not have caused the creation of extremist groups in the Muslim world; our biggest offense is going into the Middle Eastern countries in pursuit of oil and bringing along with us our western values. In the eyes of many Muslims, not just the Jihadists, America is an immoral society that allows drinking, gambling, sexual immorality, and a host of other offenses. We also give women certain rights (the vote, drivers' licenses, etc.) that they would never allow. It was bad enough, in their eyes, that we brought these disgusting values with us when we came for the oil, but when we invaded Afghanistan and Iraq, we threatened to upend all of Muslim culture. We were the infidel, the Satan, who had to be killed.

You can see, then, that when we know some of the back story of America's history in the Middle East, we can better understand the intensity with which we are hated by Islamic extremists today and why groups such as Al Qaeda and ISIS have pulled off barbaric attacks such as 9/11 and the bombings in Paris and Brussels.

The issue of the Syrian refugees has heightened the crisis between Islam and the West in a way that is also not new to anyone who knows American history. Even though we have always been a nation of immigrants and a haven for people seeking refuge from turmoil and persecution, we have also been a country that has been capable of showing very real hostility to immigrants who we believe to be a threat.

The American or Know-Nothing Party of the 1850s came into existence in response to the increased Irish immigration. The party feared that the Irish, who were desperately coming into the country to flee the potato famine, were a threat to the American culture, with their Roman Catholicism.

In the late nineteenth century, many Americans were very hostile to the new immigrants from southern and eastern Europe who, Americans feared, were socialists and anarchists. Those fears came to full flower after the Wall Street bombings in 1920 and the Sacco and Vanzetti case in 1921. The explosion of a bomb on Wall Street killed thirty-eight people and sent a shock wave across the country. People believed there were terrorists all around—anarchists, socialists, and communists— who would strike again. The following year, when Sacco and Vanzetti, two Italian anarchists, were accused of murder, many people, including the judge at their trial, were convinced they were guilty. In 1921 and 1924, Congress passed restrictive immigration laws that set rigid quotas for the number of immigrants who could come into the United States from countries that were likely sources of terrorists: Italy, Russia, and other eastern European nations.

Meanwhile, Asian immigration had been practically stopped cold with the Chinese Exclusion Act of 1882 and the Gentlemen's Agreement with Japan in 1907, which kept Japanese workers from immigrating. During World War II, President Roosevelt authorized the relocation of Japanese-Americans on the West Coast, out of fear they might help the enemy.

What is less known is that Jews from Europe were held to strict quotas even though they were in desperate need to flee the Nazi Holocaust. The reason was that there was a fear in top government circles that German Nazi agents and saboteurs might be among the refugees.

When we see many Americans, then, including some of the major presidential candidates in 2016, calling for prohibiting the Syrian refugees from coming into the United States because Islamic jihadists might be among them, we are witnessing nothing very new. Donald Trump has brought the idea to new levels by advocating that no Muslims at all be allowed into the country. This kind of xenophobia (fear of foreigners) has reared its ugly head many times before. As someone familiar with the history of those incidents, I know that, years later, when cooler thinking prevailed, we looked back at those xenophobic attitudes with regret. Surely, if we were true to the words on the Statue of Liberty, we would have allowed the Irish fleeing famine, the Chinese seeking opportunity, the Italians seeking a better life, and the Jews seeking escape from the Holocaust to come into our country. Surely, today, when thousands of terrorized Syrians are fleeing the very jihadists we are fighting, we can allow them to seek refuge among us.

The *Boston Globe*, November 24, 2015:

> **FDA targets flawed medical tests, citing dangers, costs;**
>
> **Patients harmed by wrong results, Congress told**

Most Americans take the Food and Drug Administration for granted, if they know what it is. When I hear a story such as this, I find it helpful to know how the FDA came into existence and what its purpose is. In this instance, the FDA has found that many tests that are administered to patients, such as X-rays, are often more dangerous than people think and should sometimes be skipped. I have often shared this thought. I realize that doctors don't want to leave something undetected and risk getting sued by the patient or his or her family, but sometimes it seems I am being put through more trials than are necessary. I am glad the FDA is there to keep tabs on this kind of thing.

I am even happier that the FDA is there to check on the validity of drug claims, the possible consequences of taking certain drugs that help some symptoms but have terrible side effects, and the purity of food products. The FDA's greatest achievement occurred in the 1960s, when it denied approval of a drug called Thalidomide. It was widely used in Great Britain to help women deal with pregnancy discomforts, but the FDA would not license it in the United States until it was tested further. Ultimately, it was discovered that the women who used the drug did have more comfortable pregnancies, but they gave birth to babies that were horribly deformed: babies with no arms or legs, and other terrible deformities. American women, and their husbands and babies, were spared these horrors because of the FDA.

The FDA exists because President Theodore Roosevelt was disgusted by the conditions in the meat packing plants in Chicago that he had read about in the novel *The Jungle*. Ground up rats in his sausages was a little more than this president could bear, so he got Congress to pass the first legislation to create a federal agency to check on the factories owned by private capitalists. In an age of unbridled free enterprise, this was a bold step. Laissez-faire capitalists saw it as a step toward socialism, where the government would actually own and run the food industries. Upton Sinclair, the socialist who wrote *The Jungle*, was upset that TR and Congress didn't go full out and take over the meat packing companies and all the other food processors.

It is certainly true that you do not have to know how and why the FDA was created to enjoy its protection, but I think that knowing about the FDA and why it was created helps you to have an informed opinion about what the government should, and should not, do. Why is it important to have an informed opinion about this? Because this is the basic argument we have in this country between Republicans, who want as much free enterprise as possible, and Democrats, who look to the federal government to take care of most problems. If you have any interest in being an informed citizen who participates in the political process by supporting candidates and voting, then you need to know as much as possible about the debate that has gone on for well over a hundred years between those who favor free enterprise and those who favor government regulation or even socialism.

The *Boston Globe,* November 29, 2015:

Clinton to propose billions in infrastructure spending

Hillary Clinton, a Democratic candidate for president in 2016, says if she is elected president she will propose a bill to spend billions to repair the nation's roadways, bridges, and railroads. Republicans, of course, react to her idea with horror because they see more federal government involvement in the economy, and more taxes to pay for the program. Democrats like her idea because this kind of government spending creates jobs and helps the economy by facilitating commerce.

Historically, the concept of federal involvement in infrastructure (internal improvements in the early days) was fairly unpopular. The National Road through the Appalachian Mountains was about the only significant federal enterprise. Such major connecting thoroughfares as the Erie Canal were all state projects.

After the Civil War—in fact, during the Civil War, with the South out of the Union—the thinking changed dramatically, and the federal government got involved in creating infrastructure in a big way, with the construction of the Transcontinental Railroad. Soon after came the gigantic Panama Canal project and the Boulder Dam (Hoover Dam) in Southern Nevada. Interestingly, all of these projects were presided over by Republican presidents who wanted to expand the economy and strengthen national defense; then, in the 1950s, the greatest infrastructure project of them all, the Interstate Highway System, was guided through Congress by yet another Republican, Dwight D. Eisenhower.

The Democrats finally got into the act of creating infrastructure during FDR's years. The WPA projects were seen mostly as jobs programs, but the Tennessee Valley Authority (TVA) created the biggest electric power producer in the country. Today, it's the Democrats who are pushing for infrastructure projects not just for job creation, but for the positive effect they will have on commerce and industry. It will be interesting to see how the Republicans approach this issue. Everyone can see that the country's roads and bridges are in disrepair, and a number of tragic bridge collapses have caused numerous fatalities. The Republicans, however, are loathe to raise taxes or send the country further into debt, especially to give a "win" to a Democrat, especially a Democrat named Clinton.

Knowing the history of internal improvements, or public works, or infrastructure, or whatever name you choose to call them, enables me to evaluate what the candidates are saying on the subject and to develop an informed opinion about it. I think the Republicans, at least until now, have always been on the right side of this issue. Abraham Lincoln was thrilled to sign the Pacific Railway Act in 1862 because he knew it would spur the development of the West and promote a lively East-West trade. Dwight Eisenhower saw the poor condition of our roads during a 1919 trip across the country with the Army. He saw what real highways could look like in Germany during World War II, and as president, he couldn't wait to get that kind of network of superhighways going in his own country.

The American economy has always benefitted from improvement in the country's infrastructure, and those improvements have almost always come about because of Republican leadership. It will be a shame if the

Republicans leave behind their sensible approach to *investment* in roads and bridges only to score questionable political points against a hated adversary. I think infrastructure projects, even ones that seem very wasteful, such as the "big dig" central artery tunnel in Boston, almost always benefit the economy substantially. History shows that to be true.

The *Boston Globe*, December 5, 2015:

Good Nov. jobs report means rate rise likely

This story explains how the Federal Reserve Bank will probably raise interest rates because the economy is doing much better over the past six years. In 2009, when the recession hit, the Fed lowered interest rates to make loans readily available and to increase the money supply. This action, along with other factors, has improved people's ability to make purchases, and the economy has rebounded to the extent that the unemployment rate is at five percent; it was at ten percent in 2009.

The Federal Reserve Bank was created in 1913 as the long-awaited answer to the question of how the government could regulate the money supply. Earlier, national banks in the nineteenth century had only lasted for twenty years because of widespread hostility to those banks as tools of the rich and powerful. Andrew Jackson famously made war against the national bank and destroyed it in the mid-1830s. Other concepts, such as the free and unlimited coinage of silver, were pushed hard by the farmers and debtors of the late nineteenth century, but those ideas met resistance from the wealthy people who feared inflation. The Federal Reserve Bank, with its power to set interest rates and require banks to keep certain amounts of their assets on deposit at the Fed, can increase the money supply during hard times and tighten the money supply when inflation occurs.

The *Boston Globe*, December 3, 2015

NATO invites Montenegro to join military defense pact;
Russia responds with threats of retaliation

The *Boston Globe*, December 4, 2015:

Russia-Turkey feud deepens

Many stories have appeared in the news lately about NATO, and they have been troubling. In 1949, the United States took the lead in organizing the North Atlantic Treaty Organization, a military alliance formed predominantly to defend Western Europe from a Soviet attack. The alliance was the centerpiece of our containment policy. The Soviet Union disintegrated in 1991, and Russia is no longer a communist country, but as the story about Montenegro shows, the Russians still consider NATO to be an alliance against them. The threats of retaliation are probably just bluster ... so far.

The dust-up between Turkey and Russia is very concerning for the United States because Turkey is a member of NATO. Article V of the NATO Treaty commits each member to defend a member if it is attacked: an attack against one will be regarded as an attack on all. If the crisis escalates and Russia attacks Turkey, we will be obliged to come to Turkey's defense.

All of this began because the Turks shot down a Russian warplane that they claim flew over Turkish territory. Currently, no one thinks this crisis will escalate to a shooting war, but very few people thought the crisis in the summer of 1914, when the Austrian archduke was assassinated, would lead to anything either; of course, it did lead to World War I when the alliance system of that time swung into action.

Complicating the current crisis is the fact that Turkey is a major player in the containment of ISIS, the Muslim jihadist group of fanatics that control territory (what they call a caliphate) in Syria and Iraq, right next to the Turkish border. Russia has troops and bombers in Syria supposedly to attack ISIS, but more likely to support the Syrian dictator, Bashar Assad. Russian President Vladimir Putin yearns for the glory days of the Soviet Union, and he would probably very much like to teach Turkey, a long-standing Russian enemy, a lesson. In so doing, he could stick it to NATO a bit. Would he be so bold as to order an air strike on Turkey?

Conservatives in the United States think it is possible that Putin will do something drastic, because he doesn't respect President Obama. Putin knows he's not dealing with a president like Ronald Reagan who, like the cowboys he played in the movies, was ready to draw and shoot at the slightest provocation. Obama always orders military action reluctantly and usually sets a date when the action will be over, thereby telling the enemy how long they need to hold out.

Obama's liberal supporters, and there are many, argue that he is wisely avoiding the kind of heavy-handed intrusion into the Middle East that has gotten our country into so much trouble during the last thirty years, and especially since the invasion of Iraq in 2003. Obama and his supporters believe that every bomb we drop on the Middle East creates more jihadists who will attack us there and even in our own country.

I hope it is obvious that a clear understanding of what has happened in history since the end of the Second World War is essential to an understanding of what is happening today in the Middle East. As citizens, we need to understand the forces and events that could result in another war that would require our involvement. Candidates running for office make many claims about how they will keep the country safe. It's impossible to evaluate who has the best workable plan unless we know the history involved. The 2016 presidential candidates talk loosely about the ISIS situation, the Russian threat, and many other issues. We can spot the demagogues if we know the history.

The *Boston Globe*, December 7, 2015:

> **Obama vows victory over terror; says strategy will succeed, cautions against succumbing to fear**

The most deadly terrorist attack on the United States since 9/11 occurred in San Bernardino, California, on December 2, 2015, when a husband and wife team armed with automatic weapons killed fourteen people and wounded twenty others at a conference center. Before they were killed by police, the assailants pledged their allegiance to ISIS. Evidence indicates this was their own personal jihad; they were not under orders from ISIS, but their attack was inspired by the extremist group. Police found a large arsenal of weaponry in the couple's apartment.

In an effort to calm the nation and restore confidence in his strategy to defeat terrorism, President Obama delivered a speech in which he emphasized that "our military, with its bombing program and support for the forces of the government of Iraq, has contained the geographic spread of ISIS and even restored Iraqi rule to some cities that ISIS had once taken. With the help of the moderate Muslim nations in the Middle East and our European allies, we will continue to degrade ISIS by shrinking its territory, destroying its ability to make money, and killing its leaders.

"In the meantime, Obama continued, "we have to be vigilant at home against jihadi attacks such as the one in San Bernardino, but we cannot become so fearful that we abandon our principles of freedom. We should not hold all Muslims responsible for the horrid acts of a few, and we should not lock out refugees who are desperately trying to flee the terror in their own countries. We *do* need to restrict one freedom, however, and that is the right to bear arms. More effective gun control legislation is absolutely needed to make it more difficult for fanatics who have become violent to secure automatic weapons and huge ammunition clips capable of killing dozens of people without reloading."

As I listened to the president's speech, I thought of the many parallels to other eras and events in American history, and I hoped that if any of my former students were watching that they could see the same. I thought of the Red Scare after the Wall Street bombings and the Palmer Raids that followed, when Attorney General A. Mitchel Palmer ordered federal agents to bust into the homes of hundreds of suspected radicals. The Feds garnered nary a single real terrorist in those raids, but many people were victimized by the brusque intruders without warrants. President Obama may have had this grim history in mind when he warned against overreaction. I also thought of President George W. Bush who, after the horrific attacks of September 11, 2001, made it a point in several speeches to warn Americans against thinking that all Muslims were responsible for the attacks. The Palmer Raids are a cautionary tale; Bush's high-minded approach is admirable.

Many Americans, especially those Republicans running for president, are calling for a more aggressive approach than President Obama is providing. They want more vigorous bombing; they want "boots on the ground" in Syria to get the job done; they want us to "light up the sand" with our bombs. Those hawks should remember how much hatred we stirred up when we had soldiers in Iraq after our invasion in 2003. The story of Iraq, and before that Vietnam, should always warn us, as noted in Chapter XI, that we can often make a situation worse by inserting ourselves into a culture that does not share our values.

As for bombing, both Obama and his critics should remember that bombing has historically not been effective in winning wars; in fact, it has often strengthened the enemy's will to fight. In World War II, we practically annihilated many German cities, but the Nazis fought on until the bitter end and rebuilt the factories, railroads, and bridges that had been destroyed. Similarly, in Vietnam, where we dropped more tonnage of bombs on that tiny country than we did in all of World War II, we not only failed to bring the communists to their knees, we lost the war!

There are no easy answers to the problems in the Middle East or the threat of terrorism, but one thing is certain: having an understanding of the times in American history when we had to deal with wars, terrorist attacks, and a crises in confidence, helps us evaluate what we are doing now and decide who is offering the best approach to take us safely into the future. I don't necessarily fully ascribe to the George Santayana's axiom, "Those who cannot remember the past are condemned to repeat it," but I do believe that knowing history helps us know simplistic, overly emotional talk when we hear it. Candidate Donald Trump shouted recently that if he were president, he would "bomb the crap out of ISIS."

That drew big cheers, and it was emotionally satisfying to many people who were, quite rightly, upset by the terrorist attacks that have taken place lately. As a policy, though, his rant doesn't stand up to any kind of scrutiny; if you know your history, you can see that.

This chapter could go on for hundreds of pages, as almost everything that is happening in our country today has a backstory in our history. If we know about our country's history, especially if we have personalized it and taken the time to really understand those involved and why they acted as they did, then we can understand what is going on today. When I see what is happening in our country today, it makes me think, "I've seen this movie before." Sometimes that is alarming, but oftentimes it is comforting. It is always helpful to know that we are not floating out to sea, leaving the shore we have left invisible in the mist. Knowing history, we can see where we've been and have some idea where we are going.

P O S T S C R I P T

A PEEK INTO
THE FUTURE

Having spent forever thinking about the past, I decided it was time to try to peer into the future, so I arranged to meet with Dr. Roger Peekham, the noted futurist. We met at Starbucks; he sat with an enormous cup of their brew and I had a bottle of water. He was a short bald man who wore round metal-rimmed glasses, and he had an impish look on his face. I liked him immediately, but he sort of gave me the creeps.

I had some specific questions in mind, so I got right to it.

"Will the war with Islamic terrorists end anytime soon?" I asked.

"Oh, yes," he said with some enthusiasm. "It will be over by the year 2020."

"How will that happen?" I asked hopefully.

"The CIA will develop an app that they will be able to encrypt into any iPhone, iPad, or computer they target. This app will cause anyone who turns on the device to enter a virtual reality of the CIA's choosing. Every jihadist with an iPhone (which means all of them) will enter a world in which radical Islam has WON the global jihad. Every person the jihadists see will be a true believer of Islam. Every woman will be wearing a burka; every man will have a callus on his forehead from touching the ground in prayer five times a day. Any church they go into will be a mosque. They could walk into St. Peter's in Rome and think it's a mosque. Their entire world will be Muslim, so they will have *won* the global jihad and they will have no more need to kill infidels. Men who were once scowling, bearded terrorists will be walking around smiling at everyone in their totally Muslim world."

"Sounds great," I responded, "but how will we know that *they* didn't come up with this kind of app first and that *we* are not the ones living in a virtual world?"

He laughed with a witch-like cackle and fixed me with a cynical smile.

"At this point, what difference does it make?" he said with annoyance.

"This all seems pretty weird," I said, "but let me run another one by you. Will there be any progress in the obesity epidemic?"

"Yes, indeed. That will be resolved with a virtual world as well. For a small fee, obese people will be able to obtain a virtual reality app that will cause them to see every plate of salad as an enormous dinner of their favorite food, let's say a steak with mashed potatoes and a large slice of pie with ice cream. They will feel full after eating the salad, just as if they had eaten the steak and pie. Fat people will lose weight by the tons, and by the middle of the century, it will be very rare to see a fat person on the street.

"So, I can assure you," he went on, "that by the mid-twenty-first century, most of our major problems will be resolved through the use of virtual reality. Not only that, most of the hard labor will be done by robots that will be perfected to the point where they will be indistinguishable from real human beings. You will even be able to buy the perfect wife or husband for yourself on line!"

At this point, I wished we were in a pub so I could order a stiff drink.

"This description you have given me of the not-so-distant future makes me very uncomfortable, I have to say," I told him.

Dr. Peekham peered at me sympathetically (condescendingly?) over his glasses.

"Don't be alarmed," he soothed. "People such as yourself who have not fully left the twentieth century behind will be provided for. There will be special reality villages set up for you in which everyone is a real person and no one has a device of any kind. You will be able to have actual conversations and even read real paper newspapers and books. It will be just as you remembered it, and you will be able to enjoy it until the last one of you is gone. Then we will shut down the reality villages and the virtual world will be all there is. It will be wonderful. There will be no wars, no diseases, no loneliness, nothing to interfere with total happiness. All the terrible things that happened in the years and centuries before will be forgotten!"

Now I really needed a drink. The "forgotten" part was already happening. I had seen people wearing virtual reality glasses who believed they were riding a roller coaster; it was invisible to everyone but them. Dr. Peekham's predictions seemed all too possible. What bothered me the most was that Dr. Peekham seemed totally adjusted to the future he was predicting. He wasn't much younger than I was and yet he was all aboard for the virtual world.

After we parted, I went down the street to the pub, and even though it was only eleven in the morning, I ordered a tall draft of Guinness stout. As I sipped the delicious foam off the top I thought of Santayana's aphorism, "Those who forget the past are doomed to repeat it." Maybe, I thought, it should be amended to say, "Those who remember the past are doomed to miss it."

I set the glass down and watched as a young couple came in and sat at a table in the corner, talking excitedly as they ordered their lunch. It reminded me of so many times my wife, Diane, and I have done the same thing throughout the years. In many ways, I felt comforted, as real life does still go on and our memories of the past still help us live today and plan for tomorrow.

I picked up my second Guinness for another sip. A short time ago, I had imagined a meeting with a guy named Peekham, and now, happy that the conversation with the futurist was *only* in my mind, I silently toasted the young couple in the corner, put my glass down, and continued waiting for Diane to join me.

I N D E X